Philosophy of Religion

Philosophy of Religion

The Basics

Richard E. Creel

WILEY Blackwell

This edition first published 2014
© 2014 John Wiley & Sons, Inc.

Registered Office
John Wiley & Sons Ltd, The Atrium, Southern Gate, Chichester, West Sussex, PO19 8SQ, UK

Editorial Offices
350 Main Street, Malden, MA 02148–5020, USA
9600 Garsington Road, Oxford, OX4 2DQ, UK
The Atrium, Southern Gate, Chichester, West Sussex, PO19 8SQ, UK

For details of our global editorial offices, for customer services, and for information about how to apply for permission to reuse the copyright material in this book please see our website at www.wiley.com/wiley-blackwell.

The right of Richard E. Creel to be identified as the author of this work has been asserted in accordance with the UK Copyright, Designs and Patents Act 1988.

Library of Congress Cataloging-in-Publication Data

Creel, Richard E., 1940–
Philosophy of religion : the basics / Richard E. Creel.
        pages   cm
    Includes bibliographical references and index.
    ISBN 978-1-118-61957-5 (cloth) – ISBN 978-1-118-61943-8 (pbk.)
1. Religion–Philosophy.   2. Christianity.   I. Title.
    BL51.C693 2013
    210–dc23

                                                    2013016695

A catalogue record for this book is available from the British Library.

Cover image: *Time for Reflection.* © Lou Wall/Corbis
Cover design by Simon Levy Associates.

Set in 10/13pt Palatino LT Std by SPi Publisher Services, Pondicherry, India
Printed in Malaysia by Ho Printing (M) Sdn Bhd

1   2014

Dedicated
with deep appreciation for encouragement and support
to
William P. Alston, Philosopher
Jeffrey T. Dean, Editor
Sharon T. LaRose, Physician

Contents

Preface for Teachers   xi
Acknowledgements   xii

Introduction   1

1   **What Is Religion?**   **6**
    1.1   Creed   6
    1.2   Code   7
    1.3   Cult   8
    1.4   Community   9
    1.5   Toward a Definition of Religion   11
    1.6   Ze, Zer, Mer   13

2   **Six Conceptions of God**   **17**
    2.1   Experiential Sources of Concepts of God   17
    2.2   Six Conceptions of God   21
    2.3   Religious Naturalism   21
    2.4   Pantheism   23
    2.5   Panentheism (Process Theism)   25
    2.6   Deism   28
    2.7   Classical *Biblical* Theism is based on divine
          revelation   29
    2.8   Classical *Philosophical* Theism   31

3   **Divine Attributes and Dilemmas**   **34**
    3.1   What Is a Dilemma?   39
    3.2   Ways to Respond to a Dilemma   40
    3.3   Divine Attribute Dilemmas   41

3.4	Proposed Solutions to the Preceding Dilemmas		45
	3.4.1	Unsurpassability	45
	3.4.2	Omnipotence	46
	3.4.3	Are Omnipotence and Omnibenevolence Incompatible?	47
	3.4.4	Immutability and Personhood	48
	3.4.5	Divine Omniscience and Human Freedom	49
3.5	Open Theism		53

4   Human Language and Talk about God   57

5   Arguments about the Existence of God   72

6   The Ontological Argument   77
| 6.1 | Is Anselm's Argument Decisive? | 82 |
| 6.2 | A Version of Duns Scotus' Ontological Argument | 83 |

7   The Cosmological Arguments   88
7.1	The First Three of "The Five Ways" of Thomas Aquinas		89
7.2	Paul Edwards' Infinite Regress Argument against the Cosmological Argument		92
	7.2.1	Two Criticisms of Edwards	93
7.3	The Oscillatory Theory		93
	7.3.1	Criticism of the Oscillatory Theory	94
7.4	The Kalam Cosmological Argument		95

8   The Teleological or Design Arguments   101
| 8.1 | The Anthropic Principle | 108 |
| 8.2 | The Multiverse | 109 |

9   God and Morality   118
9.1	Two Arguments from Morality for Belief in the Existence of God		118
9.2	The Relation of Morality to God		119
	9.2.1	The Divine Command Theory	119
	9.2.2	Theocentric Ethics	120
	9.2.3	Natural Law Ethics	121

10 Religious Experience and Belief in God   **128**
   10.1 The Principle of Credulity and the Rationality of
         Belief in God   128
   10.2 Religious Experience as Evidence for the
         Existence of God   132
   10.3 Toward a Cumulative Argument for God   134

11 Arguments against Belief in the Existence of God   **137**
   11.1 Evidentialism and the Burden of Proof   137
   11.2 Conceptual Arguments: Analysis of the
         Concept of God   138
         11.2.1 The Argument from Meaninglessness   138
         11.2.2 The Arguments from Incoherence and
                 Self-Contradiction   138
   11.3 Arguments from Science   139
         11.3.1 The Natural Sciences: The Adequacy of
                 Science   139
         11.3.2 Criticisms of Naturalism   141
         11.3.3 The Social Sciences: Religion and Emotion   142
   11.4 The Problem of Divine Hiddenness   145
   11.5 The Problem of Many Religions   147

12 The Problem of Evil   **152**
   12.1 G.W. Leibniz (1646–1716)   153
   12.2 The Logical Argument from Evil: Arthur
         Schopenhauer (1788–1860)   153
   12.3 The Evidential Argument from Evil: Edward
         Madden, Peter Hare, William Rowe   153
         12.3.1 Criticisms of Arguments from Evil against
                 the Existence of God   154
   12.4 Charles Hartshorne's Panentheist or Process
         Theodicy   156

13 God and Life after Death   **164**
   13.1 Cessationism   165
   13.2 Immortalism   167
   13.3 Resurrectionism   170
   13.4 Personal Identity and Continuity   173

14 Miracles, Revelation, and Prayer   **179**
    14.1 Miracles   179
    14.2 Revelation   182
    14.3 Prayer   183

15 Rationality without Evidence   **185**
    15.1 Pascal's Wager   185
    15.2 Evidentialism vs. the Right to Believe   187
    15.3 Fideism   188
        15.3.1 Faith as Action or Leap   188
        15.3.2 Faith as Passion or Gift   189
    15.4 Agathism, Agatheism, and Religious Hope   190

Glossary   194
Biographical Notes   203
Index   209

Preface for Teachers

A fellow teacher once asked me, "If I use your text, what does that leave for *me* to do in class?" What this book freed me to do was have more discussion in class of the issues in the book, and it freed up time for me to take in short primary source handouts for study and discussion. To help guide review and evoke discussion, I have provided at the end of each chapter a section titled "For Review, Reflection, and Discussion." Then follows a section "For Further Reading." In the latter section, I make many recommendations from the first two books mentioned next, citing the relevant sections for the chapter just ended. It would be excellent for students to have a copy of the Zagzebski/Miller *Readings* or some other volume of readings (or at least have such available on reserve), and it will be helpful if Taliaferro's *Companion* and Eshleman's *East Meets West* are on reserve for students. In addition, I recommend highly that students be informed of Stanford University's online philosophical encyclopedia: http://plato.stanford.edu/contents.html. Here are references for the texts just mentioned:

Zagzebski, Linda, and Miller, Timothy, eds., *Readings in Philosophy of Religion: Ancient to Contemporary* (Wiley-Blackwell: 2009).
Taliaferro, Charles, Draper, Paul, et al., eds., *A Companion to Philosophy of Religion*, 2nd ed. (Wiley-Blackwell: 2010).

For students who want to read more about Asian philosophy of religion, I recommend *Readings in the Philosophy of Religion: East Meets West*, edited by Andrew Eshleman (Wiley-Blackwell: 2008).

Finally, at the end of this volume students will find a glossary and biographical notes. In the glossary, I alphabetize and summarize many of the distinctions and conceptual tools that I introduce to help students become more perceptive and analytic. Some of this material, and more, is available online for mobile access by your students.

Acknowledgments

For valuable criticisms, corrections, and suggestions regarding my original manuscript, I would like to thank the anonymous reviewers whom Wiley-Blackwell secured.

In addition, I extend special thanks to James Keller, Emeritus Professor at Wofford College, for splendid supererogatory help.

Introduction

When most people graduate from high school, they are already familiar with history, literature, mathematics, science, and social studies, but it is rare for philosophy to be taught in high school, so most people's first exposure to philosophy is in college. Or perhaps you graduated from college without taking a philosophy course or reading a philosophy book but have decided it's time to do so. Good for you! Or perhaps you are a bright high school student! In all of these cases, I think you will appreciate it if I spend a little time answering the question "What is philosophy?" before we plunge into "philosophy of religion."

Philosophy is an *activity* that goes all the way back to 600 BC in ancient Greece. It includes in its foundations such brilliant thinkers as Socrates, Plato, and Aristotle. Over the centuries we must add giants such as St. Augustine, St. Thomas Aquinas, René Descartes, Benedict Spinoza, G.W. Leibniz, John Locke, David Hume, Immanuel Kant, G.W.F. Hegel, John Stuart Mill, Soren Kierkegaard, Friedrich Nietzsche, Bertrand Russell, Ludwig Wittgenstein, and many others. (No – you do not have to memorize all those names!) As I mentioned, philosophy is an activity, not a static thing, so we have to ask, "What have philosophers been *doing* over the last 2600 years, right up to the present moment?" Most basically they have been trying to understand the nature of reality, the nature of the human situation, good and evil, right and wrong. Additional concerns are spin-offs of those basic concerns. For example, the issue about the nature and existence of God is one facet of the question of the nature of reality; the question of the meaning of life is one aspect of the philosophical attempt to understand the human

Philosophy of Religion: The Basics, First Edition. Richard E. Creel.
© 2014 John Wiley & Sons, Inc. Published 2014 by John Wiley & Sons, Inc.

situation; the issue of the morality of abortion pertains to the question of right and wrong. For a brief but useful *definition* of philosophy consider the following: we humans are passionate and meticulous in our pursuit of answers to the preceding kinds of issues, so philosophy is *the passionate, systematic pursuit of knowledge of the real and the good.* Such pursuit certainly involves solitary reflection, but ultimately philosophy is not a solitary pursuit. Philosophy proceeds most fruitfully in dialogue, when people communicate with one another, whether by face to face discussion or by reading and responding to one another's writings. One thing I have learned for certain over the decades is that *we* are smarter than I am! So formulate your own thoughts, then discuss them with others.

Now that we know a little of what *philosophy* is, let's ask what a philosophy *of* something is? A philosophy of something is an effort to identify and explore the basic concepts, positions, issues, and controversies in a field of activity. For example, there is philosophy of art, philosophy of history, philosophy of law, philosophy of mathematics, philosophy of psychology, philosophy of science, and more. Philosophy itself is a first-order activity (it has its own unique concerns, such as metaphysics and ethics), but philosophy *of* something is a second-order activity (in it philosophy focuses on something other than philosophy), and there can be a philosophy of (a philosophical study of) anything! In addition, to the "philosophies of" mentioned earlier there are books on philosophy of sport, philosophy of architecture, philosophy of love and sex, and much more. Pick a topic of interest and you will almost certainly find a philosophy book on it.

A philosophy of something is always an attempt to identify the central concepts, concerns, issues, and positions in a field. To that extent it is an attempt to be objective and simply set things forth the way things are in some field. Sometimes, however, a philosopher of something wants to add his or her personal insights, conclusions, and convictions about some issue in the field; that is perfectly fine, but readers should be sensitive to when a writer is setting forth material and when he or she is critiquing some position or trying to add something new to the field. In this volume, I will try to present an objective, balanced treatment of various positions, but no doubt some of my preferences will bleed through – and that's okay. This book is not a compendium of truths for you to accept. It is a *tool* to help you develop your *own* thoughts whether they agree with mine or not.

Now, that we know what a philosophy of something is, what is *philosophy of religion*? Philosophy of religion consists of identifying some of the most basic concepts, positions, issues, and controversies in or about religion. A "comparative philosophy of religion" would examine such things in all the great world religions, not just Judaism, Christianity, and Islam, but also Taoism, Confucianism, Hinduism, Buddhism, Sikhism, etc. But alas, that would make this book too long for its intended purpose and it would push me beyond my current levels of expertise regarding Asian religions. Consequently, in this volume we will focus on philosophical issues in Judaism, Christianity, and Islam, with a few references to other religions – though I encourage you to study Asian religions (one good reason to do that is because they are no longer confined to Asia – there is a Buddhist temple in my small southern hometown!).

It is important to note that *philosophy of religion* is not the same thing as *comparative religion* or a study of *world religions*. The fields of world religions and comparative religion examine the history of a religion, its founders and formative figures, its rituals, symbols, dress, architecture, geographical distribution, etc. Our focus will be limited to philosophical issues. What those issues are you will find out soon. Meanwhile, keep in mind also that philosophy is not the same thing as *theology*. Theology is the clarification of the beliefs of a specific religion, plus a defense of those beliefs; it is conducted by specially trained intellectuals *within* that religion. Moreover, theology is usually based on some purported source of *divine revelation*, such as the Bible, the Koran, the Book of Mormon, or the Vedas of Hinduism – a source that is taken as authoritative within that religion. Philosophy of religion, by contrast, does not require that one belong to the religion being examined, nor does philosophy appeal to divine revelation for authority. Philosophy is limited to using the tools of reason and experience that are common to everyone.

Speaking of experience, obviously someone is going to be better prepared to be a "philosopher of" something if he or she, in addition to studying philosophy, is intimately familiar with the area of activity to be examined. A philosopher of art, for example, will have a richer, more sensitive background for doing philosophy of art if he or she has been an artist or studied art history. As a philosopher of religion I, in addition to a Ph.D. in philosophy from Southern Illinois University, have a Master of Divinity degree in ministerial studies from Yale Divinity School, served full-time in the ministry before going to graduate school in philosophy, taught basic religion courses, as well as basic and advanced philosophy courses, have remained involved with religion in various ways over the decades, and philosophy of religion has been my specialty for forty years.

Now, in our "passionate, systematic pursuit of knowledge of the real and the good," let's begin to identify and explore some of the philosophical concepts, positions, issues, and controversies in western religion. We will pursue this objective by means of the various chapters that follow. Let's take a quick look at their contents before we begin.

In chapter 1, we will examine features that are common to nearly all religions; then we will formulate from our observations a working definition of religion to keep in mind as we proceed through the rest of the book. Having gotten a deeper sense of what religion is about, we will in Chapter 2 explore six conceptions of God that have been influential in western, and to some extent, eastern, religions. We will culminate this survey with a widely influential *philosophical* conception of God. In chapter 3, we will examine a wide range of characteristics or attributes that are typically ascribed to God – and we will discover that some of these attributes are controversial, even contradictory, and lead to puzzling questions about the nature of God. Having in Chapters 2 and 3 gotten a rather sophisticated grasp of the nature of God, in Chapter 4 we will ask how (and even whether) it is possible for human language to describe God. After all, human language developed to describe the things of *this* world – physical things and subjective experiences – so we can't ignore questions as to how our language can possibly describe anything other than the physical world and its contents.

Next we will examine arguments for and against the existence of God – which is what most students want to get to without all the preliminaries! First, though, in Chapter 5, we need to think carefully about what an argument is and how, for example, it is different from a discussion or a quarrel. Then in Chapters 6–10 we finally explore some of the most influential arguments *for* the existence of God, including the ontological argument, the cosmological argument, the teleological argument (with a side look at the relation of God to morality), and the argument from religious experience. Criticisms of those arguments will also be examined. In Chapters 11 and 12, we will examine arguments *against* the existence of God, including the most influential argument against the existence of God, namely, the argument from the existence of evil. Again, we will see what some critics of those arguments have to say. In Chapter 13, we will examine the issue of life after death and ask what bearing God has on that possibility. In Chapter 14, we will explore miracles, revelation, and prayer. Finally, in Chapter 15, we will examine whether evidence and arguments are necessary for belief in God to be rational. Perhaps faith and hope are viable foundations of religious life? Given all that you will be exposed to in the course of our time together, I suspect you will conclude with me that whatever conclusion we arrive at, it should be held with thoughtful, open-minded humility.

In closing this introduction, I mention that in addition to teaching many new concepts and positions to you, I want to equip you with valuable distinctions and new tools of thought that are useful outside of philosophy as well as in it, so from our study please try to take away a good grasp of these: the nature of a dilemma; the differences between univocal, equivocal, and analogical uses of language; the differences between a discussion, a quarrel, an argument, and a debate; the differences between possibility, plausibility, probability, and proof; the differences between necessary and sufficient conditions; Ockham's Razor; the principle of credulity; running out permutations; the principle of evidentialism; the differences between knowledge, belief, faith, and hope; and more. Now let's begin!

For Review, Reflection, and Discussion

1. What is philosophy? How is it different from what you thought it would be?
2. What is "philosophy of" something?
3. What is the something that you would most like to read a philosophy of?

For Further Reading

For an introduction to the basics of philosophy see Creel, Richard E., *Thinking Philosophically: An Introduction to Critical Reflection and Rational Dialogue* (Blackwell Publishers: 2006).

Chapter 1

What Is Religion?

The two main concerns of philosophy of religion are God and religion. In this chapter, we will focus on the nature of religion. Before we attempt to formulate a definition of religion, let's look at four of its major facets: creed, code, cult, and community. Notice the mneumonic device: 4 C's! (a mneumonic device is a strategy for helping you remember something). These four characteristics can be found in nearly everything that is identified as a religion. Ask yourself how well they fit with the religion with which you are most familiar. (I was alerted to these features by Peter Slater, who says in his *Dynamics of Religion* that a religion is "a personal way of life informed by traditional elements of creed, code, and cult and directed toward the realization of some transcendent end." He adds that "A personal way of life is both individual and communal" (Harper & Row, 1978, 6–7)).

1.1 Creed

A religious creed is a religion's way of summarizing, expressing, and transmitting in words its most important beliefs about reality and history. It is a religion's way of saying, "This is how we understand who we are, what our lives are about, and what reality is like."

Examples of creeds are the Shema in Judaism ("Hear O Israel, the Lord our God, the Lord is one," Deuteronomy 6:4); the Nicene Creed in Christianity; The four Noble Truths in Buddhism; and in Islam the statement that "There is no God but Allah, and Mohammed is His prophet."

Philosophy of Religion: The Basics, First Edition. Richard E. Creel.
© 2014 John Wiley & Sons, Inc. Published 2014 by John Wiley & Sons, Inc.

Why does a religion have a creed? Because a religion *is* in part a way of understanding reality. The creed of a religion provides people with a point of view to gather around; it provides them with ideas by means of which to identify themselves to one another and to outsiders; it provides outsiders with something to consider and decide about. Creeds are a way whereby members of a religion can express their agreements with one another and can discover their disagreements.

I know of no religion which does not provide or encourage a particular understanding of reality. However, different religions differ greatly with regard to how long and detailed their creeds are, and with regard to how completely and literally members and people who would be members are expected to take their creed. Roman Catholicism and conservative protestant churches stand at one extreme; they have very detailed creeds and expect them to be understood in a certain way and accepted completely. Liberal forms of Judaism and Christianity stand at the other extreme, having briefer creeds and a much more open attitude as to how they are to be understood and how completely one is expected to believe them.

1.2   Code

A religious code is a statement of what we as humans ought to do and ought not to do. Sometimes the parts of a code are very specific, such as the Biblical command that one should not mix the flesh of a calf with the milk of its mother (Exodus 23:19). Sometimes the parts of a code are very general: Love your neighbor as yourself (Leviticus 19:18).

Examples of religious codes are the 10 Commandments of Judaism (You shall not kill, steal, bear false witness, commit adultery, or covet your neighbor's possessions; Exodus 20); the Great Commandment of Christianity (You shall love the Lord your God with all your heart and soul and mind and strength and your neighbor as yourself; Mark 12: 29–31); and the Eightfold Path of Buddhism, plus the Buddhist command, "Don't cause suffering."

Why are there religious codes? Religion is concerned with action, as well as with belief. It is concerned with the living of life, as well as with the understanding of life. Just as no religion of which I am aware is unconcerned with helping the individual toward an understanding of the nature of reality, none is unconcerned with giving to the individual, or helping the individual develop, a set of principles according to which life can be lived in a moral and fulfilling way.

1.3 Cult

The cult aspect of religion does not necessarily have anything to do with bizarre, mysterious, or secret practices (though it may). Cult, as that word is used here, is simply the external aspect of religion whereby through symbols, rituals, ceremonies, music, architecture, clothing, hair styles, and more, a religion expresses its beliefs and values and the way it perceives and feels the world. By means of these symbols and practices, a religion tries to cultivate a vivid sense of the reality and presence of the sacred. These practices and symbols help focus and refocus the attention of members on the beliefs and values of the religion; they help bring young people and converts into the religion, and they identify the religion and its members to those who do not belong to it.

Examples are: Jewish circumcision of infant males; bar/bas mitzvah initiation of young people into Judaism; Christian baptism of infants or adults by immersion, pouring, or sprinkling; saying the Lord's Prayer together; confession of sins to a priest in Roman Catholicism; taking communion in Christianity; bowing to the ground in prayer (Islam); blowing the ram's horn to signal the beginning of Yom Kippur (Judaism); the whirling dance of the dervishes of Islam.

Why are there cultic practices? People have a need for structure, rhythm, texture, and focus in their lives, as opposed to disorganization, emptiness, and aimlessness. The daily, weekly, annual rites and celebrations of a religion help provide structure and rhythm to life. They give texture and qualitative richness to life. They help give one a sense of the reality and presence of the sacred. They give life a special feeling or texture (there is something it *feels* like to be a Southern Baptist or a Sikh or a Pure Land Buddhist). Cultic practices give people something to remember fondly and to look forward to (e.g., Christmas and Easter; Hanukkah and Passover). They help people focus on what the religion considers to be important, and they help people refocus on it after they have been diverted from it by the distractions, temptations, trials, failures, and tragedies of life.

With regard to these objectives, consider the impact of the daily prayers of a devout Muslim male who five times every day bows on his knees toward Mecca and prays to Allah; or consider the weekly worship and the annual holy days of Jews and Christians. Such practices and celebrations give to the individual and the community a sense of structure, cohesion, rhythm, and flow which keeps things in perspective from the point of view of the particular religion involved.

People also need rituals that help them achieve and maintain social solidarity with one another, and which give them identity as members of a special group. Consider again the dramatic influence of the Muslim practice of daily prayer. Five times every day every practicing Muslim male knows that he is joining with millions of other Muslims who are bowing and praying to Allah; indeed, there is a continual bowing of millions of Muslims as the earth rotates on its axis; the individual Muslim male can sense himself as part of a continuous wave of worshippers – a wave that never stops. (The wave at a football game is nothing compared to the wave of Islam. The Muslim "wave" goes on 24 hours a day, every day of the year!)

Finally, I mention that the *symbols* of a religion can enhance the significance of life, giving to life a sense of depth or transcendence or mystery or richness that is foreign to the secular point of view. Further, these symbols, as external artifacts, can visually remind people in moving ways of the beliefs and values of their religion.

Examples of religious symbols are the Star of David and the yarmulke (Judaism), the cross (Christianity), the yin/yang symbol (Taoism), and the lotus flower (Buddhism).

Religious *rites of passage* are symbolic acts that honor important events in life, such as birth, maturity, marriage, ordination, and death, from the point of view of the religion. Examples are Christian baptism of infants and Jewish bar mitzvah of mature boys.

1.4 Community

Nearly all religions are highly communal, recognizing and emphasizing the social needs of individuals and bringing them into relation with one another. However, the ways in which the individuals in religions are organized vary greatly, ranging from very hierarchical forms to nonhierarchical forms.

Why is there communal organization in religions? *First*, there needs to be some way of exercising authority within a community so as to define its essence and make decisions. If an organization doesn't stand for something, then it stands for nothing, in which case, it isn't really an organization. *Second*, people need companionship, friendship, and a nourishing web of social relationships. We find these kinds of relationships most readily with people with whom we are like-minded. With such people we can relax, feel accepted, and share our thoughts and feelings because we are bound together by common beliefs and values. The members of a religious community will not agree on everything, but they agree on what they consider most important, and that helps keep disagreements among them from becoming disagreeable or destructive. (Episcopalians have a saying: "Agree on essentials; disagree on nonessentials; be charitable in all things.")

Third, religious communities provide religious *education* to children and outsiders, helping to form their values and their understanding of themselves, other people, and the world. *Fourth*, being an organized community provides a religion with a more effective means of outreach – whether to share the good news that they believe their religion contains or to help those in need of charitable aid. *Fifth*, many people find that communal worship and prayer (worship and prayer with others) contain special values in addition to the values of solitary prayer, meditation, or worship.

Some people try to reduce religion to one or the other of the preceding four aspects of religion. For example, some think of religion solely in terms of beliefs. "A religion," they say, "is just a bunch of beliefs." Other people think of religion as "morality tinged by emotion." They emphasize the code aspect of religion – sometimes parodying religion as "just a bunch of rules to live by." Still others think of religion in terms of bizarre or boring practices. Finally, some think of religion as just a kind of social organization.

I believe that each of those ways of portraying religion is misleading and inadequate. Anyone who thinks of religion in only one of those ways will have a one-dimensional understanding of a four-dimensional object. To be sure, the four dimensions are combined in different proportions in different religions. For example, the cultic aspect is especially prominent in Eastern Orthodox Churches. The creedal aspect is especially prominent in Roman Catholicism. The code aspect is especially prominent in Orthodox Judaism. The communal aspect is especially prominent in liberal Protestantism. But every religion is concerned with reality, morality, the texture, flow, and rhythm of life, and the solidarity of people with one another. To fail to notice and appreciate any of those four facets of a religion would be to fail to appreciate the richness of religion in its most enduring and influential forms.

1.5   Toward a Definition of Religion

Before attempting to formulate a definition of religion, let's think about the religious search that leads to the emergence of religion. The religious search is motivated by discontentment with our lives. It is a search for something to liberate, integrate, elevate, and transform our lives. Paul Tillich, a twentieth-century philosophical theologian, said that the religious search is a search for that which is ultimately real and ultimately valuable because only that which is ultimately real and ultimately valuable is worthy of our whole-hearted, unqualified devotion and can unify and transform our lives in the ways we most deeply desire. *Religion* is a response to the religious search. It is an answer to the haunting spiritual questions and unhappiness that motivate the religious search. Religion *interprets* the nature of spiritual unhappiness, *identifies* the cause or causes of it, *affirms* that the problem can be overcome, and *sets forth* a way of life whereby spiritual unhappiness can be overcome and spiritual peace can be found. The nature and cause of spiritual unhappiness is, of course, understood in different ways in different religious traditions. In Biblical traditions, spiritual unhappiness is often understood as alienation from our Creator, resulting from sin or rebellion against God. In Hinduism, it is often understood as alienation from one's true self, caused by ignorance of who one truly is. In Buddhism, it is often understood as the unhappiness caused by craving things that cannot satisfy us. In naturalistic traditions, it is often understood as resulting from a lack of a sense of worthy things to live for.

Keeping the preceding analysis in mind, I would like to articulate a definition of religion for your consideration. Keep in mind, however, that there is no universally accepted definition of religion that I can just hand to you. Any definition of religion will be controversial, including mine. But to understand ourselves and humankind better, we need to try to understand religion better, so what I propose is to provide you with a working explanation and definition of religion which you can accept, reject, or modify as you see fit. Before I begin, recall Peter Slater's definition, given at the beginning of this chapter: a religion is "a personal way of life informed by traditional elements of creed, code, and cult and directed toward the realization of some transcendent end." Then consider this definition by Erich Fromm, who says that a religion is "any system of thought and action shared by a group that gives to the individual a frame of orientation and an object of devotion" (*Psychoanalysis and Religion* [Bantam Books: 1950], p. 22).

Now I want to summarize some of the preceding points with a definition that I hope you find illuminating and helpful: A religion is a way of understanding, feeling, and living life that consists of (i) *beliefs about* the nature of one's self, others, nature, history, and ultimate reality; (ii) *belief in* something or someone thought to be the highest good; (iii) *a way of life* expressive of how one should live one's life given one's beliefs about reality and the highest good; and (iv) *stories, symbols, and practices* that are intended to help the individual, the community of believers, and outside seekers to achieve, remain, and progress in appropriate relationships to that which is believed to be the highest good. The preceding is "quite a mouthful," but if you read it slowly and thoughtfully several times, I think you will begin to get a rich sense of the various aspects of religion and how they function in human life. Meanwhile, for a briefer definition try this: *religion is a way of thinking and living that involves devotion to a supreme being or value.*

By the way, in my longer definition I have spoken about "the highest good" rather than "God" because there are, as we will soon see, two basic kinds of religion: naturalistic and supernaturalistic. Naturalism is the belief that nothing exists beyond nature. *Naturalistic religions* agree that nothing exists beyond nature, but they also hold that nature itself or certain parts or possibilities of nature are sacred and should be treated with reverence and devotion. *Supernaturalistic* religions hold that there is some being, force, realm, or dimension that transcends nature and gives it its meaning. The opposite of religion in either of the preceding forms is usually called "secularism," which holds that nothing exists beyond nature, and nothing in nature is sacred or worthy of worship or single-minded devotion. Rather, the secularist holds, there are various limited goods in life that compete with one another for our attention – food, shelter, health, family, friends, work, freedom, creativity, etc.

Now we turn our primary focus from religion to God, but the two will continue to be closely related. As we go along ask yourself how different conceptions of God lead to different forms of religion, and how different forms of religion lead to different conceptions of God.

1.6   Ze, Zer, Mer

As we begin to focus on God in the rest of this book, you will find me using three new words for a good reason. Other than the male pronouns "he," "his," and "him," there are no singular pronouns in the English language that are commonly used without regard to gender to refer to humans, androgenous creatures (such as we find in science fiction and perhaps will find in fact on other planets), and persons without a gender (such as God and angels, according to some important religious traditions). For excellent reasons, this practice of using male pronouns generically is becoming less and less common. Indeed, some individuals and professional societies have begun to use "she" and "her" generically, rather than "he," "his," and "him." That change has been fitting and illuminating, but ultimately it suffers from the same problem from which the generic use of male pronouns suffers, viz., it is grammatically incorrect and can be confusing or misleading. Efforts have been made to avoid the unfair and ungrammatical nature of the preceding alternatives, but they have proven awkward and do not accommodate nongendered persons. To be sure, awkward or ungrammatical language is better than language that unjustly offends people, and especially women, who have borne the brunt of linguistic and other injustices for millennia. Fortunately, there is, I think, a better way.

To get beyond the preceding difficulties, we need to come up with a set of nongendered personal pronouns that are widely adopted, and the sooner the better. More specifically, we need to go beyond: (i) the confusion and incorrectness of using male pronouns generically for all persons, for example, "Everyone who pays his taxes by check should write his social security number on his check" (ditto for the generic use of female pronouns); (ii) the awkwardness of written and spoken locutions such as "he/she" and "he or she," for example, "Everyone who pays his or her taxes by check should put his or her social security number on his or her check" or "Everyone who pays her/his taxes by check should put her/his social security number on her/his check" (also, this locution does not accommodate nongendered persons such as God; of course God doesn't pay taxes, but he/she should); (iii) the incorrectness of using a plural pronoun to refer to an individual, for example, "When an individual is in distress, we should help them"; and (iv) the incorrectness of referring to nongendered persons, such as the God of monotheism, as "he" or "she" or "it," for example, "If we are faithful to God, he will bless us."

To capture in language the richness of actuality and possibility, we need non-gendered personal pronouns that refer indifferently to persons whether they are female, male, or – as in the case of God, some angels, robots, science-fiction creatures, and perhaps extra-terrestrials – none of the aforementioned. I propose "ze," "zer," and "mer" as non-gendered personal pronouns for general use. I propose "ze" for the nominative case, "zer" for the possessive case, and "mer" for the accusative case. "Mer" is a blend of the last letter of "hi*m*" and the last two letters of "he*r*," "ze" is a blend of "*s*he" and "h*e*" ("se" with a modification to be explained); "zer" is a blend of "his" and "h*er*" ("ser" with a modification to be explained).

"Z" has been substituted for the "s" in "se" and "ser" to avoid such homophones as "see" and "sea," in the case of "se," and "sir" in the case of "ser." Using these new pronouns and making the appropriate substitutions, the illustrative sentences earlier would read: "If we are faithful to God, ze will bless us"; "Everyone who pays zer taxes by check should write zer social security number on zer check"; "When an individual is in distress, we should help mer."

"Ze," "zer," and "mer" may seem awkward now, but if we use them regularly and the usage becomes widespread, they will soon seem quite natural. Meanwhile, we will have enriched the categories of our language and improved our ability to communicate clearly, precisely, and grammatically. "She," "her," "he," "his," and "him" should, of course, continue to be used when appropriate. "Ze," "zer," and "mer" will supplement them, not supplant them.

To close on a personal note: in my philosophy of religion courses I explain these terms to my students, and then I use them when I speak of God, which of course I do a lot. My students are not required to use these terms, yet many of them are intrigued, attracted, and choose to do so, at first with self-conscious good-humor. My female students seem especially appreciative of an opportunity to speak of God without being forced to use a gendered pronoun or an awkward strategy designed to evade the use of pronouns altogether. Similar benefits accrue for general discussions of the nature of a person, whether in philosophy of religion, philosophy of mind, or other areas of philosophy (must a person be gendered?). Hence, even if "ze," "zer," and "mer" do not enter into common usage (obviously the odds are against that), nonetheless they can be very useful in religious and philosophical discussions.

For Review, Reflection, and Discussion

1. Having read this chapter, are you satisfied with my definition of religion? If not, how would you change or replace it, and why? (Note: giving examples is not to give a definition. To say, "Religion is Judaism, Christianity, Islam, Hinduism, etc." would be to gives examples of religion, not to give a definition of religion. To define something is to state the essence of it – an essence by means of which genuine examples can be identified and pretenders can be excluded. In terms of terminology to be discussed more later, what are the *necessary* and *sufficient* conditions of something being a religion? Or is the designation of something as a religion completely conventional or arbitrary?)
2. What would you add to or subtract from the four aspects of religion?
3. Is there a hierarchy of importance among the four aspects of religion? If so, what do you think is their order of importance and why?
4. Could a group without a creed, or a philosophy of life, be a religion? If yes, how so? Can you identify one? If no, then is a creed or a philosophy of life a necessary condition of something being a religion?
5. Some people think that religion is an effort to respond to spiritual unhappiness. How is spiritual unhappiness different from other kinds of unhappiness?
6. What is now your understanding of the differences between philosophy and religion? How are they alike?

For Further Reading

Holley, David, *Meaning and Mystery* (Wiley-Blackwell: 2010). Holley explains religions as "life-orienting stories" that should be judged not on the basis of objective, public evidence but on the basis of how well they help us understand, integrate, and live our lives.

Fromm, Erich, *Psychoanalysis and Religion* (Yale University Press: 1950, or Bantam Books: 1967). Sensitive, helpful insights from a philosophical psychoanalyst.

Noss, David S., *A History of World Religions*, 12th ed. (Prentice-Hall: 2007). This is one of the most inclusive and detailed surveys of world religions in one volume.

Sharma, Arvind, ed., *Our Religions* (HarperCollins: 1993). Each chapter is on a different religion by an expert from that tradition. Sharma writes about Hinduism.

Slater, Peter, *The Dynamics of Religion* (Harper & Row: 1978). Readable. Insightful. Brief.

Smith, Huston, *The World's Religions, Revised and Updated*, (HarperOne: 2009). Smith is a marvelous writer and also has an illustrated version of his *World's Religions*.

Chapter 2

Six Conceptions of God

In the nineteenth century, the philosopher Friedrich Nietzsche said "God is dead!" In the twentieth century, the philosopher and playwright Jean-Paul Sartre took up Nietzsche's chant: "God is dead!" When people say "God is dead" I am reminded of the saying, "The king is dead. Long live the king!" What that meant in ages past was that as soon as the king died, a new person automatically became king by inheritance, so as long as there was an heir there was always a king. Similarly, it seems that in many cases as soon as a conception of God becomes discredited or unacceptable, a new conception of God emerges to replace it. Rumor once spread that the American humorist Mark Twain had died, but he hadn't. In his humorous way, he corrected the error by making the following public statement: "Reports of my death have been greatly exaggerated." Similarly, reports of the death of God have been greatly exaggerated. Belief in God has been around for thousands of years and gives no signs of vanishing. To be sure, participation in institutional Judaism and Christianity has declined considerably over the last century, but belief in God has not declined at the same rate and seems to be somewhat independent of that decline.

2.1 Experiential Sources of Concepts of God

Before looking at six diverse conceptions of God, let's think about how the concept of God might have arisen and why it has been so resilient. What is it that accounts for the emergence, survival, and vitality of the

Philosophy of Religion: The Basics, First Edition. Richard E. Creel.
© 2014 John Wiley & Sons, Inc. Published 2014 by John Wiley & Sons, Inc.

idea of God? Many believers say, "Just as we need names for trees and dogs and lakes and hills, we need a name for God. To be sure, God is not a physical object, like the Rock of Gibraltar, that we can just point to and say, 'We need a name for *that*.' But God has *revealed* merself to us in various clear and dramatic ways, so we need a name for God just as surely as we need a name for the Rock of Gibraltar."

Perhaps the revelatory explanation of names for God is true, but even apart from revelation we can, philosophically, account for fundamental aspects of the concept of God by reflecting on certain human experiences. Insofar as ideas of God can be explained in terms of human experience, they are usually based on one or more of the following concepts, each of which is deeply rooted in human experience and very important to us: being, power, knowledge, goodness, and companionship.

First, there are people who think of God as the supreme *being* or the ultimate reality. To them, the idea of God is the idea of whatever has always existed and will always exist; it is the idea of an eternal being that stands in sharp contrast to all of the other beings with which we are familiar – beings which are finite and transient, which come into existence and go out of existence, whether soap bubbles or mountains. Along this line, Paul Tillich said that God is not *a* being but is *the Ground of Being*. God is the eternal source of being which stands beyond the realm of finite beings. God is Being-Itself.

Second, there are those who think of God as the supreme *power*. God is the one that is ultimately or most fully responsible for all that exists in the universe. God is the creator, sustainer, mover, healer, shaker, and destroyer. God is the one most able to help or hurt us. This idea is dominant in the Hindu conception of Shiva.

Third, there are those who think of God as the supreme *knower*. God is the one, and the only one, who knows all possibilities, all actualities, past, present, and future. We humans do not like ignorance. We like to think that even when *we* do not know the truth about something, *someone* does. Here enters the idea of God as the one who knows the truth even when we do not. Belief in God assures believers that there is an explanation for all things and that, therefore, we should never despair in our search for answers. All things do make sense. God understands even when we do not.

This belief is one of the ways in which western religion encouraged the development of modern science: the world is the creation of an intelligent being, and that being has given us intelligence by which to understand how ze has structured the world. Indeed, Enlightenment thinkers in the seventeenth and eighteenth centuries thought of science as a study of the mind of God. By means of scientific exploration, they thought of themselves as "thinking the thoughts of God," discovering how God decided to structure the world.

Fourth, there are those who think of God as the supreme *good*. Their idea of God is the idea of objective goodness, of perfect goodness, of something which or someone who can guide us to what is truly good and truly right. It is the idea of that which is worthy of our ultimate commitment and wholehearted devotion.

Fifth, there are those who think of God primarily as the supreme *companion*. This idea of God is the idea and experience of a spiritual being who is always with us, to strengthen us, encourage us, comfort us, grieve with us, and rejoice with us. As one of my students once wrote, "I like the idea of having someone to talk to and watch over me."

Now I want to make some observations about the kind of religion that each of these ideas of God can to lead to when it is taken in isolation from the other ideas.

The idea of God as the *supreme being* and nothing more tends to lead to a sense of awe and mystery about God together with the idea that we can know nothing about God by means of reason except that God exists. Hence, according to this approach, we should humbly acknowledge the reality of God, but we should not presume to know *what* God is like or what the *will* of God is – unless God *reveals* zer nature and will to us. Apart from revelation we know nothing about God except that God exists. (We will return to this idea in Chapter 4 when we discuss the *via negativa*, and in Chapter 14 we will discuss revelation at more length.)

The idea of God as the *supreme power* tends to lead to a calculating religious attitude according to which one tries to find out the will of God and do it to avoid harm and be rewarded. This view of God or the gods can be seen clearly in ancient religions in which rituals and sacrifices were aimed at getting God or the gods to help worshippers or to refrain or cease from harming them. Insofar as such practices involve rituals that have to be performed in very exact ways by learned people (priests), we see a forerunner of the scientific practice of looking for things we can do that will get the results we want. This is religion-as-technology.

The idea of God as *supreme knower* tends, when taken in isolation, to lead to fatalism in people who assume that since God knows every-thing, therefore God also knows the future, and therefore the future is unchangeable and there is nothing we can do to change what God knows will happen. This notion tends to lead to various efforts, by prayer, sacrifice, rituals, etc., to gain knowledge from God that we desire and cannot gain otherwise – knowledge about when or how we will die, what will happen in a certain battle, whether we will marry, etc.

The idea of God as *supreme goodness*, when taken in isolation from the notion of power, tends to lead to the conviction that although God is entirely worthy of our reverence and is our best source of knowledge about the good, God has no power other than the power of inspira-tion. Hence, although God is real, God cannot help us except by providing guidance and inspiration; other than that we must help ourselves.

Finally, the idea of God as *supreme companion* can lead to a trivial-ized notion of God as a pal or buddy who is simply a very supportive and indulgent friend. This idea of God, taken in isolation, tends to lack a notion of the awesomeness and mystery of God, and of the high, stern expectations that God may have of us. An example of this atti-tude can be found in a statement attributed to the German poet Heinrich Heine. It is said that when he was on his deathbed a friend urged Heine to make his peace with God. Heine replied that he did not need to beg God for forgiveness: "God will forgive me. That is his job." (*"Dieu me pardonnera. C'est son metier."*) (Heine knew French as well as German.)

There is, of course, no single conception of God that everyone shares, but the conceptions of God in the great world religions usually contain all or most of the preceding elements – and perhaps that is why those religions have been so enduring and influential. But even in religions which have a complex conception of God, it is not unusual to find that one or two of its elements is emphasized more than the others – and that is one of the things that gives a religion its distinctiveness. Indeed, it is interesting and revealing to examine each religion or denomination of a religion to see how many of the pre-ceding elements are included in its conception of God and how prominent a role each element plays in the thoughts, feelings, and practices of its members.

2.2 Six Conceptions of God

After the preceding introduction to five *sources* of the idea of God, now let's examine six *conceptions* of God, some of which are of ancient origin, some of which are of contemporary origin, but all of which are still attractive and influential. I will use a distinction between "immanent" and "transcendent" to help distinguish these views from one another. To say that God is *immanent* is to say that God is involved in the world in some way or interacts with the world in some way, such as answering prayers or causing miracles. To say that God is *transcendent* is to say that God can exist *apart* from the world. Note that these words, as defined here, are not opposites of one another. God might be both immanent and transcendent: God might exist independently of the world yet involve merself in it. Indeed, God is portrayed this way throughout the stories in the Bible. (Finally, don't confuse the following three words with one another: Immanent (within)/Imminent (about to occur soon)/Eminent (highly regarded). They have similar pronunciations but very different meanings.)

2.3 Religious Naturalism

Religious naturalism claims that God is *immanent but not transcendent*. God is immanent in the world only as an ideal in people's minds or as a force in nature. Hence, if we define an "atheist" as "one who does not believe in a being who transcends the physical world" then religious naturalists are atheists even though they consider themselves to be religious. (Some such persons can be found in the Unitarian-Universalist Fellowship.) Perhaps the first great modern religious naturalist was Ludwig Feuerbach, a nineteenth-century German. Feuerbach said, "God is man's 'truth,' i.e., God is what man ought to be. Therefore we ought to strive towards godliness, for in and through God man aims at his true self." Also, "God is the essence of man viewed as absolute truth, i.e., as the fulfillment of what is truly human" (*The Essence of Christianity*, abridged version, Chapter 2).

Feuerbach's point is that our ideas of God and the gods are important because it has been in our thinking about God and the gods that we have been formulating our ideas of our ideal potentialities as human beings – though for centuries we did not realize that was what we were doing. At first we thought we were speaking of a personal being or beings who transcend this world, but we were not. The truth about humankind's ideal potentialities is to be found in our ideas of the *attributes* of God, attributes such as supreme knowledge, goodness, justice, power, friendship, and being. (In polytheism, which is belief in many gods, each god tends to be associated primarily with one attribute – Zeus with power; Aphrodite with love, Minerva with wisdom, etc.). What is important about God is not whether God exists (Feuerbach thought ze did not). What is important is whether we take seriously the attributes of God – whether we strive "to be perfect as our heavenly Father is perfect" – in justice, compassion, knowledge, power, etc.

John Dewey, an early twentieth century American philosopher (1859–1952), followed in Feuerbach's footsteps by denying the existence of a transcendent God but affirming the historical and social importance of the *idea* of God. In Dewey's words, God is "the unity of all ideal ends arousing us to desire and actions." God is "the active relation between the ideal and the actual." (*A Common Faith*, Yale University Press, pp. 42, 51) The idea of the Kingdom of God is really the idea of a perfect society, a society that must be constructed by humans, not by a supernatural being, and created here on earth, not in heaven. Once we realize this, the idea of the Kingdom of God inspires us to focus on this life rather than on a fictitious next life. It inspires us to understand prayer as a way of focusing ourselves and gathering strength to do what needs to be done by ourselves, rather than as an appeal to a fictitious being. As a Unitarian-Universalist aphorism puts it: "Prayer doesn't change things. Prayer changes people, and people change things."

Finally, Henry Nelson Wieman, a mid twentieth century American philosopher (1884–1975), used the word "God" to refer to the *natural force* that creates and enriches human consciousness. Note: for Wieman God is not just an idea; God is real, but God is a natural force not a transcendent being. Wieman adds that this natural force or source of energy and guidance is not a personal being and may not be eternal or omnipotent. But for now it is real because it sustains us, enriches and transforms us, so it is what we should call "God." We should seek it out and learn how to gain the most benefit from it, just as we are doing with other natural forces such as electricity and nuclear fission. But it is not a force that we can manipulate. Rather, it is a force to which we must submit ourselves in order that it might transform us for the good in ways in which we cannot transform ourselves. (See Wieman, *The Source of Human Good*; William Rowe, *Philosophy of Religion*, Chapter 13; M. Scott Peck, *The Road Less Traveled*.)

2.4 Pantheism

(Benedict Spinoza; G.W.F. Hegel; Shankara and Advaita Vedanta Hinduism)

According to pantheism, God is neither immanent nor transcendent. God is the creator and that which is created.

According to pantheism, God is *identical* to all of reality; God and the world are one and the same thing ("world" in philosophy ordinarily stands not just for the planet Earth but for the entire universe). The word "pantheism" literally means "all" (pan) "God" (theism). All is God and God is all. The world is God, and God is the world. This position implies that God neither transcends the world, that is, God does not exist independently of the world and did not create it from nothing, nor is God immanent in the world in the sense that a stone or a tree is in the world. Consider that water and H_2O are the same thing. Therefore, water cannot transcend H_2O. Similarly, it would be a mistake to say that water is *in* H_2O. Water is H_2O and H_2O is water. In like manner, God is not *in* the world; God is the world.

Note also that according to pantheism, and unlike the religious naturalism of Feuerbach and Dewey, the word "God" refers to an *actuality* rather than merely to an *ideal possibility*, and unlike Wieman, the pantheist's God is not a force *within* nature (like wind or waves); it *is* Nature – and Nature is all there is to reality. However, you might be wondering, "What's the difference between saying that God is the world and saying that there is no God and that only the world exists? Isn't it the case that if God is the world, then there is no God? So isn't pantheism atheistic?" Not really. There is a profound difference in belief and attitude between the pantheist and the secular atheist. The pantheist feels that the Nature is sacred and should be revered; it inspires a sense of awe before the divine. The pantheist believes that the world is not a mere mass of mindless matter and energy but is, rather, something which is fundamentally spiritual rather than material. Nature is considered to be divine.

The former description primarily fits western pantheism. Some pantheists, however, believe that matter is an illusion and only pure spirit exists. The world of separate objects and things, they say, is a dream from which we wake up when we become enlightened. See, for example, the Advaita Vedanta tradition of Hinduism. An implication of Hindu pantheism is that every individual is identical with God. The reasoning goes like this: God and the world are identical. I am part of the world. Therefore I am identical to God. Therefore I am God, and it is an illusion to think I am not. Breaking free from that illusion and realizing one's oneness with *Brahman* (the Hindu word for the absolute) is the way to salvation. Hence, the goal of life is to realize one's identity with God and thereby enter pure, eternal bliss. (This conclusion is, of course, blasphemous to Jews, Christians, and Muslims, who believe that God existed before the world existed and could have continued to exist without ever creating a world.) Hindu pantheism also means that I am identical to you and you to me, since we are all identical to God, and only God exists. Such a belief has obvious ethical implications for how we should treat one another, all animals, and nature in general.

A western version of pantheism was set forth brilliantly by G.W.F. Hegel, a nineteenth-century German philosopher. Hegel reasoned that the whole of reality is a single individual beyond which nothing else does exist or could possibly exist, since the whole of reality includes everything that is. Hegel considered the whole of reality to be a single Absolute Spirit that is eternally in the process of actualizing its potentialities. Therefore, all things that exist at this moment, including you and me and the planets and stars, are forms that the Absolute (God) is taking at this moment in order to actualize itself. But the potentialities of the Absolute are infinite, so it can never actualize all its possibilities. Rather, it actualizes its potentialities on higher and higher levels of achievement for ever and ever – and that is why history shows progress and is evolutionary. History is the creative activity of an infinitely resourceful spirit.

According to Hegel reality is a supreme mind aspiring to ever and ever higher levels of achievement. To be sure, you and I and each planet and star will eventually perish, but we and they will be succeeded by new individuals as the Absolute continues to actualize and evolve itself through time. The *forms* that the Absolute takes disappear, but the Absolute never does – just as the different shapes that a lump of clay is molded into disappear while the lump of clay continues to exist and always takes some shape (as does the Absolute). But note that you and I are not things that the Absolute has *created*, as though we were separate from the Absolute; rather, we are forms that the Absolute is taking at this moment; we *are* the Absolute as it has created itself at this moment and is moving toward the next moment.

2.5　Panentheism (Process Theism)

God is immanent but not transcendent.

For the *pan*theist, God is all that exists (remember: "pan" means "all"); God is the absolute. For the pan*en*theist, there is more to reality than God. Reality (the Absolute) consists of God *and* the world. God is different from the world and the world is different from God. God and the world are not identical. They are distinct from one another, but God is "in" all of the world.

However, according to panentheists, God and the world are *not separable*. God could not exist apart from the world, and the world could not exist apart from God. God and the world need one another. The world would not be a *uni*verse without a central organizing force within it; rather, it would be chaos. God is necessary to bring about the unity and orderliness that make the difference between chaos and cosmos. Similarly, God is by nature a creator, so God would not be God without a creation, that is, without a world. The world gives God something to create from, to work with, to transform. From this we can infer that since God has always existed, so has the world, and since the universe has always existed, so has God. Hence, God both is and is not the creator of the universe – as a sculptor is and is not the creator of a statue (the sculptor creates the *form* of the statue but not the *matter* of which the statue is made).

According to panentheism, God did not start the world or create it at some point in time. God did not create the world *ex nihilo* (from nothing) any more than an artist creates an artwork from nothing. An artist creates a work of art by acting upon a medium that already exists, such as wood or marble or canvas. Similarly, God "creates" the world only in the sense of transforming a world that already exists. God "creates" the world by acting upon the things that constitute it. (The idea of creating something from absolutely nothing is, according to the panentheists, incoherent, i.e., does not make sense. Nothing has no potentiality from which anything could be created. One thing can be created only from something else.) Furthermore, just as the sculptor does not create the characteristics of the wood upon which ze works but, rather, has to take advantage of those characteristics or work around them, God does not create all of the characteristics of the world. Rather, ze has to work with things as they are and from them try to bring out the best results possible.

To summarize, God is by nature a creator, and so God could not be God without a world to transform any more than a human could be an artist without a medium to act upon. God has always been acting upon the world, and the world has always been responding to and influencing God. God and the world have both always existed and been acting upon and influencing one another. Their relationship is a two-way street. God and the world are the ultimate partners in the dance of creativity, and the world influences God as much as God influences the world. So although God is distinct from the world and is immanent in the world, God does not transcend the world. The world is just as immanent in God as God is in the world. God and the world are wholly involved in one another.

Now let's turn to one of the most distinctive and intriguing aspects of panentheism. According to panentheism the world (as distinguished from God) consists of nothing but finite individuals, each of which has some degree of freedom to choose among alternatives. Consequently, *reality*, which consists of God *and* the individuals that make up the world, reality is a society of free individuals. God has the most freedom of any individual. Other individuals have different degrees of freedom, but every individual has some options and makes choices. For example, a human has a wider range of freedom than does an eagle, but the eagle, too, has some options, including some that humans do not have, such as flying unaided and strafing the water to catch fish.

God is related to the individuals that constitute the world in a manner analogous to the way in which a political leader in a democracy is related to its citizens, or an orchestra leader is related to the members of the orchestra. God does bring order into the world, but like the politician in a democracy or the orchestra leader, ze cannot do it by coercion. Zer only power is indirect, such as the power of persuasion or example. But persuasion and example can, of course, be very powerful. Consider the influence of Gandhi or Hitler, Buddha or John F. Kennedy, Mother Theresa or Martin Luther King, Jr. As Alfred North Whitehead put it, "The power of God is the worship he inspires" (*Science and the Modern World*, Chapter 12, last paragraph). It is only through the devotion which God inspires that ze has influence upon the world. Hence, the extent of God's influence in the world depends on the degree to which creatures follow the inspirations they receive from God.

God does not exercise zer power by giving speeches, however. God influences the citizens of the universe by holding visions of truth, beauty, and goodness before them – by attempting to touch them in ways that inspire them to freely decide to seek what is true, create what is beautiful, and do what is good. God's power is the power of inspiration, not of threat or coercion. "God's role [in the universe] is not the combat of productive force with productive force, of destructive force with destructive force; it lies in the patient operation of the over-powering rationality of his conceptual harmonization [of all things]. He does not create the world, he saves it: or, more accurately, he is the poet of the world with tender patience leading it by his vision of truth, beauty, and goodness" (*Process and Reality*, Part V, Chapter 2, Section 4). God has no body. God is pure spirit. Because God is not physical, God cannot physically coerce us or punish us or bully us, nor would ze want to. God does not act on the world by force and aggression. Ze can only influence our mind and heart and soul.

The preceding means there are strict limits to God's influence on the world. God cannot destroy the world or overrule the freedom of the individuals that make it up or send anyone to hell, as there is no life after death (according to Whitehead and Charles Hartshorne but not all panentheists). Any individual can always choose to ignore or resist God rather than follow zer leading. Nonetheless, God is always with us, calling and luring us to seek what is true, do what is good, and create what is beautiful, rejoicing with us in our joys, and abiding with us as a sympathetic companion when we suffer. Moreover, although there is no life after death for the creatures of the world, God, the only individual who will endure forever, will forever remember each of us and our contributions to the world – eternally remembering and cherishing the good that we do, eternally remembering and regretting our misdeeds and indifference. Consequently, Hartshorne has said, the most enduring contribution of our lives is to the joy or sorrow of God, who with deep and appropriate feelings eternally remembers each of us and the life we have led.

[A kind of panentheism can be found also in Plato's dialogue, *Timaeus*, in which he speaks of God as acting on eternal matter according to eternal forms, neither of which God created.]

2.6   Deism

God is transcendent but not immanent (John Toland, Voltaire, Jean-Jacques Rousseau, Immanuel Kant, Ben Franklin, Thomas Jefferson).

Deism has been around in various forms since ancient Greece, but it flourished in eighteenth-century Europe as a result of the emergence of modern science. Deism was an effort to bring religion in line with the emerging understanding of nature as governed wholly by natural laws. According to eighteenth century deism, God created the world from nothing (*ex nihilo*), set it running according to natural laws which ze created, gave us intelligence by means of which to discover and understand the laws of nature, gave us a sense of moral right and wrong by which to guide our behavior, and then "backed away" from the world to let it run on its own and to let us live our lives according to our own decisions. God is somewhat like a parent who sends a daughter or son to college and says, "I'll pay for you to go to college, but I'll not be involved or available. I've given you everything you need to be a successful college student; now you've got to live your life on your own and make your own decisions. All I ask is that you behave intelligently and morally. But do keep in mind that I will keep up with how you are doing, and one day I will ask you to account for how you have used the gifts that I have given to you!"

According to deism, then, since the creation of the world, God continues to maintain the world in existence, but ze is not involved in the world in any way. There are no miracles and never were. Belief in miracles is a result of ignorance and superstition. Moreover, God has not directly revealed merself to humans, as ze is said to have revealed merself to Adam and Eve in the Garden of Eden, for example, or to Moses on Mount Sinai. Furthermore, God does not answer prayers. Hence, petitionary prayers are a waste of effort (more about miracles, revelation, and prayer in Chapter 14). God's will is simply that we live our lives according to the faculty of intelligence and the sense of morality that ze has given us. Hence, science and morality are enough for the living of a good, God-approved life.

To be sure, God is *aware* of everything that goes on in the world, and God is great and generous, so prayers of praise and gratitude are appropriate, but they are not necessary to salvation. Moreover, institutional religion is not important, except insofar as it helps promote moral behavior. However, there is life after death, so obedience to the moral law of God is important because we will be judged by God and rewarded or punished based on how seriously we have taken our obligation to live according to God's moral law. But we will not be judged according to whether we have belonged to the right religion or worshipped in the right way. Rather, we will be judged on the basis of the universal principles of morality that God has implanted in all of our minds and hearts. (Theories of the relation of God and morality will be taken up in Chapter 9.)

Classical Theism: God is transcendent and immanent

1. biblical theism (based on revelation)
2. philosophical theism (based on reason).

2.7   Classical *Biblical* Theism is based on divine revelation

This is the position of many Jews, Christians, and Muslims (the Koran is the most important book of revelation to Muslims but they also believe that much in the Bible is divine revelation). Classical biblical theism might more helpfully be described as: "Historical Ethical Monotheism." Each of those three words needs to be elaborated.

Historical (God is fully involved in the beginning, the continuance, and the end of world history):

Creation (God transcends the world. That is, God exists outside or beyond the world.): God created the world, including the laws of nature, *ex nihilo* (out of nothing). (That is the traditional understanding of theologians, but recent biblical scholarship, such as in the Anchor Bible commentary on Genesis, points out that the doctrine of creation *ex nihilo* is nowhere affirmed explicitly in the Bible – which of course is not to say that that doctrine is not true, but if it is not true, that would favor the panentheist philosophy of God's creation of the world.)

Providence (God is immanent, i.e., involved in the world): God guides history, performs miracles, answers prayers, provides propositional revelations (i.e., literally speaks to some people, such as Moses and Isaiah, providing prophecies about the future and declarations, such as the Ten Commandments), and God causes religious experiences of different kinds, for example, God is experienced as companion, comforter, judge, forgiver, and majestic being.

Consummation: God will bring history to an end, resurrect the dead, judge all, and reward or punish appropriately.

Ethical:

God is morally good and demands moral behavior from us. Ze is not indifferent to how we live our lives (compare the ancient Greeks Aristotle and Epicurus who thought that God or the gods had better things to do than be concerned with us). God holds us responsible for how we live our lives. To be sure, God is merciful and forgiving. The opening words of the Koran are: "In the name of Allah, the merciful, the beneficent [gracious]." However, God is also demanding and zer mercy is not to be taken for granted. That would be an insult to God and a grievous mistake on our part. Hence, when Heinrich Heine quipped that he did not need to worry about God's forgiveness, "God will forgive me. That is his job!," Heine was stomping on thin ice!

Mono ("mono" means "one," "theos" means "God," so monotheism is belief in one and only one God):

God is absolutely unique. There is and can be only one God. The Bible says: "Thou shalt have no other Gods before me" (Exodus 20:3). There is also the Shema, "Hear, O Israel, the Lord our God, the Lord is One." (Deuteronomy 6:4) The Koran says "There is no God but Allah" (II.254; XVI.51). All of these statements represent an emphatic rejection of polytheism, which means belief in more than one god ("poly" means "many").

Theism: God is not an impersonal natural force (Wieman) or the tension that we feel between the ideal and the actual (Dewey) or merely an ideal conception in the minds of humans (Feuerbach). God is a personal being, an intelligent agent who considers alternatives, makes choices, and acts on them.

Readers who want to know more about theism that is based on revelation need to turn to the writings of the various religions that are based on revelation, writings such as the Torah of Judaism, The New Testament of Christianity, The Koran of Islam, the Bhagavadgita of Hinduism, the Book of Mormon, and Science and Health with Key to the Scriptures (by Mary Baker Eddy, the founder of Christian Science). Our job in philosophy is to see what human *reason* can reveal about God, so for the rest of this book, we turn our attention to philosophical theism.

2.8 Classical *Philosophical* Theism

To appreciate where philosophical theism is coming from or what it is about, let's first consider different ways to find out the nature of something:

1. Revelation and faith [Biblical theism]. God tells us how things are.
2. Observation and description. Our senses and introspection reveal how things are. This applies to physical objects and mental phenomena (such as emotions) that can be observed directly.
3. Observation and induction. From what our senses and introspection reveal directly we infer things that are not experienced directly. Consider detective work; for example, figuring out who committed a crime or who painted an old anonymous work of art.
4. Definition and deduction. We start with a definition or concept and then purely by means of reason infer conclusions from it. For example, if we start with the concept of a Euclidean triangle, then from it, by just thinking about it, we can figure out that the sum of the internal angles must always equal 180 degrees. If we reflect on the concept of a Euclidean chiliagon (a thousand sided figure with equal sides and angles) we can figure out what the degree of each angle must be. The typical way of exploring the concept of God in philosophy is this third way because the development of the idea of God over the centuries has been toward what Immanuel Kant called "a limiting ideal," that is, an idea of something which sets a limit because it cannot be surpassed. As a result of this kind of thinking, most philosophers have come to think of the concept of God as the concept of "a supremely perfect being" (René Descartes) or as "a being than which none greater can be conceived" (St. Anselm).

Here are some quotations to give you a taste of the kind of thinking that led to Anselm's and Descartes' definitions of God:

St. Anselm, *Proslogion*, Chapter 2: God is " something than which nothing greater can be thought." Chapter 15: "Therefore, O Lord,"

Anselm said in prayer, "not only are You that than which a greater cannot be thought, but You are also something greater than can be thought. For since something of this kind can be thought [viz., something which is greater than can be thought], if You were not this being then something greater than You could be thought – a consequence which is impossible." Translated by Hopkins and Richardson (Edwin Mellen Press: 1975).

Thomas Aquinas, *Summa Contra Gentiles*, I, 5: "... then only do we know God truly when we believe Him to be above everything that it is possible for people to think about Him." (Here the word "above" means "superior to," not "different from" – a point to which we will return in Chapter 4.)

A Muslim chant: "God is greater!" (explained in Chapter 4)

A Hindu scripture: "The Lord's pre-eminence is altogether without anything equal to it or excelling it" (Vyasa, *Yogabhaya*, I, 24).

Plato, *Epinomis* 985a: Lesser deities are not exempt from pain whereas "a god who enjoys the fullness of deity is clearly above both pain and pleasure, though possessed of all-embracing wisdom and knowledge."

It is impressive that the concept of God that was captured so well by Anselm and Descartes has parallels in diverse cultures and religions.

For Review, Reflection, and Discussion

1. Participation in religious institutions is declining in western Europe and the United States. Do you think belief in God is declining at the same rate, faster, or slower? How do you account for these declines? (See the Pew Forum on Religion and Public Life, "'Nones' on the Rise," October 9, 2012, for a good example of sociology of religion.)
2. In addition to the five sources of the concept of God that I mentioned, such as power and companionship, can you think of additional sources of the concept of God in human experience?
3. Which of the six concepts of God (naturalism, pantheism, etc.) do you find most attractive and why? Which concept do you find least attractive and why?
4. Why do you think Ludwig Feuerbach described the one-dimensional idea of God as "ultimate being which can only be known by revelation" as "atheism in disguise?"

5.   Immanuel Kant formulated the concept of "a limiting ideal." What does the concept of God have to do with the concept of a limiting ideal?

For Further Reading

Feuerbach, Ludwig, *The Essence of Christianity* (Harper: 1957). Ungar Publishing has an abridged version by the same title (1957).

Dewey, John, *A Common Faith* (Yale: 1934). A short classic by one of the founders of American pragmatism.

Wieman, Henry Nelson, *The Source of Human Good* (Southern Illinois University Press: 1946). Also, *Man's Ultimate Commitment* (Southern Illinois University Press: 1958).

Spinoza, Benedict, *The Ethics*. Perhaps the greatest expression of western pantheism. Numerous editions are available.

Levine, Michael, "Pantheism," *A Companion to Philosophy of Religion*, 2nd ed. (Wiley-Blackwell: 2010).

Shankara is a Hindu pantheist in the Advaita Vedanta tradition. His important pantheistic commentary on the Vedanta Sutras is available on several internet sites, e.g., http://www.bergen.edu/phr/121/ShankaraGC.pdf. For a book of philosophy of religion readings which includes many selections from Asia see: *Readings in the Philosophy of Religion: East Meets West* (Wiley-Blackwell: 2008), edited by Andrew Eschleman. Panentheism is expressed brilliantly in *Process and Reality* by Alfred North Whitehead (1861–1947), but that is a very difficult book. Start with his *Religion in the Making*. Panentheism was developed more fully in the work of Whitehead's colleague and admirer Charles Hartshorne (1897–2000). See Hartshorne's *Man's Vision of God*. For a presentation of panentheism on a popular level see Rabbi Harold Kushner's book *When Bad Things Happen to Good People*.

Frazer, Gregg L., *The Religious Beliefs of America's Founders: Reason, Revelation, Revolution* (Kansas University: 2012). A historical examination as to whether Franklin and Jefferson were deists.

Anselm of Canterbury, *Monologium* and *Proslogium*. Anselm elaborates the classical philosophical conception of God in these two brief works.

Descartes, René, *Meditations*. See the third meditation for an elaboration of the classical concept of God, beginning about the middle of the meditation.

Chapter 3

Divine Attributes and Dilemmas

Having given a basic definition of God in the classical philosophical
sense, what we are going to do now is consider more specifically what
kinds of characteristics such a being would have to have. I am going to
open up this exploration by listing 22 *pairs* of attributes or characteristics. Because each pair consists of opposites (in logic we call them
"contradictories"), one of each pair must apply to God and therefore
the other cannot. (But of course you want to consider whether these
pairs really are contradictories or whether there might be a third possibility in addition to the two listed.) On the *left* of each pair I am going
to place the attribute that is *traditionally* attributed to God by philosophers and theologians, but some of these attributions are controversial;
indeed, some are very controversial. Later we will explore some of
these controversies, but for now (i) try to understand each side of these
pairs, (ii) try to understand why someone who thinks of God as a
supremely perfect being would think that God must be the one way
rather than the other way, and (iii) ask yourself which way *you* think is
more appropriate and why.

Attributes of God
A Supremely Perfect being
—René Descartes

A Being than which None Greater can be Conceived
—St. Anselm

Philosophy of Religion: The Basics, First Edition. Richard E. Creel.
© 2014 John Wiley & Sons, Inc. Published 2014 by John Wiley & Sons, Inc.

Another way to describe God is to say that God is *omniperfect*. That is, "all perfect," "perfect in all ways." Which, then, of the following attributes do you think would more accurately describe an omniperfect being?

1. Infinite/Finite (here the prefix "in" means "not"; "finite" means "limited")

   That which is finite is limited in at least one respect, such as size or power or knowledge, and perhaps in all respects. That which is infinite is unlimited in at least one respect and perhaps all. Would God be finite or infinite? In only some respects or all? If some, which and why?

2. Unsurpassable/Surpassable

   That which is surpassable either is or can be exceeded in some respect, such as power, goodness, or knowledge. That which is unsurpassable cannot be exceeded in a certain respect or perhaps in any respect. Would God be surpassable or unsurpassable? In all respects or only some? If some, which and why?

3. Unequallable/Equallable

   Just because something cannot be surpassed does not mean that it cannot be equalled. That which is equallable can be equalled by something else in some respect, such as power. That which is unequallable is superior in some respect and nothing can be equal to it in that respect. Is God unequallable in all respects or can God be equalled in some or all respects? Could there be two Gods who are equal in all respects?

4. Unique/not Unique

   That which is not unique can have a counterpart or twin that is very or even exactly like it except for being numerically different. Think of two eight balls produced on the same factory line, one after the other; they are indistinguishable except for being two in number. By contrast, that which is unique does not have and cannot have a twin or even a close counterpart. In common discussion, we use the word "unique" loosely for something that is the first of its kind or that is rare. By contrast, there can be only one of that which is truly unique; hence the Bible and the Koran claim that "God is one," that monotheism is true ("mono" means "one"; "theos" means "God"). In this strict sense only God is unique, and ze has no close competitors. Moreover, if God is unique, then God has no equal.

5.   Omnipotent/not Omnipotent ("omni" means "all"; "potens" means "power"; something that is potent is powerful).
     That which is omnipotent can do everything. That which is not omnipotent cannot do everything; there is at least one thing that it cannot do. Would God be omnipotent or less than omnipotent?

6.   Omniscient/not Omniscient ("omni" means "all"; "science" means "knowledge")
     That which is omniscient knows everything. That which is not omniscient is ignorant of at least one thing that an omniscient being would know. Would God know *everything*? If not, what would God not know and why?

7.   Omnipresent (Ubiquitous)/not Omnipresent
     An omnipresent or ubiquitous being is present everywhere or, to put it a bit differently, everything is present to it. There is nowhere that it is not (there is nothing that is not present to it). If a being is not omnipresent, then there is somewhere that it is not or something that is not present to it. Would God be omnipresent? If not, where would ze not be? Or, what would not be present to God? What would be the connection between omnipresence and omniscience?

8.   Omnibenevolent/not Omnibenevolent ("omni" means "all"; "bene" means "good"; "volent," like the word "volition," means "to will")
     An omnibenevolent being wills nothing but what is good. Such a being is perfectly good. A being that is not omnibenevolent does not have a perfectly good will. Would God be omnibenevolent? (Note: we are not asking if God *is* omnibenevolent. We are asking whether the concept of a supremely perfect being *implies* that such a being would be omnibenevolent.)

9.   Free/not Free
     A being which is absolutely free can choose between alternatives without being constrained by external or internal factors to choose one way or its opposite. Would God be perfectly free to choose any alternative or would there be restrictions, external or internal, on what God could choose?

10. Independent (Transcendent)/Dependent on the world ("in" here means "not")
     The issue here is whether God depends on the world in any way. To say in this context that God transcends the world is to say that God exists outside the world (is not an entity in the universe) and

does not depend on the universe for zer existence or attributes. Could God exist without the universe? Do God and the universe require one another? You will remember that the panentheists say: "Without God the *uni*verse could not exist (there would be chaos or nothing). Without the universe God would not be a creator and therefore would not be God."

11. Immanent (Involved in the world)/Uninvolved

   The question here is whether God acts in the world, guiding and influencing history, such as by revelation or miracles or answering prayers (all three of which we will discuss in Chapter 14), or whether God refrains from acting in the world. Beware of the following words that look and sound like "immanent": "*imminent*" (meaning about to happen soon), and "*eminent*" (meaning outstanding of its kind, such as an eminent philosopher). Would a supremely perfect being be immanent in the world, as biblical theists claim, or not be involved in the world, as deists claim?

12. Uncreated (has Aseity)/Created

   Something which is created depends on something other than itself for its existence; a statue depends on a sculptor for its existence. Something which has the property of aseity does not depend on anything for its existence. It exists because it is its very nature to exist. Would God have the property of aseity? Would God exist by virtue of zer own nature and nothing else?

13. Indestructible/Destructible

   Something which is destructible can be destroyed by an external force. Even if it is never destroyed, the point is that it could be destroyed. Something that is indestructible cannot be destroyed. Would God be destructible or indestructible?

14. Imperishable/Perishable ("im" here means "not")

   Destruction, as explained earlier, implies an external force that does the destroying. But something might perish from within, from some flaw or weakness that it possesses; machines rust, tomatoes rot, animals deteriorate and die. For a thing to be imperishable, means for it to be such that nothing internal will or can cause it to cease to exist or function. Would God be imperishable or perishable?

15. Everlasting/Transient

   Something that is transient exists for a time and then ceases to exist (or is such that it could cease to exist because it is dependent on something else for its existence – something that could "pull the plug" on its existence). Something that is everlasting exists from forever to forever because it has the property of aseity. Would God be everlasting or transient?

16.   Atemporal (Eternal)/Temporal ("a" here means "not")

Something that is temporal exists in time; it has a past which is no longer, a present which is, and a future which is not yet. Something atemporal does not exist in time. Consider the number 3; it does not have a past, present, or future; it exists outside of time (though we in time can become aware of it). Would God be atemporal, existing in an eternal now without a past, present, or future? Or would God be temporal and limited by time?

17.   Incorporeal (Pure spirit)/Corporeal ("corpus" means "body")

That which is corporeal is physical and exists in space. That which is incorporeal does not have a body or exist in space. The number 3 is incorporeal and a-spatial – but of course a written symbol of the number 3, such as iii, is corporeal. Would God be incorporeal and a-spatial or corporeal and spatial? (Mormons claim the latter for God the Father and God the Son.)

18.   Simple/Composite

That which is composite consists of parts that are joined together to make a whole, such as an automobile engine. That which is simple, in this special philosophical sense, has no parts. It is simple in a radical way. It is one thing but it has no parts. Would God be simple or composite? If composite, what would be the parts that compose God and how would they be held together? If simple, how can we understand something that exists but has no parts?

19.   Immutable/Mutable

That which is mutable can change in some respect. That which is immutable cannot change in a certain respect or perhaps in any respect. The number 3 is immutable with respect to its being odd rather than even. Would God be immutable? If yes, why? Or would God be mutable? If yes, in what respect or respects would God be changeable?

20.   Personal/Nonpersonal

To be a person in the fullest sense is, among other things, to have the attributes of consciousness, self-consciousness, knowledge, rationality, emotion, freedom of choice, and agency (the ability to act). Are all of the preceding attributes necessary characteristics of a person? Taken together are they sufficient for something to be a person, or is something more needed? Would a supremely perfect being be a person or would ze be other than a person, or perhaps transcend personhood? If other than a person, what would that mean? (N.B.: a person is not necessarily a human. A person, such as God or an angel, mighty be incorporeal whereas a human is corporeal.) ("N.B." is an abbreviation for "nota bene" which in Latin literally means "note well," that is, pay special attention.)

21. Impassible/Passible

There are two issues here. First, is God passible, that is, subject to influence by the world in any respect, or is God impassible, that is, beyond being affected by what goes on in the world? (Aristotle believed and some Hindus believe that God is not affected by what goes on in the world.)

Second, is God subject to being caused to suffer or feel sorrow by what goes on in the world, or is God not subject to being caused to suffer by what goes on in the world? Is God above the turmoil of the world? Is God always perfectly blissful or not? Remember the earlier quotation from Plato's *Epinomis* 985a: "a god who enjoys the fullness of deity is clearly above both pain and pleasure, though possessed of all-embracing wisdom and knowledge." So would God be passible or impassible with regard to being influenced at all by the world and especially with regard to being touched emotionally by human joy and suffering? (N.B.: Don't confuse the word "impassible" with "impassable." A river is impassable if people cannot pass over it. A poker player is impassible if nothing can make zer facial expression change.)

22. Worthy of worship/Not worthy of worship

To be worthy of worship is to be of such great goodness or wisdom or majesty as to be worthy of whole-hearted devotion, praise, and adoration. Would God be worthy of worship? Why or why not? (Remember: we are asking about God as defined by Anselm and Descartes.)

3.1 What Is a Dilemma?

Now let's examine some of the controversies that have been generated by the preceding attributes. We will do this by exploring *dilemmas* that are generated by these attributes. A dilemma is a *forced choice* between alternatives. The choice isn't forced in the sense that you have to choose one alternative or the other; it is "forced" because *not* choosing will result in something worse than choosing either alternative. (There might be more than two alternatives, but to keep things simple, I will speak of dilemmas that have only two alternatives.) Fortunately, there are good or happy dilemmas as well as bad or unhappy dilemmas. In *a happy dilemma*, you would like to have both alternatives but can have only one. Failure to choose between the alternatives will result in losing both. For example, if you live in Chicago and someone gives to you a ticket to Hawaii and a ticket to Paris and the planes leave at the same time, you will lose *both* opportunities if you cannot decide which trip to take. In *an unhappy dilemma*, you would like to *avoid* both alternatives but can avoid only one. The judge says, "$5000 or 5 weeks in jail. Your choice." Hence the expression: "Caught on the horns of a dilemma." If one horn doesn't gore you, the other one will. You don't want to pay $5000 *or* spend five weeks in jail! Our focus will be on unhappy dilemmas because they are the ones that claim to reveal problems with the classical concept of God.

3.2   Ways to Respond to a Dilemma

1. If an unhappy dilemma is genuine, then you cannot avoid all of its unhappy alternatives. At best you can avoid all but one of those alternatives by choosing which alternative to be afflicted by. In such a situation, you want to *choose the least evil of the alternatives*, if there is a lesser evil. If your alternatives are equally undesirable, then you still want to choose one rather than the other or you may be afflicted by both! For example, if you go home and find your house is burning, and you have two dogs, each of which is in a different part of the house, and it is clear that you do not have time to save both, you must decide which one to save or you will lose both of them. (Here is the famous Dilemma of Buridan's Ass: a hungry donkey, equidistant between two equally attractive bales of hay, cannot decide which to eat, and so starves to death between them!)

   However, not everything that appears to be a dilemma really is a dilemma. So if you have time, examine a seeming dilemma to see if it really is a dilemma for you. Two strategies here are to attempt to "break a horn" of the dilemma or to try to "go between the horns" of the dilemma.

2. To *break a horn* of a dilemma is to show or discover that one alternative of the dilemma is not really a problem. For example, say your boss tells you "Fire Jane or fire John. We cannot afford both of them." You don't want to fire either. You interview both and discover that John is planning to quit for a new job soon! Hence, you are no longer in a dilemma because the "fire John" horn of the dilemma ceases to be a problem. You can break off that horn without feeling bad.

3. To *go between the horns* of a dilemma means to find a third alternative that is not as undesirable as the original alternatives (which means to discover that you are not in a true dilemma). For example, let's say you love philosophy and religion equally but do not have time to major in both, so, alas, you are forced to major in one and abandon the other. But you don't want to abandon either. Then you discover that there is a new "Joint Major in Philosophy and Religion" so you will be able to complete a major in time and won't have to abandon either discipline!

But remember: if an unhappy dilemma is a real dilemma, you *cannot* escape both alternatives – though you might be gored by both horns if you don't take timely action (as in, for example, the burning house in which you have two dogs). Here's another example: the judge says "$5000 or 5 weeks in jail. Which do you want?" You don't want either, so you hem and haw until finally the judge says, "You've got 60 seconds to make a decision. If you haven't given me a decision by then, you must pay $5000 *and* go to jail for 5 weeks!"

3.3   Divine Attribute Dilemmas

Now let's look at three attribute dilemmas, but keep the following in mind: my objective throughout this book is not to lay out the unvarnished truth. Virtually everything in philosophy is controversial. My objectives are to show you (i) how philosophical reasoning is done and (ii) what are some of the conclusions that have been arrived at. I have my own convictions and I will share some of them with you, but that is not to say that I am right. It is to say that I have thought about these things, want to share my reasoning and conclusions with you, and invite you to use *your* reasoning and experience to respond to what I or others have said. Now let's take up the debate that centers around the attribute of unsurpassability.

1. The Problem: A single divine attribute is said to be *incoherent* in itself.
   A. Unsurpassability: (The Dilemma: the believer must concede that God does not exist or that God is surpassable.)

   Explanation: The critic of the attribute of unsurpassability says that the notion of "a being than which none greater can be conceived" is as incoherent as the notion of a whole number than which none greater can be conceived. No matter how great a whole number is, we can think of a greater. Hence, there cannot be an unsurpassable whole number. Similarly, no matter how great a being is, we can think of a greater one. Hence, it is impossible for a being to be unsurpassable. But God must be unsurpassable or God would not be God; that is, God would not be a being than which none greater can be conceived. Hence, a believer must either cease to believe that God exists (since nothing that exists can be unsurpassable) or the believer must concede that God is not unsurpassable (which is to concede that God is not God). The first alternative requires that the believer cease to be a believer; the second alternative requires that the believer cease to believe that God is a supremely perfect being. Hence, the attribute of unsurpassability puts the believer right in front of the horns of a dilemma. (We will look at possible responses later.)

   Now let's look at a dilemma regarding omnipotence:

   B. Omnipotence: (Dilemma: the believer must conclude either that God does not exist or that God is not omnipotent.)

   Explanation: God, a supremely perfect being, must be omnipotent, that is, all-powerful, or ze would not be God. Therefore, God can do anything. Therefore, God can do what is impossible. But the impossible is that which cannot be done. Therefore, God cannot do the impossible. Therefore, there is something that God cannot do. Therefore, God is not omnipotent. But if God is not omnipotent, then God is not God. If God is God, then God is omnipotent, but if God is omnipotent, then God cannot exist, since nothing can exist which can do what is impossible. Hence, the believer must conclude either that God does not exist (since nothing can exist which can do that which is impossible) or that God is not omnipotent (in which case God is not God).

By the way, if God exists, then yes God can do many things that are impossible *for us*, but surely there are some things that no one, not even God, can do. Consider the following.

   i. Can God create a squircle (a two dimensional figure that has all the properties of both a square and a circle)? No. Such an entity would have to have four straight sides, intersecting at right angles (as does a square) and a point within it that is equidistant from all the points on its perimeter (as does a circle), but it is impossible to create such a figure. Therefore, there is a geometrical figure that God cannot create.

  ii. Can God change the past? No. Once an event has occurred, it is forever and unchangeably the case that it occurred. Not even God can make that which has occurred to not have occurred. Therefore, God is not omnipotent. Also, if God exists, ze cannot make it the case that ze never existed.

 iii. Can God create a stone so big or heavy ze cannot move it? If God *can* create such a stone, then God is not omnipotent because ze cannot move it. If God *cannot* create such a stone, then ze is not omnipotent because there is a stone ze cannot create. Hence, whether or not God can create such a stone, ze is not omnipotent.

The preceding section focused on single attributes that don't make sense in themselves, according to some critics. Now let's look at some attributes that other critics think make sense in themselves but which, they also think, contradict one another and therefore cannot both be true of God.

2. The Problem: One Divine Attribute is said to be Incompatible with Another Divine Attribute.

   A. It is said that God *cannot be both omnipotent and omnibenevolent.*

       Explanation: It is said that a supremely perfect being must be both omnipotent and omnibenevolent, but a being which is omnibenevolent (perfectly good) cannot do evil whereas a being which is omnipotent (all-powerful) can do evil. Hence, God cannot be both omnipotent and omnibenevolent. But as a supremely perfect being, God must be both; therefore, the concept of God is self-contradictory; consequently, either God does not exist because nothing with contradictory properties can exist, or God is not both omnipotent and omnibenevolent, in which case God is not God according to the traditional conception. Hence, the believer is forced to choose between (i) ceasing to believe that God exists and (ii) ceasing to believe that God is both omnipotent and omnibenevolent. If the believer chooses the first alternative, ze ceases to be a believer. If the believer chooses the second alternative, ze must somehow decide whether to give up omnipotence or omnibenevolence.

B. It is said that God *cannot be both immutable and a person.*

Explanation: That which is absolutely perfect cannot get better and cannot deteriorate; therefore it cannot change. Therefore, God must be immutable. However, God must also be a person. A person is a being with awareness of self, awareness of the world, the power of reason, the ability to make and implement choices, and the ability to interact with other persons. Obviously, anything less than a person would not be a supremely perfect being. Therefore, God must be a person. However, if God is immutable, then God cannot be a person because an immutable being cannot act (i.e., cannot go from not acting to acting and cannot begin an action and then stop it) or respond to changes in the world or interact with other persons, since all of those things require change. Hence, the believer must conclude that God is not a person or that God is not immutable. But if God is not immutable, then God is not perfect, and if God is not a person, then God is inferior to ourselves.

3. The Problem: A Divine Attribute is said to be Incompatible with A Human Attribute.

Two examples:

A. It is said that Divine Omniscience and Human Freedom are incompatible. Dilemma: either God is not omniscient or humans are not free.

Explanation: If God is omniscient, then God knows everything and therefore has always known everything that will happen in the future. Therefore, God has always known, even before we were conceived, every decision that we will ever make. Hence, there was never a time at which we could have chosen differently than God knows we will choose. Therefore, we have never had an opportunity to choose otherwise than we have chosen and will choose. By contrast, if we are free, then God cannot be omniscient because ze cannot know the decisions that we will make in the future, since until the moment of decision arrives, we are genuinely free to choose, to do a certain thing, or choose not to do it. Thus, either we are free and God is not omniscient or God is omniscient and we are not free.

B. It is said that Divine Omnipotence and Human Freedom are incompatible. Dilemma: either God is not omnipotent or we are not free.

Explanation: If we are free, then God cannot make us do what ze wants us to do. To be free, means that what you choose is entirely up to you. Therefore, if we are free, then God is not omnipotent, that is, God does not have the power to make us do something or refrain from it. If we are free, then whether we do something or refrain from it is entirely up to us. By contrast, if God is omnipotent, then ze can make us do whatever ze wants us to do and therefore we are not free; we are like puppets or robots or characters in a play. Hence, either God is omnipotent and we are not free or we are free and God is not omnipotent.

3.4 Proposed Solutions to the Preceding Dilemmas

Having gone on the offensive for a while, now let's see how someone might critique the preceding dilemmas.

3.4.1 Unsurpassability

It is true that some properties are infinitely surpassable. For example, length. No matter how long a straight line is, we can conceive of a longer line. Also, whole numbers: no matter how large a whole number someone proposes, we can think of a bigger one. However, there are some properties that have a maximum possible state that is unsurpassable. For example, a two-dimensional arc with a consistent degree of curvature cannot reach more than 360 degrees because when it reaches 360 degrees it becomes a closed circle. That is how the divine attributes are: each has an unsurpassably maximal state. Consider, for example, omniscience. To be omniscient means to know all there is to be known. Obviously, then, nothing can be *more* than omniscient because nothing can know more than all there is to know. Similarly, nothing can be more than omnipotent. To be omnipotent is to be able to do all that can be done, and nothing can be capable of doing *more* than all that can possibly be done, so nothing can be more than omnipotent. Hence, it is intelligible that God could be unsurpassable. (Recall that Immanuel Kant's concept of God is the concept of a limiting ideal. Also see William Wainwright on properties with intrinsic maxima, *Philosophy of Religion*, 2nd ed., p. 8)

3.4.2   Omnipotence

To the claim that God cannot do that which is impossible, some people reply that just because something is impossible for humans does not mean that it is impossible for God. Often they document that claim by quoting Mark 10:27 in the New Testament. Just prior to that verse in the New Testament, Jesus described the difficulty of achieving salvation in such a way that it made his disciples despair of being saved. To which Jesus replied, "For men it is impossible, but not for God; to God all things are possible" (New English Bible). And surely a supremely perfect being could do things that are impossible for any human to do. That, however, does not mean that God can do what is "*logically impossible.*" That which is logically impossible is absolutely impossible because the concept of it is self-contradictory, and therefore it would have to both be and not be a certain way at the same time in the same respect. But nothing can both have and not have a property at one and the same time in the same respect. A ball cannot at the same time in the same respect both be and not be completely red. It is true, then, that God cannot create things that are logically impossible, but that is because things that are logically impossible are not things that could possibly exist. They are not things that God cannot create; they are things that cannot exist. Anything that can exist, God can create. Hence, God's inability to actualize things that are logically impossible is not incompatible with God's omnipotence. God can do all that can possibly be done. Just as omniscience cannot include more than there is to know, omnipotence cannot include more than can possibly be done. Now let's apply this analysis to the specific problems mentioned earlier.

1. First, it is true that God cannot create a squircle, but that is because a squircle is not a thing that can possibly exist. Nothing can exist with simultaneous contradictory properties because it would have to be a certain way and not be that way in the same respect at the same time, which is impossible. Hence, a squircle is merely, as Benedict Spinoza put it, "a word thing." Because we know what a square is and what a circle is, the word "squircle" seems to stand for something that could exist, but it does not. Hence, the fact that God cannot create a squircle does not entail that God is not omnipotent.
2. Second, to change the past would mean to make something that happened to not have happened, but that is impossible. If something happened, then it happened, and it can never be made not to have happened. But that does not mean that God is not omnipotent. Omnipotence extends only to things that make sense, things that are logically possible, that don't involve a contradiction. The idea of changing the past is self-contradictory because it would mean making what was past not to have been past.
3. Third, does the paradox of the stone produce a real dilemma? No. Because God is omnipotent, God can create a stone of any size or weight, and because God is omnipotent ze can move a stone of any size or weight. Hence, it is *because* God is omnipotent that ze cannot create a stone so large that ze cannot move it.

3.4.3   Are Omnipotence and Omnibenevolence Incompatible?

The response to this dilemma has two parts. The first part says that even though God, a supremely perfect being, *would* not do evil, ze could still be omnipotent. How? Because, it is said, *if* God chose to perform actions that would constitute doing evil, God could do them – such as inflicting meaningless, pointless suffering on an innocent child. Hence, God has the *power* to do evil things even though ze would not *choose* to do them. Hence, God can be both omnipotent and perfectly good.

Omnipotence pertains to one's *ability* to do something, not to one's *willingness* to do it.

A critic might reply that the preceding defense addresses only a weak version of the omnipotence/omnibenevolence dilemma. The strong version points out that God *could not* choose to do evil. Yes, the critic says, if God chose to do something evil, ze would have the power to do it, but the point of the dilemma is that God, being perfectly good, *cannot* choose to do evil and therefore is not omnipotent (alternatively, one might argue that what this means is that God is not perfectly free to choose to do anything that can be done). The theist's response to this stronger version of the dilemma focuses on the question, "Why do persons do evil?" or "What enables a person to do evil?" The answer is that doing evil is an expression of a defect of some kind, for example, ignorance of the good, weakness of will, or perversity of character (being inclined to willfully choose that which one knows is not good). Therefore, only an imperfect being can do evil. Because God is supremely perfect ze is neither ignorant, nor weak, nor perverse. Therefore, it is *because* God is perfect that ze cannot do evil. Hence, because God is perfectly good, God not only *would* not do evil but *could* not do evil.

3.4.4   Immutability and Personhood

The rebuttal here also consists of two points. First, if we must choose between personhood and immutability, it seems clearly more important that God be a person than that God be immutable. Second, not all kinds of change are incompatible with perfection. In fact, perfection seems to *require* the ability to change in certain ways. For example, to be a perfect being one must be a person (as that was defined earlier); to be a person means to be an agent, and to be an agent requires that one be able to change from not acting to acting and from acting to not acting. Furthermore, personhood requires change by way of being able to interact with other persons by responding to them. Hence, some say, the way out of this dilemma is to *break the horn of immutability* – specifically, to show that perfection requires immutability in some respects, for example, with regard to omnipotence and moral character, but requires mutability in other respects, such as agency – being able to begin and end an action and to know what is going on as things change in the world.

3.4.5   Divine Omniscience and Human Freedom

Four diverse solutions:

1. Give up human freedom (John Calvin and Jonathan Edwards)

    God is omniscient, and therefore God must know the future, as well as the past and the present. But the only way to *know* before something happens that it *will* happen is if it *has* to happen. If it is possible that it won't happen, then it can't be foreknown that it will happen. Hence, divine *fore*knowledge is *in*compatible with human freewill. Divine omniscience is nonnegotiable; therefore, we must give up belief in human free will in order to honor divine omniscience. God is The Divine Playwright: God knows all that will happen in history because ze has decided all that will happen in history, just as the human playwright knows what will happen in the play because ze has written it. So we break off the horn of human free will.

2. Give up divine omniscience (Socinus, 1539–1604)

    Socinus reasoned that because humans are free and because free actions cannot be foreknown (how could they be foreknown given that they have not yet been decided!), therefore God does not know our future free actions; therefore, there is something to be known that God does not know; therefore, God is not omniscient. Hence, Socinus broke off the horn of omniscience, that is, he gave up omniscience. (Future free actions are sometimes called "future contingents" because whether they will happen is contingent, that is, dependent, on our free choice at that future time.)

3. Go between the horns (Boethius, Aquinas, Norman Kretzmann, Eleonore Stump)

    Classical theists like Boethius and Thomas Aquinas, and contemporary philosophers like Eleonore Stump and Norman Kretzmann think there is a way between the horns of this dilemma, that is, a third way that is not problematic. God as supremely perfect must be omniscient and know all things, including, therefore, the future. If God didn't know the future, then God would be ignorant of something, but God, who is supremely perfect, cannot be ignorant of anything, therefore God must know the future. But it is equally true that human beings are free and that free actions (future contingents) cannot be *fore*known. The solution to this dilemma, according to Stump and Kretzmann, lies in realizing that because God's existence is very different from our existence, God's knowledge is very different from our knowledge. We are temporal beings who exist *in* time. Consequently, our knowledge of time is from inside time; we always exist in the temporal present, between the past (which no longer exists) and the future (which is not yet), always moving out of the past to the present and into the future.

God, by contrast, is an atemporal being who exists outside of time in the eternal present. This means that all of time is always simultaneously present to God. In other words, all of time is timelessly present to God. Time to God is like an historical diorama that ze sees all at once whereas we see the diorama only a little at a time through a slowly moving peephole. Hence, God has eternal knowledge of time. God's eternal knowledge of what to us is in the future is not *fore*knowledge to God. What is future to us is always *present* to God, and being aware of what *is* happening does not interfere with its being free or require that it not be free in the way that *fore*knowledge would. For example, if I have foreknowledge from before you are born that you will marry a certain person, then it must be determined that you will do so. If it were not determined, then it would be possible for you to choose not to marry that person, and that possibility would prevent me from fore*knowing* that you would do so (a lucky guess on my part would not be the same thing as fore*knowledge*!). But if instead of having such foreknowledge, I simply attend your wedding and observe you marrying that person at that time in that place as you are doing so, then that in no way would undermine the possibility that you are doing so freely – and that is the kind of knowledge that God has of our future free actions. Though they are future to us, they are present to God. Hence, because God has eternal rather than temporal knowledge of time, it can be true both that humans are free and God is omniscient.

4. Break a horn (Gersonides, 1288–1344; Charles Hartshorne, 1897–2000)

Is the notion of atemporal knowledge of future free actions an intelligible notion? Is it possible for our *future* free actions to be present to God like the present is present to us? Some thinkers say "no." They argue that the concept of eternal knowledge generates serious difficulties for our concepts of God and time.

First, in order for God to know atemporally in the eternal present what we *will* do, it has to be the case that we are already doing what we have not yet done (remember: God as eternal doesn't *fore*know what we will do; ze observes our actually doing it). But the idea of knowing something as existing which does not yet exist is incoherent, say critics. (Or else our belief that the future has not yet happened is an illusion on our part – and if the future is an illusion, then so is the past, and there is only the present – but isn't the belief that the passage of time is an illusion too high a price to pay for saving God's knowledge of our future free actions?)

As we have seen, a future free action can be *fore*known only if it *has* to happen and therefore is not free. Hence, on the assumption that we are free, God cannot have foreknowledge of what we will do, and because our future free actions do not exist now and will not exist until we decide them, God cannot know our future free actions in the temporal present or in an eternal present, as they do not yet exist to be known. Hence, it is argued, the eternality solution does not work because if the future is real, then God cannot know our future free actions, and if the future is not real, then our actions cannot be free because there was never a time before which we could have chosen differently than we do choose. (Note: Insofar as the future is *determined*, God can *fore*know the future even though the future does not yet exist – just as we foreknow that the sun will first appear in the east tomorrow morning, and that salt will melt the ice we put it on.)

The exercise of free will by a human requires at least three moments of time: one moment in which we are *aware* of alternatives, a second moment in which we *evaluate* them, and a third moment in which we *choose* one of those alternatives rather than the others. If the future is an illusion, however, then there is never more than one moment of time; there is only a single, immutable, eternal present – which is incompatible with both the notion that we are free beings and the notion that change takes place, since change requires at least two moments – one moment when a thing *is* a certain way, and a second moment when it is no longer that way. If there are no such moments, then change is an illusion and so is freedom of choice.

Second, if God has a timeless knowledge of time, then all events – past, present, and future – are equally actual to God, so

God has no way of knowing which of those events are happening *now*, and which are in the past and which in the future. God would be like a playwright who knows everything that happens in zer play and when it happens, but who does not know which part of the play is occurring now in a production of it to which ze is not privy. Surely, though, an omniscient being will know of what is happening now that it is happening now (and of other things that they are no longer happening or have not happened yet). Hence, the critic says, God's knowledge must not be atemporal.

Third, if God has a timeless and therefore immutable knowledge of time, then God cannot know the world as it is. Why? Because things in the world are changing, so in order for God to know the world as it is, God's knowledge of things must change as they change, but if God were immutable, God's knowledge could not change, so God could not know the world as it is. Surely, however, God, who is omniscient, knows the world as it is, and therefore zer knowledge must change as the world changes.

The solution to all of these difficulties, according to Gersonides and Charles Hartshorne, is to give up the idea that God's knowledge is immutable and to realize that although God cannot know what we will do in our freedom in the future, that does not mean that God is not omniscient. Part of what it means for us to be free is that right up to the moment of decision we are able to do a certain thing or not do it, so until the moment of decision arrives and we make our decision, *there is no such thing as what we will do*. (That, again, is why future free actions are also called "future contingents.")Therefore, of course God cannot foreknow or know eternally what we will do in our freedom. Future free actions do not exist, so they cannot be known as actual (therefore, there is no eternal present in which they are known), and future free actions are not determined, so they cannot be foreknown by knowing a causal chain that will produce them. This does not mean, however, that there is something to be known of which God is ignorant. God always knows everything there *is* to know: all possibilities, all of the past, all of the present, and all of the future insofar as the future is determined (such as when a certain star will explode or bubble will burst), and that is all that can be asked of omniscience. Therefore, God's omniscience and our freedom are compatible. Hence, Gersonides and Hartshorne broke the horn of traditional omniscience which says "If God does not know future free actions, then God is not omniscient." They showed, or at least argued, that accepting that humans are free and that God does not know future free actions does not in the least diminish divine omniscience.

3.5 Open Theism

It might be helpful at this point to see that debate over the preceding attributes has not subsided and has even given rise to a new yet old position on the nature of God. "Open theism" is a movement that began to gain serious momentum in the 1990s. It claims that the classical philosophical conception of God that has dominated western thought for nearly two thousand years is problematic and inconsistent with the Bible. This is not merely a yearning for the past or a reversion to "that old time religion." "Open theists" claim that their conception of God is superior to the classical philosophical conception and, most important to them, is consistent with the Bible. Theologians influenced by Greek philosophy conjured a conception of God as immutable, impassible, and timeless. But the biblical picture of God is a picture of a personal being who interacts with us in time, who engages in give and take with us, who responds to prayers, who sometimes repents of decisions ze has made, who is emotionally affected by our actions and afflictions, and who doesn't know all of the future because, after all, we have free wills. Hence, the future is open, that is, it is not yet fully determined what the future will be insofar as it involves the decisions of free creatures, such as humans and perhaps other creatures such as angels and extra-terrestrial beings (consequently some think "open theism" should be called "open futurism").

God's relation to us, according to open theism, is dynamic – God must wait on our prayers, decisions, and actions to decide what ze will do in response because ze does not and cannot know in advance what we in our freedom will choose to do. That is why there are passages in the Bible which make it clear that the Israelites sometimes disappointed God's expectations and that consequently God repented of decisions ze had made. For example, after Moses went up on Mount Sinai and the people of Israel made a golden calf to worship, God decided to destroy the Israelites – but Moses tried to talk God out of that intention: "And the Lord changed his mind about the disaster that he planned to bring on his people" (Exodus 32:7–14). It seems clear from that passage, according to open theists, that God did not know in advance what the people of Israel would do while Moses was on Mount Sinai. After God saw what they did ze was disappointed, angered, and decided to destroy the Israelites, but Moses convinced God to change zer mind! And, of course, there are other passages which speak of God's expectations being disappointed and of God repenting of some decision ze had made. See, for example, Genesis 6:5–7; Exodus 13:17, 33:4–5; Isaiah 5:4–7, 38:1–5.

Critics counter the preceding passages by quoting other biblical passages, for example, Malachi 3:6 in which God says, "I am the Lord, I change not," and Numbers 23:19 in which it is said, "God is not a human being, that he should lie; or a mortal, that he should change his mind." Open theists counter this by saying that in such passages God is speaking only of zer moral character and faithfulness – not of everything, such as zer knowledge of a changing world or zer decisions that are contingent on what we do in our freedom.

Does open theism mean that God is not omniscient because ze does not know what we are going to decide in the future? Not at all. Remember: God always knows everything that *can* be known, but our future free decisions (technically called "future contingents," i.e., future decisions that depend on a free will) do not exist to be known until we make them. Does this mean that God is not omnipresent because God does not exist in the future or because the future is not present to God? Not at all. God always knows everything that will *necessarily* happen in the future (such as a wildflower blooming or a star imploding), but the future itself does not *exist* to be known until the laws of nature, perhaps together with free decisions, cause future possibilities to jell into present actualities. Again, free choices are not made necessarily, so God, like ourselves, must wait to see what they will be – that is part of what it means for God to give free will to humans. God has to wait to see what we will do with our freedom, and of course our free actions will have *consequences in the physical world* that cannot be known in advance, depending, for example, on whether we decide to sculpt a piece of wood or burn it or ignore it.

Finally, in disagreement with the classical philosophical conception of God, open theists say that God is not emotionally frozen and uninfluenced by our emotions, as the doctrines of immutability and impassibility, respectively, claim. Rather, as the Bible claims, God is just and loving and emotionally involved with us; God is influenced by our victories and defeats, joys and sufferings, sins and virtues, just as we are influenced by those things in those we love. Does this mean we are anthropomorphizing God – making God too much like a human being? No. We are recognizing that to be a person is superior to being a nonperson; a person has intelligence, sensitivity, and free will, is influenced by other persons and interacts with them. Hence, the biblical notion of God is superior to the classical philosophical notion of God, not the other way around. Or so the open theists argue.

Critics of open theism say that passages such as Malachi 3:6, "I am the Lord, I change not," should be taken literally and not interpreted in a weak way. Furthermore, it is unseemly to think of God as ignorant of anything, for example, the future, or being limited in power or presence, or having to wait on human decisions to respond to them, and to be hampered and foiled by them. Such a conception, they say, undermines the way we should think of God. We should think of God as majestic, resplendent, serene, and sovereign.

For Review, Reflection, and Discussion

1. Could God be the greatest being that there is but not be a being than which none greater can be conceived? Would such a being be worthy of the title "God?" Why? Why not?
2. What is an attribute?
3. What is a dilemma?
4. Of all the attributes listed, which ones do you think definitely apply to God, which do you think definitely do not apply to God, and which ones are you uncertain about?
5. Which of the attribute dilemmas do you think were solved satisfactorily and which were not (explain)?
6. Humans can get lost. God cannot get lost. Therefore, humans can do something that God cannot do. Therefore God is not omnipotent. Right?
7. Can you think of an additional divine dilemma? Please state and explain it.
8. Is open theism superior to the classical philosophical conception of God? Why? Why not?

For Further Reading

For numerous articles on different attributes of God see Taliaferro, Charles, Draper, Paul, et al., eds., *A Companion to Philosophy of Religion*, 2nd ed. (Wiley-Blackwell: 2010), Part IV. Some of the attributes written about (each by a different author in a separate article) are omnipotence, omniscience, omnipresence, goodness, simplicity, eternity, incorporeality, holiness, beauty, and more.

Creel, Richard E., "Immutability and Impassibility," in Taliaferro, Charles, Draper, Paul, et al., eds., *A Companion to Philosophy of Religion*, 2nd ed. (Wiley-Blackwell: 2010). A fuller discussion of these controversial attributes.

Peterson, Michael, *Philosophy of Religion: Selected Readings*, 2nd ed (Oxford University: 2001). Part III consists of readings on the divine attributes by Maimonides, Aquinas, and others, including contemporary writers and a selection from the Hindu *Upanishads*.

Rowe, William, *Philosophy of Religion*, 2nd ed. (Wadsworth: 1993), pp. 6–7. A very good discussion of the omnipotence/goodness dilemma.

Zagzebski, Linda, "Foreknowledge and Human Freedom," in Taliaferro, Charles, Draper, Paul, et al., eds., *A Companion to Philosophy of Religion*, 2nd ed. (Wiley-Blackwell: 2010). A sophisticated article by an authority.

Chapter 4

Human Language and Talk about God

Some folks say, "People made up the idea of God. Therefore, God is just an idea." That reasoning is unsound. To see why, let's distinguish *word*, *concept*, and *thing*. There is the *word* "God," the *concept* (or idea) of a supremely perfect being (which we designate by the word "God"), and perhaps there is a *thing* (or being) which *is* a supremely perfect being. Just because we make up the idea or concept of something does not mean that it is not an idea of something that actually exists. For example, we made up the idea of extra-terrestrial life (ETL), but that doesn't mean that therefore ETL is just an idea and there is no such thing. Of course, there may not be ETL, but just because we made up the concept of ETL does not mean that therefore there is no ETL. Most people now believe there probably is.

Returning to the topic of the previous chapter (the attributes of God), it is clear that no matter which forks in the road we take on the divine attribute dilemmas, we wind up with a most unusual concept. On most accounts God, the supremely perfect being, is absolutely unique, that is, is unlike anything else in reality because ze is simple (nondivisible), incorporeal (nonphysical), nonspatial (without spatial characteristics), and perhaps immutable (nonchanging) and atemporal (not in time). Notice that the preceding attributes tell us only what God is not like. But if we know only that God is not like this and not like that, how can we talk about what God *is* like? Moreover, if we only know what God is not like, how can we know it is God we are talking about when we presume to be talking about God? In brief, how can we know what we are talking about when we talk about God if we only know what God

Philosophy of Religion: The Basics, First Edition. Richard E. Creel.
© 2014 John Wiley & Sons, Inc. Published 2014 by John Wiley & Sons, Inc.

is not like? These are important questions that deserve answers. We will proceed by examining four answers to the question: "Does talk about what God is like make sense, and if so, what sense does it make?"

1. Logical Positivism: Talk about God is Meaningless (A.J. Ayer; Ludwig Wittgenstein)

According to logical positivists like A.J. Ayer and the early Ludwig Wittgenstein, human language developed as humans learned to communicate about the things that concerned them most – things such as food, shelter, and dangers in the environment. Consequently, the basic categories of language are public, physical categories, such as color, shape, sound, smell, size, and movement. Even when we learned to speak to one another of our inner experiences, we had to do so by using physical categories in a metaphorical way, as when we say that a pain is sharp or dull, or that we are feeling weighed down by our responsibilities, or that we "smell a rat!"

Hence, language can be used to identify and communicate about things in nature, but, according to the logical positivists, it is not suited to speak of things that are supposedly beyond the realm of nature. As British philosopher Bertrand Russell said, "We must attach some meaning to the words we use, if we are to speak significantly and not utter mere noise; and the meaning we attach to our words must be something with which we are acquainted" (and we are only acquainted with the physical environment and our inner experiences). Russell added, "The fundamental principle in the analysis of propositions containing descriptions is this: Every proposition we can understand must be composed wholly of constituents with which we are acquainted" (*The Problems of Philosophy* [Oxford University Press: 1912], p. 58 in the 1959 edition). By "acquainted," in the first quotation, Russell means acquainted by means of our senses. We know what we mean when we speak of a thing being red, long, fast, etc., but words like "pure spirit," "metaphysically simple," "omnipresent," "timeless," "nonspatial," etc., do not make sense when we presume to apply them to an entity. Therefore, the concept of any so-called entity to which they are supposed to apply cannot make sense. Indeed, there is no concept here, just a word. Hence, talk about God does not make sense. The idea of God is "nonsense" because we cannot use our senses to make sense of the idea of a simple, omnipresent, incorporeal spirit, and things only get worse if we add that this pure spirit is immutable and atemporal. We are acquainted with no such thing.

It is important to note that the positivists are not saying that God is "beyond our comprehension." Their point is that the word "God" does not stand for anything that is intelligible. We cannot understand anything that is not either conveyed to us by our senses, such as a horse, or imaginatively composed of things that are conveyed to us by our senses, such as a unicorn, so none of our words can possibly refer to anything beyond the world as we know it by sensation and introspection. Hence, to presume to talk about a supernatural being is a nonsensical delusion. If I tell you I have a pizzle in my pocket, and you say "Neat – show it to me!," and I reach my hand into my pocket, pull it out, open it, and you see nothing, and say, "Where's the pizzle?," and I say, "It's right there in my hand," and you say, "But I don't see anything," and I say, "Well of course you don't; pizzles don't have physical properties," then you will rightly conclude that the word "pizzle" doesn't stand for anything and that I am either insane or playing a joke on you (or both!).

To be sure, say the positivists, talk about God is "meaningful nonsense," but its meaningfulness is emotive (emotional), not cognitive (intellectual). Because of childhood experiences at Hannukah or Christmas, for example, the *word* "God" arouses in us images of family gatherings and exchanging presents and nine-stick candelabras or the baby Jesus, and perhaps feelings of happiness and notions of kindness and generosity, but all of those images, notions, and feelings are natural, not supernatural. That's why they make sense and why the word "God" has emotive meaning for many people, but in order for a word to have cognitive meaning, it must stand for something that we can understand, and since "God" stands for a nonsensible being, it is nonsensical, and therefore cognitively meaningless.

In brief, insofar as talk about God is cognitively meaningful, that is, is intelligible or comprehensible, it is not talk about God, and insofar as it is talk about God, it doesn't make sense – though it may seem to, as does Lewis Carroll's poem "Jabberwocky." In that poem Carroll says, "Twas brillig, and the slithy toves did gyre and gimble in the wabe. All mimsy were the borogoves, and the mome raths outgrabe." "Jabberwocky" is an amusing piece that is fun to read, but talk about God is not amusing because people take it seriously; they think it makes sense when it doesn't. Moreover, say the positivists, it is because talk about God doesn't make any objective sense that there are so many different ideas of what God is like; people are free to use the word "God" to mean anything they want because there is no objective reality against which we can check the correctness of different descriptions of God. Hence, rather than injecting into the word "God" whatever we want, we should follow the recommendation of Ludwig Wittgenstein, who said: "That whereof we cannot speak, we should be silent." (In his German: "Wovon man nicht sprechen kann, daruber muss man schweigen.")

A point worth repeating before we move on is that the logical positivist is not saying that God is beyond our comprehension. Ze is saying that the idea of God simply does not make sense, any more than it makes sense to say that a brillig twuncle weighs more than a fresseled vunch. Hence, the logical positivist is not an atheist. An atheist says to the theist, "I understand what you mean by 'God,' but I don't think there is any such being." The logical positivist says, "I don't know what you mean by 'God,' and I don't think you do either, so there can be no meaningful response to the question, 'Does God exist?'" There is nothing to be comprehended so there is nothing to affirm or deny. Similarly, the logical positivist is not an agnostic. An agnostic says, "Maybe God exists. Maybe God doesn't exist. I don't know," and that means the agnostic presumes to understand what it is the existence of which the theist affirms and the atheist denies, but that presumption of understanding is precisely what the logical positivist rejects.

2.   Reductionism: Talk about God is Oblique (Ludwig Feuerbach; John Dewey; Henry Nelson Wieman)

Reductionists think the positivists have gone too far. Reductionists do not necessarily reject the intelligibility of the traditional concept of God (though they may), and they say that talk about God must have some cognitive meaning or it would not have survived for so long among so many intelligent people. However, the reductionists say, the positivists are right that talk about God is not talk about a supernatural being. The reason that talk about God makes sense, say the reductionists, is that it is really talk about natural phenomena. However, those who engage in religious talk usually do not realize that they are *not* talking about a supernatural being but, rather, are talking about some aspect of life in this world. Hence, the reductionists "reduce" the meaning of "God" from an otherworldly being to something in this world. Ludwig Feuerbach, for example, said that talk about God is really talk about the ideal potentialities and aspirations of humankind. For thousands of year humans have unwittingly carried on their thinking about their own ideal potentialities by projecting them onto an ideal supernatural being (or beings). This, Feuerbach would say, is the reality behind Jesus' statement, "Be ye therefore perfect as your father in heaven is perfect" (Matthew 5:48). Why should we seek to be perfect as our heavenly father is perfect? Because our conception of our heavenly father is really a conception of how we humans ought to be.

John Dewey thought that talk about the Kingdom of God is really talk about the social ideals that are so inspiring as to motivate us to commit ourselves to them and even sacrifice ourselves for them. Henry Nelson Wieman took talk about God to be talk about that force in nature which transforms us for the good in ways in which we cannot transform ourselves.

In brief, according to reductionists, talk about God is really indirect talk about something else, so when it is properly understood, talk about God can be "reduced" to direct talk about that something else, for example, the ideal essence of humankind, or the vision of an ideal society, or the natural force that transforms us from being selfish to being altruistic, from being closed-minded to open-minded, from being destructive to creative. Hence, a cognitively meaningful usage of "God" can be saved.

3. The *Via Negativa*: Meaningful Talk about God is Negative (Moses Maimonides, also known as "RAMBAM"; see his *Guide for the Perplexed*, Part I, Chapters L–LX)

According to Moses Maimonides, the greatest Jewish philosopher of the Middle Ages, talk about God is not meaningless or indirect; it really is talk about a supernatural being, but because God is so radically different from everything in this world, the positivists are correct that human language is not able to describe God. Our language is fit to give accurate descriptions of things in this world only. Furthermore, our minds are too limited to be able to understand the nature of God. Hence, it is not because the concept of God is meaningless that we cannot say what God is like; rather, it is because God is so radically different from anything in our experience and because God so radically transcends the limits of our minds. God is "wholly other" than anything we can experience with our senses or grasp with our minds. Consequently, any positive description of God that we attempt to make will be infected by the limitations of the human mind and the objects of our experience. The inevitable result, if we attempt to describe God, will be a misunderstanding and a misdescription. Consequently, it is better for us to be silent and humble before the awesome mystery of God than to make incompetent assertions about what God is like.

To go at this point another way, the positive assertions of language can capture and communicate cognitive meaning only by being based on general properties (or "universals") that can be shared by any number of individuals – properties such as color, shape, and size. We like to think of various things as "unique," but no physical entity is absolutely unique; any physical entity shares some characteristic with other things and can be duplicated or cloned; that is what makes descriptive language possible. We see the redness of an object, so we can understand what it would mean to say that another object is red or could be red. Because descriptive terms refer to general properties ("universals"), they can be used to describe an individual only when that individual is not unique, that is, only when that individual has properties that do describe or could describe other individuals. But in contrast to physical entities, God is utterly unique. There is absolutely nothing in our experience or our imaginations like God, nor could there be, so language cannot be used to describe God.

Nonetheless, Maimonides said, language is not totally useless as a tool for speaking of God. We can use it to say what God is *not* like, and that is important because it can keep us from having a defective or misleading understanding of God (the most important of all beings to not misunderstand!). By contrast, if we make a positive statement about God, such as, "God is mighty," then in the background of our thinking we must have the image of an awesome storm or a massive animal or some such thing, since we derive our concept of power from our experiences with such things. But, inescapably, physical things have limits. Storms and animals, no matter how awesome, eventually weaken and die. Hence, to say "God is mighty" is to infect our notion of God with a sense of finitude. Positive statements about God cannot escape this problem. Consequently, Maimonides said, other than the positive statement "God exists," we should limit ourselves to negative statements about God (not negative in the sense of "critical," but in the sense of saying "God is not a certain way"). For example, rather than saying that God is mighty, and running into the problems mentioned earlier, we should say, "God is not weak." That way of describing God should not distort our thinking about God because it does not tell us how to think of God; it tells us how not to think of God. It tells us that God is in no way like anything that is weak; it tells us that no kind of weakness is to be associated with God.

Consider another example: "God is wise." Our notion of wisdom has inescapably been cobbled together from examples of wise people whom we know or have learned about. But human wisdom is usually acquired as a result of tragedy or suffering or failure or trial and error. And sometimes, as with Socrates, people's wisdom consists of realizing and admitting the extent of their ignorance (see the account of Socrates' wisdom in Plato's *Apology*). Hence, our concept of wisdom is saturated with a sense of insight arising from the sufferings and failures imposed upon us by our physical, mental, and spiritual limitations. Consequently, it is better to say that God is not foolish or is not ignorant than to say that ze is wise. The negative statement preserves all that needs to be said, and it does not generate misleading images or needless worries on the part of the believer, nor does it elicit silly questions and objections on the part of the unbeliever (such as thinking of God as a wise old man with a long white beard!).

Consider also "God is omnipresent" vs. "God is not absent." We cannot think of "present" except in a physical, spatial sense, so when we make the positive statement, "God is present everywhere," we cannot help but think of God as being in space with us and therefore being contained in and limited by space. But anything contained in space is not worthy of being called "God." Hence, it is better to say "God is not absent" or "There is nowhere that God is not."

As a concession to ordinary language, Maimonides said that it is okay to make a positive assertion about God as long as it is meant in a negative way. It is okay to say, "God is loving," if what you mean is something like, "God is not cruel or indifferent." If you say, "The Lord God is a living God," you should explain that that means that God should not be thought of as dead or inanimate. In other words, it is okay to make positive statements about God as long as you know better and can explain yourself correctly, just as when we say, "The sun is rising," yet know and can explain that the sun is not really rising but merely appears to be rising as a result of the rotation of the earth.

By applying this distinction to positive talk about God, we can enter into ordinary discourse with untutored people yet at crucial moments help them understand why positive talk about God should always be meant negatively and used only rarely.

As an aside I would like to point out a difference between the *via negativa* (literally "the negative way") in Hinduism and in Maimonides. The Hindu application of the expression "neti, neti" (literally "neither this nor that") to *Brahman* (the Hindu word for the highest being) seems intended to lead ultimately to a positive understanding of Brahman. The child asks, "Is Brahman like an elephant?" And the teacher answers "no." A tiger? No. A snake? No. And so on until the child (perhaps by then an adult!) begins to understand what Brahman is like. By contrast, Maimonides seemed to be saying that the *via negativa* does not lead us finally to a positive understanding of God. Rather, it only helps us avoid misunderstandings of God. These different results are understandable in light of the pantheism of advaita vedanta Hinduism and the theism of Maimonides. According to advaita you *are* Brahman, and so by means of the *via negativa* you are coming to understand yourself, and there should be no ultimate obstacle to understanding yourself. By contrast, according to Maimonides the divine is radically different from ourselves. God is "the wholly other" whom we can never comprehend but only acknowledge in awe and humility. Maimonides does say that the *fewer* things a person can correctly negate of God, the more remote ze is from understanding God, and the *more* things a person can correctly negate of God, the closer ze is to understanding God, but he is emphatic that no creature can ever cross the great divide to an understanding of what God is like.

Criticisms of the *Via Negativa*:

Maimonides was a classical theist, but many classical theists do not agree with his conviction that we should refrain from trying to understand what God is like and from making positive statements about God. Here are three reasons for their disagreement.

First, if Maimonides is correct, then negative as well as positive statements about God are problematic so that the *via negativa* renders the meaning of the word "God" meaningless. Why? Because Maimonides says we should not say "God is strong" but, rather, "God is not weak," but to say that someone is not weak is just as certain to arouse worldly visions of strength as saying that someone is strong. Similarly, Maimonides' theory implies that as well as not saying "God is wise" we should not say "God is not foolish," for the latter as well as the former will arouse visions of worldly wisdom. Hence, if we follow the logic of Maimonides' position we are left without anything positive or negative to say or even think about God.

Maimonides' one concession was to say that it is okay to say "God exists." That, according to Maimonides, doesn't describe God; it doesn't assert a characteristic of God that could be misunderstood; it merely asserts God's existence without saying what God is like. Given the logic of Maimonides' position, however, it seems that he should not have allowed us to say even that much, since our conception of existence is based on our experiences of the world just as much as are our concepts of power, wisdom, and so on. Specifically, our conception of existence is based on our experience of physical objects and physical properties that come into existence and go out of existence and depend on other things for their existence, so Maimonides should have also forbad us to say, "God exists." (Paul Tillich, a twentieth-century philosophical theologian, agreed that for such reasons as the preceding we should not say "God exists" or "God is a being," but he thought we could still say "God is the Ground of Being" or "God is Being-Itself." See his *Systematic Theology*.)

The ultimate result of Maimonides' *via negativa*, say some critics, is that we cannot know in the least what we mean when we use the word "God." Logical positivists would be happy with that conclusion and say, "Yes! That's what we've been saying! The word 'God' is cognitively meaningless!" Theists who reject the *via negativa* say, "No! The word 'God' is not cognitively meaningless! Therefore, any theory which implies that 'God' is meaningless is defective and needs to be replaced."

Second, the *via negativa* destroys the justification for worship. If we do not know what God is like in a positive sense, then how can we justify standing in awe of God or being devoted to God or worshipping God? As F.H. Bradley put it: If we do not know what God is like, then in worshipping God, we do not know what the devil we might be worshipping! Indeed, if God is totally unlike anything that we can understand, how can we justify any response to God other than ignoring mer and getting on with our lives? Perhaps this is why Ludwig Feuerbach said that the *via negativa* is "atheism in disguise." Positivists and atheists will like Feuerbach's and Bradley's points, but theistic critics of the *via negativa* blame and reject that theory because it undermines our understanding of God and our justification for worshipping God.

Third, some say we could not say what God is *not* like if we had no understanding of what God *is* like. More generally, it does not seem possible to meaningfully say what something is not like unless we have some idea of what it is like. If I ask you, "What is a spuggle not like?" how could you possibly answer me unless you have some idea of what a spuggle *is* like? Similarly, it is only because we do have some positive idea, however vague and obscure, of what God *is* like that we can say what God is not like. To be sure, as Maimonides insisted, it is important not to make mistakes in our thinking about God, but we can say what God is not like only in contrast to our understanding of what God is like, so we should not shy away from attempting to understand God or from attempting to give positive descriptions of God. Rather, we should try to formulate an illuminating theory as to how it is that human language can be used to make literally correct descriptions of God.

4. The *via analogia*: Meaningful Talk about God is Analogical (Thomas Aquinas)

Thomas Aquinas thought that Maimonides was wrong in thinking that we cannot make literally accurate positive statements about God. However, he agreed with Maimonides that when we say that God is powerful, intelligent, just, loving, etc., we should not mean the very same thing we mean when we say that humans or other creatures are powerful, intelligent, just, loving, etc. To understand what we should mean, and how it is related to but different from what we ordinarily mean, we need to explore three different ways in which a word can be used when it is used more than once: the univocal way, the equivocal way, and the analogical way.

Ways in which the same term can be used more than once:

1. *Univocally* (the very same meaning each usage)

The word "thumb" is used univocally in the following two sentences:

> "I have a thumb on my right hand."
> "You have a thumb on your right hand."

(The univocal way of talking about God leads to anthropomorphic deities such as those of ancient Greece and Rome because, if we are speaking univocally when we say that God is strong or wise we mean the same sort of thing that we mean when we say that an animal or a human is strong or wise.)

2. *Equivocally* (completely different meaning each usage)

The word "eagle" is used equivocally in the following two sentences:

> "I shot an eagle in the summer of 1988." (camera/bird)
> "I shot an eagle in the summer of 1988." (golf/score)

or

> "I bought a lemon in the fall of 1979." (citrus fruit)
> "I bought a lemon in the fall of 1979." (troublesome car)

This is the way of the *via negativa* and leads to a completely incomprehensible deity because whatever we mean by a term applied to anything in this world, when we use that word to speak of God we must mean something completely different. But how can we mean by a word something completely different from what it means in ordinary usage?

3. *Analogically* (related but incommensurable meanings)

The word "smart" is used analogically in the following sentences:

> "My dogs are smart."
> "My students are smart."

(Each statement is talking about the same thing, intelligence, the ability to understand things and solve problems, but it is recognized that the intelligence of students is of a higher order than that of dogs. The difference isn't just a matter of degree, such as one dog being smarter than another; it is a difference in kind.)

According to the *via analogia* the properties we attribute to God – such as power, knowledge, justice, love, and wisdom – are experienced by us first in the things that make up the world. But those properties (power, knowledge, justice, love, and wisdom) existed in God, according to Aquinas, before they existed in the world because God existed before the world (and, indeed, God created it). Moreover, the properties we find in the world that are worthy of attribution to God do not exist in God in the same form in which they exist in the things of this world. In God, those attributes exist in absolute perfection, and we cannot imagine or conceive of what infinitely perfect existence or power or knowledge or love or wisdom or goodness or justice would be like. But that does not mean we cannot understand anything about God; nor does it mean we cannot meaningfully, literally, and correctly ascribe those attributes to God. It just means we cannot comprehend the fullness of those attributes as they exist in God. They go off the graph of our minds, so to say, but we can see the direction in which they go off the graph; we can extrapolate toward where they are going, though we cannot follow them to where they culminate. We have examples of this kind of transcendence among ourselves, in, for example, the scientific genius of Albert Einstein, the musical genius of J.S. Bach, and the artistic genius of Michelangelo. Hence, the *via analogia*, according to its supporters, enables us to honor both our conviction that we know, at least in part and to some extent, what God is like, and Maimonides' conviction that at some point our understanding of the attributes of God reaches a limit beyond which we cannot pass, leaving us rapt in awe and adoration of the One in whom those attributes are eternally and perfectly fulfilled and united.

Baron Friedrich von Hügel illustrated this divine/human analogy in the following way. A dog, he said, is an intelligent creature; it can understand numerous things about its owner – such as when ze is going to feed the dog, when ze is going to take the dog for a walk, when ze wants the dog to heel or sit or chase a stick, and when ze wants to be left alone. But there is no reason to think the dog understands or could understand what zer owner is doing when ze is writing a poem or solving a problem in calculus or repairing a clock. From such experiences we understand that one level of intelligence can surpass another level of intelligence in such a way that a creature of the lower level of intelligence cannot at all understand the higher level of intelligence, even though creatures on both levels are intelligent. By analogy, we can understand that just as intelligent dogs cannot at all understand certain aspects of human intelligence, it is possible that there is a being who is so much more intelligent than every actual or even possible creature that no creature could even begin to understand certain levels and aspects of that being's intelligence – and that, says Aquinas, is what God's attributes are like in relation to creaturely powers of comprehension.

To summarize, we should not speak univocally of creaturely attributes and divine attributes (anymore than we should speak univocally of canine intelligence and human intelligence), but that does not mean we must speak equivocally of creaturely attributes and divine attributes. Certain attributes that we find in creatures, such as power and intelligence, seem worthy of attribution to a supremely perfect being, and are therefore properties which in a real, though very limited, way we share with God. Biblical theists might say that is part of what is meant by the biblical statement that humans are created in the image of God (Genesis 1:26–27). Perhaps God created humans in zer image, that is, created humans with certain properties that God also has, precisely so that humans could know in part what God is like. Hence, by analogical thinking we can know what God is like by recognizing that we share certain attributes with God but that the form which those attributes take in God exceeds anything that we can fully understand (and in some cases understand at all).

Finally, Thomas Aquinas believed it is important to point out that an analogy between a creature and God is never an analogy by proportion, that is, an analogy in which there is a specific or mathematical proportion between the creature and God. There can be a specific proportion of strength between, say, a mule and an elephant in a log pulling contest. But there can be no specific proportion between an elephant's strength and God's strength. When we draw an analogy with God, Aquinas says, rather than thinking in terms of analogy by proportion we should think in terms of analogy by proportionality. There is no definite proportion between the strength of an elephant and of God, just as there is no proportion between any whole number and infinity. Nonetheless, strength is strength so we know what we are talking about when we say that God is powerful.

Here are some quotations that may help you better understand analogy by proportionality:

Thomas Aquinas (1225–1274) articulated the *via analogia* by proportionality this way: "then only do we know God truly when we believe Him to be above everything that it is possible for people to think about Him" (*Summa Contra Gentiles*, I, 5). Note: Aquinas did not say that God is "different" from everything that it is possible for people to think about mer; that would lead to the *via negativa*. Rather, he said God is "above," meaning "superior to," everything that it is possible for humans to think about mer.

Gottfried Leibniz (1646–1716) says in *Monadology and Other Philosophical Essays*, ed. Schrecker, p. 140: "Though it be true that before the infinite God we appear as nothing, it is precisely a privilege of his infinite wisdom to be able to take perfect care of what is infinitely below him. Certainly there is no assignable proportion between the creatures and God; nevertheless, they [creatures] keep certain proportions among themselves and tend toward the order which God has instituted."

Robert Adams says in his *Finite and Infinite Goods* (Oxford University Press: 1999, p. 52), "God's superiority exceeds our cognitive grasp in a positive direction, and is not exhausted by negative or universalizing operations familiar to us. The divine knowledge, love, beauty are not just free from defects we can identify; they contain a richness we can hardly name. To us this richness is bound to be alien in ways we may find uncomfortable."

Finally, consider the Muslim chant: "God is greater. God is greater. God is greater!" When I first heard that chant I didn't think it made sense. It sounded like an incomplete sentence – God is greater than *what*??? Now I get it: Whatever *we* can think of, no matter how great, God is greater!

For Review, Reflection, and Discussion

1. Explain the differences between a word, a concept, and a thing. Give an example of each that was not given in this chapter.
2. Give an example of your own of each of the following uses of a word: univocal, equivocal, analogical.
3. How do the *via negativa* and *via analogia* theories of talk about God differ from one another? How do they agree?
4. What is the difference between the logical positivist theory of talk about God and the reductionist theory? What do they agree on?
5. What concession did Maimonides make for the use of positive talk about God?

6. Assuming the classical conception of God as a supremely perfect being, which of the four theories of the relation of human language to talk about God (naturalism, reductionism, *via negativa, via analogia*) do you think makes the most sense? Explain why that is your choice.

For Further Reading

Soskice, Janet, "Religious Language," in Taliaferro, Charles, Draper, Paul, et al., eds., *A Companion to Philosophy of Religion*, 2nd ed. (Wiley-Blackwell: 2010).

Peterson, Michael, *Philosophy of Religion: Selected Readings*, 2nd ed. (Oxford University: 2001). Part VII, "Religious Language," includes selections from Aquinas, Antony Flew, Wm. Alston, and others.

Davies, Brian, ed., *Philosophy of Religion: A Guide and Anthology* (Oxford University: 2000), Part II, includes selections from Augustine, Aquinas, Ayer, Richard Swinburne, and Flew. "Notes on Contributors" gives brief background on each philosopher.

Chapter 5

Arguments about the Existence of God

Soon we will begin looking at arguments for and against the existence of God. However, in order to understand more adequately what we are doing when we argue for or against the existence of God we need to distinguish between the following things:

1. A *discussion* (an exploration of a topic by two or more people)
2. A *disagreement* (people expressing opposite opinions or beliefs about some topic)
3. A *quarrel* (a disagreement in which people become angry or insulting)
4. An *argument* (in ordinary usage "argument" means a disagreement or a quarrel; in philosophy "an argument" means *one or more reasons given in support of a conclusion*)
5. A *debate* (consists of two opposed arguments – one person presenting an argument for a certain conclusion and the other person presenting an argument against the preceding argument)

When you engage in verbal exchanges with other people, or hear other people engage in such exchanges, pause and ask yourself what is going on. Is it a simple exchange of information ("It's going to rain." "Yes, but it won't be heavy."), or a discussion, or a disagreement, or a quarrel, or a debate, or is someone presenting an argument in the philosophical sense? Note that whereas in ordinary conversation the word "argument" is used to mean a quarrel, a debate, or a heated disagreement, in philosophy the word "argument" has a technical

Philosophy of Religion: The Basics, First Edition. Richard E. Creel.
© 2014 John Wiley & Sons, Inc. Published 2014 by John Wiley & Sons, Inc.

meaning, as defined earlier: one or more reasons presented in support of a conclusion. Philosophers frequently debate with one another, and when they debate they present arguments to each other. What we are about to do is examine and evaluate some of their arguments for and against belief in the existence of God. When I present a criticism of an argument what I am doing is presenting an argument against the original argument. If each of two people were to present one of those arguments to the other person (one argument for a certain conclusion and another argument against that conclusion), they would be having a debate.

The *objective* of an argument regarding the existence of God is, for the most part, either

1. To show that God does not exist, or
2. To show that God does exist, or
3. To show that God is different from what someone has claimed, or
4. To show that we do not or cannot know whether God exists.

The *strength* of an argument regarding the existence of God will be one of the following:

1. Proof (100% or 0%) (Necessary or Impossible)
2. Probability (>50% <100%; more likely true than not)
3. Plausibility (>0% ≤50%; less than probable but some reason to think it is true)
4. Possibility (>0%)/Impossibility (0%); ("possible" means "not impossible"; "impossible" means "not possible")

When examining an argument, first you want to ask how strong an argument the arguer is *claiming* to make. Is the arguer claiming that zer argument shows proof, probability, plausibility, or possibility? (It would not be fair to criticize an argument because it is not a proof when the presenter of the argument only claimed that the argument showed that its conclusion was plausible. The appropriate response, if you disagree, would be to argue that the conclusion is not plausible.) Having determined how strong a claim the arguer is making, then you want to determine whether the argument is really as strong as the arguer has claimed. A proof shows definitively that God does or does not exist. (Of course there is a difference between an argument *being* a proof and someone *thinking* it is a proof.) A probability argument aims at showing that God probably does exist or probably does not exist, given the evidence at hand. A plausibility argument is an attempt to show that there is some reason to believe that God does or does not exist even if it is not probable. The weakest argument is simply an attempt to show that it is possible that God exists or does not exist (a point to which we will return in the next chapter).

To help you further understand these points, consider the following diagrams. The first one tries to capture the difference between the extremes of certainly true and certainly false, with 50% representing "neither probable nor improbable."

100% (definitely true)........50%.........(definitely false) 0%
(neither probable $\updownarrow$ nor improbable)
99% ←← (probable) ←← 50% →→ (improbable) →→ 1%

Hard and *Soft* outcomes of arguments: here is some more terminology to help you distinguish the positions that people take regarding the existence of God:

```
                        Hard Theism – proves that God exists
                      /
    a. Theism
                      \
                        Soft Theism – shows that God probably exists


                        Hard Atheism – proves that God does not exist
                      /
    b. Atheism
                      \
                        Soft Atheism– shows that God probably does not exist


                        Hard Agnosticism – proves that we can't ever
                      /    know whether God exists
    c. Agnosticism
                      \
                        Soft Agnosticism – shows that we don't know now whether God
                        exists or not, but perhaps we can come to know that
```

Logical Possibility vs. Logical Impossibility:

It is logically possible for X to exist if X is cognitively meaningful and self-consistent, for example, if X is a circle.
It is logically impossible for X to exist if X is cognitively meaningless, for example, if X is a tranzel fludget.
It is logically impossible for X to exist if X is self-contradictory, for example, if X is a squircle (a square circle; see argument in Chapter 3).

Two types of argument regarding the existence of God:

An *a posteriori* argument is based on our experiences, and more specifically on our experience that there is a world, or on our experiences of the way the world is. This kind of argument, if it succeeds, achieves probability or plausibility but not proof of God's existence or nonexistence.

An *a priori* argument proceeds on the basis of pure reason; it does not appeal to experience or the way the world is; it achieves proof if it succeeds. The ontological argument, which we will examine soon, is an *a priori* argument; other arguments are *a posteriori* arguments.

Another conceptual tool that you need to understand and keep in mind is *the Principle of Sufficient Reason*. The principle of sufficient reason claims that for every thing that exists and event that occurs there is an explanation that is satisfactory to reason. This principle lies at the heart of science and is appealed to in several *a posteriori* arguments for the existence of God. Be careful to distinguish causes and reasons. There are causes, not reasons, that account for the extinction of the great dinosaurs. There are reasons, not causes, that explain why the internal angles of a Euclidean triangle must add up to exactly 180 degrees. There are causes of, not reasons for, you sneezing. There are reasons for, not causes of, your choosing to major in economics rather than history.

Keeping in mind what we mean in philosophy by "an argument," let's now begin exploring some of the major arguments for the existence of God. Later we will examine arguments against the existence of God. In each case, we will also examine criticisms of those arguments. But all along the way keep in mind this statement by Thomas Aquinas: "We must love them both: those whose opinions we share, and those whose opinions we reject. For both have labored in the search for truth, and both have helped us in finding it."

For Review, Reflection, and Discussion

1. What is the special meaning of "argument" in philosophy?
2. Explain how an argument in the philosophical sense is part of a debate.
3. Explain the differences between proof, probability, plausibility, and possibility.
4. Distinguish hard and soft outcomes of arguments.
5. What makes something logically impossible?
6. What are the differences between an *a priori* argument and an *a posteriori* argument? Which argument for the existence of God is an *a priori* argument?
7. What does the principle of sufficient reason say?
8. Do you think it is *possible* (not impossible) that God exists?

For Further Reading

Copi, Cohen, and McMahon, Kenneth, et al., *Introduction to Logic*, 14th ed. (Prentice-Hall, Inc.: 2010). A long-standing, popular introduction to the nature of argument and its various forms, including formal logic.

Schwartz, Stephen P., *Fundamentals of Reasoning* (Macmillan Publishing Company: 2005). Focuses on reasoning and informal logic. Worked out in the class room and well-tested.

Chapter 6

The Ontological Argument

The first argument for the existence of God that we will examine is the
ontological argument. It was developed in its earliest, most powerful
form by St. Anselm (1033–1109). This is an *a priori* argument, that is, it is
not based on experiences of the world; it is "prior" to or independent of
such experiences. It presumes to *prove* the existence of God simply from
analysis of the concept of God. This is a difficult, complex argument,
but thinking it through is one of the very best ways to gain an understanding of how philosophical thinking is done. I will develop this
argument by presenting several theses that build on one another,
providing replies by a critic plus responses to the critic – replies such as
Anselm did make or such as I think he would make.

Thesis 1: It is greater to exist in reality than just in the mind

St. Anselm said that the concept of God is the concept of a being than
which none greater can be conceived. Obviously, such a being must be
all-knowing, all-powerful, and eternal because, for example, it is greater
to have knowledge than to be ignorant, and it is greater to know everything than to be ignorant of anything. The same analysis applies to
power and duration of existence. Moreover, it applies not only to duration of existence but also to existence itself. Specifically, it is greater to
exist than not to exist; therefore, God must exist. If you think of God as
not existing, then you are not thinking of God, since it is possible to
think of a being greater than one which does not exist, namely, one
which does exist. It is not possible, however, to think of a being greater

Philosophy of Religion: The Basics, First Edition. Richard E. Creel.
© 2014 John Wiley & Sons, Inc. Published 2014 by John Wiley & Sons, Inc.

than a being than which none greater can be conceived. Therefore, logical analysis of the concept of God reveals that God exists! In brief, it is greater to exist than not to exist. Therefore, God – a being than which none greater can be conceived – must exist.

A critic replies: Sure, God exists, but only as an idea in people's minds.

ANSELM: Existing only as an idea in someone's mind would not be a very exalted form of existence. It is greater to exist in reality outside the mind than only as an idea in someone's mind. God is that individual than which none greater can be conceived. Therefore, if God existed only in the mind, we could think of something greater than God, but that is impossible. Therefore, if we think of God as existing only in the mind, we are not thinking of God. A being than which none greater can be conceived must exist in actuality and not merely as an idea in people's minds. Hence, we must think of God as existing in actuality or we are not thinking of a being than which none greater can be conceived.

GAUNILO: A critic named Gaunilo replied to Anselm as follows: by the preceding reasoning we could prove that a perfect anything exists, for example, a perfect island. All we need to do is say that a perfect island is an island than which none greater can be conceived. It is greater to exist than not to exist; therefore, an island than which none greater can be conceived exists! But such a conclusion is absurd ("absurd" in philosophy means obviously false or extremely questionable), and any argument which produces an absurd conclusion is fallacious. Therefore, the ontological argument is fallacious. (To show that an argument is fallacious by showing that an absurd conclusion can be drawn from it is called "the argumentum ad absurdum" – which consists of showing that the argument leads to an absurdity.)

ANSELM'S REPLY: Gaunilo's criticism is unfair to my argument. The question is whether a being than which none greater can be conceived exists. An island cannot be a being than which none greater can be conceived because it must be surrounded by water, so it must be finite, and anything that is finite can be surpassed, for example, by a bigger island, or an island with more trees or more flowers on it, or trees that are more beautiful, etc., so the notion of an unsurpassably great island is incoherent (as is also the notion of a whole number than which none greater can be conceived). Moreover, an island is by its nature contingent on other things, such as water, for its existence – no water, no island. But a being than which none greater can be conceived cannot be dependent on anything for its existence. Therefore, an island cannot be a thing than which none greater can be conceived. Hence, to believe that the ontological argument can be used to prove the existence of an island than which none greater can be conceived is mistaken. If the ontological argument works, it works only for a being than which none greater can be conceived, and such a being cannot be finite or contingent. However, any being other than God must be finite and/or contingent because any being other than God must depend on God for its existence. Hence, for any individual other than God, a greater can be conceived. (Gaunilo's criticism looks good at first, but, for the reasons just stated, even atheists agree that Gaunilo's criticism of Anselm's argument was not fair and does not work.)

IMMANUEL KANT'S CRITICISM OF THE ONTOLOGICAL ARGUMENT: A definition is a statement with two parts: *the subject* (which names that which is being defined) and *the predicate* (which lists the essential characteristics of the subject). For example:

"A Euclidean triangle is a closed, two-dimensional, geometrical figure, with three straight sides."

"Closed," "three-sided," "two-dimensional," and "geometrical" are the predicate terms which tell us what a triangle is. Kant complained that Anselm attempted to define God into existence, but nothing can be defined into existence. Existence is not a proper term in the predicate of a definition. The predicate terms in the definition of a thing establish its essence, not its existence. To say "X exists" is to say that the predicate terms which constitute the essence of X describe something that is actual. Consider this definition: "A chiliagon is a closed, two-dimensional, geometric figure with exactly 1000 sides." To say "A chiliagon exists" is to say "Something exists which is a closed, two-dimensional geometrical figure with exactly 1000 sides," but we cannot tell *from the definition* whether that statement is true, that is, whether a chiliagon exists. A definition tells us *what* to look for in order to find out whether something exists. It can't tell us whether it exists. Hence, Anselm made a fallacious move when he presumed to derive the existence of God from the definition of God. (In the language of informal logic Kant might say that Anselm "begged the question" of the existence of God by presuming the existence of God in his concept of God. That is, he *assumed* in his definition what he meant to prove rather than proving it.)

ANSELM: There are two problems with Kant's critique (Kant lived long after Anselm, so I am constructing a hypothetical response by Anselm).

First, says Anselm, I did not smuggle existence into the concept of a supremely perfect being and then pretend to find it in the predicate – like a child who hides an Easter egg for merself and later acts surprised to find it. I was as startled as anyone to discover that the concept of God entails the existence of God. My discovery was like that of the person who discovered that the internal angles of a Euclidean triangle must always add up to exactly 180 degrees. People were familiar with triangles long before anyone arrived at that insight. Similarly, people were familiar with the concept of God long before I realized that one of the essential characteristics of God – and therefore one of the necessary predicate terms in a fully developed definition of God, along with omniscience, omnipotence, etc. – is that God exists (and there were hints of this insight prior to me in Augustine and Boethius). In brief, I did not intentionally nor unwittingly hide existence in the subject of my definition of God and then, of course, find it among the predicate terms that define the essence of God. It was by sheer logical analysis of the concept of a being than which none greater can be conceived that I came to see that existence is one of the essential characteristics of such a being, just as surely as omniscience is.

Second, we should not be so quick as Kant to rule out the possibility that existence can be a predicate. After all, we can sometimes tell from the definition of a thing that existence is *not* a predicate of that thing, that is, that it *cannot* exist. For example: "A machelor is a married bachelor." We don't have to go knocking on doors to find out whether there are any machelors, and if so how many. All we have to do is think about the concept of a machelor, realize that it is self-contradictory (a machelor must simultaneously be both married to someone and not married to anyone), and we can conclude with certainty that there are no machelors. Hence, since we can prove by conceptual analysis that some things do not exist, we should not dogmatically rule out the possibility that by conceptual analysis we can prove that some other thing does exist, that is, that existence is one of the predicate terms in a proper definition of it (or is an implication of it). As was noted earlier, we need not worry that accepting this possibility will trap us into accepting the existence of all sorts of strange things. The only thing the existence of which is implied by its concept is a being than which none greater can be conceived, and that is God.

CRITIC: Anselm's thesis is correct. God cannot exist in the mind only. If God exists, God must exist outside the mind. However, that does not entail that God exists. It entails only that *if* God exists, then God must exist outside the mind. So those atheists who say "God exists only in the mind" are at worst simply mistaken (since God could not exist only in the mind), and at best they have simply misspoken (what they mean is that the *idea* of God exists, but God does not exist).

Thesis 2: It is greater to exist necessarily than contingently

ANSELM: But it's not only necessary that God exist in actuality and not merely in the mind, if God exists. If that were all there is to my argument, then the critic would be right that the nature of God does not require that God exist. However, it is greater to exist necessarily than contingently. To exist contingently means for a thing to depend on something other than itself for its existence. For an individual to exist necessarily means it has the property of *aseity*, that is, it exists solely by virtue of its own nature. It is greater to exist necessarily than in dependence on anything else. Therefore, God, a being than which none greater can be conceived, would not exist in dependence on anything else. Moreover, since God must exist necessarily, therefore God must exist because that which is necessary is that which must be the case, just as it is necessary that the internal angles of a Euclidean triangle must add up to 180 degrees. Hence, just by thinking about the nature of God, we can see that God must exist necessarily rather than contingently and therefore *must* exist in actuality, not just in someone's mind.

CRITIC: Anselm's second thesis, like his first, is correct, but once again his conclusion is unwarranted. He is correct that *if* God exists, then God must exist necessarily. But that just means that if God exists, God does not depend on anything for zer existence, so if God exists, it is impossible for God to cease to exist. Because of God's property of aseity (existence by virtue of zer own nature), God's continuance in existence cannot be contingent on anything. It is the nature of God, a supremely perfect being, to be indestructible and imperishable. Hence, because God must exist necessarily, that secures God's continuance in existence *if* God exists, but that does not imply that God exists. It implies only that *if* God exists, then God exists necessarily, that is, noncontingently. Anselm's second thesis tells us *how* God must exist *if* God exists, but it does not imply that God *must* exist and therefore does exist.

Thesis 3: It is greater to necessarily exist than to contingently exist

ANSELM: Good point. But God must not only *exist necessarily* if God exists; God must also *necessarily exist* (the different word order makes a tremendous difference). To be sure, David Hume said that anything that can be conceived to exist can also be conceived not to exist, but he was wrong. As people are fond of saying, "Every rule has its exception," and God is the exception to Hume's rule (and the only exception). Why is God an exception? Because it is greater to necessarily exist than contingently exist. Something which contingently exists is something which exists but did not have to exist; it is something which could have not existed, such as the Eiffel Tower. Obviously, God would not contingently exist, since it is not only greater to exist than not exist, it is also greater to necessarily exist, that is, to *have* to exist, than to be such that one could have not existed. Therefore, God necessarily exists, and since that which necessarily exists must exist, therefore God exists, exists necessarily, and exists in actuality and not merely in the mind.

6.1   Is Anselm's Argument Decisive?

Has Anselm proven that God exists? Some say "yes." Others, even admirers of the ontological argument, like G.W. Leibniz, say that one thing, and only one thing, remains to be done to make Anselm's argument a decisive proof of the existence of God. Before we examine what Leibniz thought was missing, let me ask a question: Do you believe it is *possible* that God exists? (Note: I am not asking if you believe that God *does* exist. I am asking only if you think it is *possible* that God exists.)

What Leibniz thought was missing from Anselm's argument and would turn it into a proof of God's existence was a demonstration that the existence of God is *possible*. Leibniz and many contemporary philosophers agree that if the existence of God is possible, then God exists, because that which necessarily exists, exists whenever it is possible for it to exist. So if it is possible for God to exist, then God exists. That argument is a two-edged sword, of course, because if it is *not* possible for God to exist, then it is *impossible* for God to exist (that which is not possible is impossible), and if it is impossible for God to exist, then, of course, God does not exist, never did, and never will. So now let's take up the question, "Is it possible for God to exist?"

Let's approach that question by doing a general analysis of what makes it possible or impossible for anything to exist. This analysis is developed along the lines of an ontological argument by Duns Scotus (1265–1308). First let's look at a schematic diagram of the argument. The general strategy of the argument is to show that the reasons why it would be impossible for something to exist do not apply to God (therefore it is not impossible for God to exist), and the reasons why something might be possible but not actual do not apply to God, so by elimination we can, according to this Scotian/Leibnizian argument, conclude that God exists.

In the diagram, I use "X" because if the analysis is correct, *everything* falls into one category or another, whether we are speaking of a rock, a watermelon, a lizard, or God. Explore the argument/diagram by first looking at "X" on the far left; then look at the two alternatives of X (impossible and possible); then look at the alternatives for "impossible" and "possible," and so on. After you study this diagram I will relate it to the question of the possibility or impossibility of the existence of God.

6.2   A Version of Duns Scotus' Ontological Argument

(The heart of Scotus's argument can be found in James Ross's *Philosophical Theology*)

I will explain the following diagram more fully later, but first explore the diagram by starting on the far left with "X is," then go up to "impossible if" and study the two alternatives. Then go down to "possible and is" and follow the various alternatives.

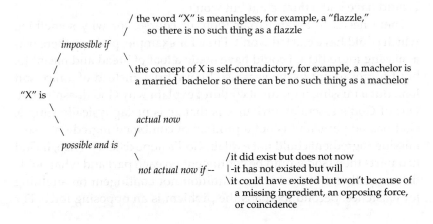

Now let's apply the preceding analysis to the question of the possibility of the existence of God.

First, unlike the word "flazzel," the word "God" is not meaningless. By "God" we mean a supremely perfect being. Therefore, it is not impossible for God to exist because the word "God" is meaningless. Second, the concept of God is not self-contradictory. Therefore, it is not impossible for God to exist because the concept of God is self-contradictory. Hence, unless we can think of some other good reason why it is impossible that God exists, we should think it is possible that God exists. (The assumption here is that the burden of proof is on those who say that the word "God" is meaningless or the concept of God is self-contradictory.)

Obviously, though, just because it is possible for something to exist does not mean that it does exist. Something which can possibly exist may be actual now or not actual now (though it must be one or the other). Hence, perhaps it is *possible* for God to exist but God does not exist. If that is true, then one of three things must be the case. First, it could be that God did exist but no longer does. Obviously, though, that cannot be true because if God ever existed God would always exist because a supremely perfect being could not pass out of existence. Second, maybe it is the case that God has never yet existed but will. Just as obviously, that cannot be true of God because a supremely perfect being would never have not existed. Moreover, anything that comes into existence depends on something to cause it to come into existence, but, as we have seen, a being than which none greater can be conceived would not depend on anything for its existence. Third, maybe God *could* have existed but just won't – just as my wife and I could have had a third child but won't.

There needs to be an explanation, of course, for why something which could have existed won't. First, for example, perhaps there was a missing ingredient. I could have made a loaf of bread and meant to, but I forgot to put in the yeast, so I got a brick instead of a nice soft loaf. But a missing ingredient couldn't explain why God doesn't exist. One of God's essential attributes is that ze is metaphysically simple; God has no parts and is not a product of combined ingredients, so a missing ingredient could not explain God's nonexistence. Also, if God had parts then God would be contingent on each part and what holds them together, but God is by definition not contingent on anything for existence. Second, perhaps the problem is an opposing force. For example, let's say I planted a tulip bulb and could have had a tulip flower in the spring, but someone dropped a big piece of glass over the place where I planted the bulb. All the ingredients were there – bulb, moisture, sun, nutrients – but the glass prevented the bulb from developing. Surely, though, an opposing force would not explain why God could have existed but will not. Such a force would have to be stronger than God, which nothing can be; moreover, it would make the existence of God contingent on the absence of something. Third, perhaps the explanation is that God could have existed but simply doesn't and won't; it's just a matter of coincidence. But that explanation makes God's existence contingent on chance – God could have existed but just didn't get lucky! Clearly, though, the existence of a being than which none greater can be conceived would not be contingent on luck or chance.

In conclusion, the preceding analysis, along lines suggested by Duns Scotus, seems to show that it is possible that God exists and that there is no good reason to think that although it is possible for God to exist that nonetheless God does not. Hence, it seems we should conclude that God exists.

The ontological argument is a formidable argument and also the most controversial of all the arguments for the existence of God. One way to reject Scotus's version is to challenge the idea that it is possible that God exists. One might agree with all that Anselm and Scotus said yet add, "So far as I *know*, the existence of God is possible, but that does not prove that God exists. It doesn't even prove that it is possible that God exists. There are many things that I *think* are possible but are not, and perhaps the existence of God is one of those things. It is true that metaphysically, that is, in terms of reality, if it is possible that God exists, then God exists. But in terms of epistemology, that is, in terms of what I know, I cannot say that I *know* that it is possible that God exists. All I can say is that *so far as I know* it is possible that God exists – and that is not enough to prove that it is possible that God exists."

To go at this a bit differently, a critic of the ontological argument might agree without qualm that if it is possible that God exists, then God exists. And the critic might agree that Scotus does a nice job of eliminating reasons why it might not be possible for God to exist. But there is a huge gap between "It is possible that God exists" and "So far as I know it is possible that God exists." According to the critic the most that Scotus has led us to is the latter, and that doesn't rule out the rationality of also saying, "But so far as I know it is also possible that God does not exist." In conclusion, if Anselm and Scotus are correct, and you believe it is possible that God exists, then you should also *believe* that God exists – but that is not the same as to *know* that God exists. Similarly, if you believe it is not possible that God exists, then of course you should believe that God does not exist – but that is not the same as to know that God does not exist – and you need to explain why you think that the arguments by Anselm and Scotus do not favor the existence of God. Meanwhile, if you are not sure *what* to think about the possibility of the existence of God, then you should join me in exploring some additional arguments for and against the existence of God.

For Review, Reflection, and Discussion

1. Anselm's ontological argument was presented by means of three theses. State the three theses in the order in which they were presented. Then explain how each thesis tries to improve upon and go beyond the previous thesis.
2. Gaunilo applied an "argumentum ad absurdum" strategy to Anselm's argument. What does an argumentum ad absurdum attempt to show? How did Gaunilo use the example of a perfect island to critique Anselm's argument?
3. What was Immanuel Kant's reason for rejecting the ontological argument? What did he say Anselm presumed to do that cannot be done?
4. What does Duns Scotus's argument try to show?
5. Does Scotus's argument succeed? If it succeeds, does it, together with Anselm's argument, prove the existence of God? If it does not succeed, why not?

For Further Reading

Anselm of Canterbury, *Monologium* and *Proslogium*. The ontological argument is in the first few chapters of the *Proslogium*, which is included in nearly every anthology of philosophy of religion. Other types of arguments are included in the *Monologium*.

Descartes, René, *Meditations*. Descartes' ontological argument is in the fifth meditation. Available in many editions.

Plantinga, Alvin, *God, Freedom, and Evil* (Eerdmans: 1977). A modal version of the ontological argument. Short, difficult, important.

Chapter 7

The Cosmological Arguments

Having explored the ontological argument at length and having been left without a proof, many would say, that it is possible that God exists (but also without a proof that it is impossible that God exists), let's look into some other arguments.

All arguments except the ontological arguments are *a posteriori* rather than *a priori*. That is, they come *after* experience of the world and are based on some characteristic of the world – either its sheer existence or some property or properties of it. Before proceeding, we need to reexamine *the principle of sufficient reason*, as all of the arguments regarding God presuppose it. There are two important aspects of that principle. First, it says, there is an explanation for everything that exists and event that occurs. To be sure, we may not know what that explanation is, but there is an explanation. This is a way of saying that reality makes sense, from top to bottom. Moreover, the existence of a thing or occurrence of an event must be explained either (i) in terms of itself, that is, its essence, or (ii) in terms of something other than itself. For example, it is by means of its essence that we explain why the angles of a Euclidean triangle must add up to 180 degrees. (Also, the ontological argument endeavors to prove the existence of God simply by appealing to the essence of a being than which none greater can be conceived.) By contrast, it is by means of something other than itself that we explain why a billiard ball changed from being at rest to being in motion (perhaps it was hit by another billiard ball or a cue stick or was moved by an earth tremor).

The second aspect of the principle of sufficient reason is its claim that more cannot come from or be gotten from less, that is, a cause

Philosophy of Religion: The Basics, First Edition. Richard E. Creel.
© 2014 John Wiley & Sons, Inc. Published 2014 by John Wiley & Sons, Inc.

must be at least as great as its effect. We can produce a shadow from the combination of light, a solid object, and a reflecting surface, but we cannot produce light or a solid object or a reflecting surface from a shadow. From the characteristics of a living animal we can produce a marble statue of the animal, but from a marble statue of an animal we cannot produce a living animal (Leibniz's *Monadology*, paragraphs 31 and 32).

Now let's turn to our first *a posteriori* arguments for the existence of God.

7.1 The First Three of "The Five Ways" of Thomas Aquinas

Thomas Aquinas is one of the most prolific and influential philosophers and theologians in western history. Among many other things he produced five short arguments for the existence of God, three of which are cosmological arguments. They are based on the existence of motion, causation, and contingency.

A. The Argument from Motion to a First Mover/an Unmoved Mover

We observe in the universe that some things are in motion. When we examine them, we discover that none is moving entirely on its own power. Everything in motion in the universe depends on something beyond itself to put it into motion – either by a push or a pull or conversion of an energy source such as food or gasoline. A is moved by B; B is moved by C; C is moved by D; and so on. A couldn't move without B, or some other mover acting upon it; B couldn't move without C, or some other mover acting upon it; and so on. Therefore, something must exist which injected movement into the universe in the first place. That is, there must be "a first mover" which is unmoved by anything else but which is capable of *initiating* movement in other things – otherwise things would not be moving. Without "an unmoved mover" we would have no explanation as to why things that are not entirely capable of self-motion are in motion. Indeed, since things at rest remain at rest and things in motion slow down and cease moving unless something external makes them move, if there were no first mover, we should expect all things in the universe to be motionless, frozen in space. But they are not; so there must be an unmoved mover.

Think of railroad boxcars. You can't make the cars move by simply adding more boxcars or attaching them in a circle. An engine (or some other powerful force) must be added to make them move. This analogy is imperfect, of course, because the engine is not an unmoved mover; it must be stoked with coal or some other source of fuel, but once it is, it is capable of temporary self-motion whereas the boxcars are not even capable of that. Hence, to initiate and sustain the chain of moved movers which constitute the universe, there must be an unmoved mover at the beginning, beyond the universe. The most plausible candidate for the first mover is God. Obviously, God, who is omnipotent, could initiate motion in a universe and is therefore the most plausible candidate for having done so. Hence, the motion we see in the universe is evidence for the existence of God. (Does this argument show that it is definite that God exists or probable or only plausible or merely possible or something else?)

B. The Argument from Causes and Effects to a First Cause/Uncaused Cause

The structure of this argument is identical to the structure of the argument from motion, but it is based on the fact that we observe in the universe that some things are effects and other things are causes of those effects. However, every cause we examine turns out to be an effect of some cause that preceded it. Nothing *in* the universe is an uncaused cause, so nothing in the universe is capable of explaining why the components of the universe are connected in cause/effect chains rather than having no effect on one another. Hence, to explain why every cause in the universe is an effect of some other cause, we must conclude that there is a first cause that kicked off the causal chain in the universe, something which pulled the trigger of the Big Bang, something which is not itself caused by anything else, and which, therefore, is an uncaused cause. The most plausible first cause, the most plausible uncaused cause of the causal chains in the universe is a being that can act independently of anything else, viz., God. Hence, the existence of causal chains in the universe is evidence for the existence of God. (Again, and as we go along, ask of each argument and criticism whether it is a proof, or a matter of probability or plausibility or something else.)

C. The Argument from Contingent Beings to a Necessary Being

When we look at the universe, we notice that things exist. When we examine the things that exist, we discover that each of them came into existence and has passed or will pass out of existence. This means the things that make up the universe are *contingent* beings, that is, they depend on something other than themselves for their existence. Hence, we need an explanation for why they exist, since they did not have to exist. Because the universe at any moment is simply the sum total of all the contingent beings which exist at that moment, therefore the universe as a whole is contingent and we need an explanation for the existence of the whole universe. Because the things which make up the universe did not have to exist, neither did the universe have to exist, so we need an explanation of its existence.

It cannot be the case that once upon a time absolutely nothing existed and then the universe popped into existence out of nothing. Why? Because something cannot come into existence out of nothing. As a famous Latin statement puts it, *Ex nihilo nihil fit*. ("From nothing nothing can be created.") Nothing has no potentiality, so where there is absolutely nothing, nothing can come into existence. Anything that has potentiality is something, not nothing. Hence, to explain the existence of the universe we must go beyond it to something that exists necessarily, not contingently. That which exists necessarily exists by virtue of its own essence or nature. That is to say, because of its nature it has to exist, just as surely as because of the nature of a triangle the internal angles of a triangle have to be equal to two right angles. The only thing we know of which by its very nature would exist necessarily and not contingently is a being than which none greater can be conceived, that is, God.

In brief, the existence of contingent beings is not self-explanatory and can be explained only by the existence of a being the existence of which *is* self-explanatory, that is, a necessary being. Therefore, from the existence of contingent beings we can infer that a necessary being exists, and the most plausible candidate for the status of necessary being is a being than which none greater can be conceived, that is, God. Hence, the existence of contingent beings is evidence for the existence of God.

7.2   Paul Edwards' Infinite Regress Argument against the Cosmological Argument

Paul Edwards (1923–2004) argued that the universe is an endless, infinite regress of caused causes. The universe has always existed, and every event in it can be explained in terms of other natural events which occurred before it. An infinite regress of caused causes does not require the existence of a first cause or an uncaused cause in order for us to have an explanation for everything that exists (hence, we can honor the principle of sufficient reason). Each thing in the universe can be explained in terms of something natural that was prior to it, so nothing in it is unexplained, yet all is explained naturalistically, without God. If this seems difficult to conceive of, think of the series of negative whole numbers, counting backwards from zero to minus one, minus two, etc. That series of numbers regresses infinitely. There is no largest negative whole number from which the series starts moving forwards toward zero. For any negative whole number there is a larger one immediately before it. Similarly, Edwards argues, for every natural event, no matter how long ago it may have happened, there is another natural event immediately before it which is the cause of it and the explanation for it. Hence, every natural event is explained by another natural event, and there is no need to bring God into the explanation.

Edwards might say that the cosmological argument commits *the fallacy of composition*. The fallacy of composition consists of assuming that because a part of something has a certain property that therefore the whole thing (the composite) must have that property, but obviously the fact that a watermelon seed is black does not mean that the watermelon has to be black. The cosmological argument, according to Edwards, commits the fallacy of composition because it assumes that because each part of the universe is caused that therefore the universe as a whole must have a cause, but that doesn't take into account the possibility of an infinite regress of events. A whole (in this case the universe) does not necessarily have to have the same properties as its parts (in this case the property of being caused). (By contrast, the *fallacy of division* is the opposite of the fallacy of composition. The fallacy of division consists of assuming that a part must have the same property as the whole of which it is a part, but just because a watermelon is green does not mean that each of its parts, for example, the meat or the seeds, must be green.)

7.2.1 Two Criticisms of Edwards

First, Edwards is correct that if the universe consists of an infinite regress of caused causes, then the existence or occurrence of each thing in the universe could be explained naturalistically. However, he is mistaken in thinking that the existence of an infinite series of contingent beings does not itself require an explanation. The whole series (even if infinite in length) could have not existed, so why does it exist? The existence of the series *as a whole* cannot be explained from within the series by a natural cause, since any such natural cause will be part of the series the whole of which needs to be explained. Hence, the existence of an infinite series of contingent beings must itself be explained by something outside the series, that is, outside the universe. (Cf. G.W. Leibniz, *Philosophical Writings*, xi–xii.) In brief, the existence of an infinite regress of caused causes would not be self-explanatory whereas the existence of God would be self-explanatory, so the existence of God, together with God's creation of the universe, would explain the existence of an infinite regress of natural causes – *if* the universe is an infinite regress of events. Without God an infinite regress of natural events would remain unexplained and the principle of sufficient reason would be unsatisfied.

Second, a few lines back I said "*if* the universe is an infinite regress" because apparently it is not. According to modern science the universe began about 12 billion years ago with "a big bang." That means there has not been an infinite regress of natural caused causes. Rather, there has been a finite regress. Hence, we need an explanation not only as to why the universe exists rather than doesn't exist (whether or not it has always existed); we also need an explanation as to why it began, since it hasn't always existed. Obviously, the Big Bang theory fits in nicely with the biblical idea that God created the universe, perhaps out of nothing (*ex nihilo*).

7.3 The Oscillatory Theory

There is, however, a scientific theory which doesn't require a supernaturalistic explanation of the Big Bang. According to the oscillatory theory, the universe has always been expanding and contracting, and always will be. The Big Bang that we know of was merely the latest explosion of the universe. There have been an infinite number of others before it. After each explosion of the universe it expands until, under the influence of the gravitational pull that the material components of the universe exert on one another, the expansion of the universe slows to a stop and then the universe begins contracting. It contracts faster and faster, and gets smaller and smaller and hotter and hotter until it reaches "critical mass" and explodes again. That process has been going on forever and will go on forever. Hence, we have a completely naturalistic explanation of the cause/effect chains and transient beings in the universe. (For an analogy, think of the material components of the universe as like a cluster of rubber balls all connected to a center by rubber bands. An explosion at the center of the cluster drives the balls apart, stretching the rubber bands which eventually stop the expansion and draw the balls back together, at which point another explosion drives them apart again.)

7.3.1   Criticism of the Oscillatory Theory

The oscillatory theory is an intriguing idea which was very attractive for a while. However, according to independent research teams at several universities, it is not true. The pivotal point seems to be that there is not enough matter – and therefore gravitational attraction – in the universe to make it "close," that is, to make it cease expanding and start contracting. According to our best evidence the universe is "open," that is, will keep expanding forever – at an accelerating rate! Moreover, even if the universe did close and contract, that would not guarantee oscillation. There could just be a Big Splat rather than another Big Bang, or there could be a series of bounces that diminish into motionlessness – and then we would need an explanation as to how the series got started.

Finally, even if the oscillatory theory were true, we would, as we saw with Edwards' depiction of the universe as an infinite regress, still need an explanation as to why an oscillating universe existed rather than a different kind of universe or nothing at all, since the existence of an oscillating universe would not be self-explanatory (all it would explain is why the universe keeps going, not why it exists).

In conclusion, according to Thomas Aquinas and contemporary Thomists the most plausible explanation of the existence of motion, causation, and contingent beings is that God, a necessary being who is an unmoved mover and an uncaused cause, exists and created them.

7.4   The Kalam Cosmological Argument

The final cosmological argument we will consider is both older than those of Thomas Aquinas (thirteenth century, CE) and yet more recent. The kalam cosmological argument originated with Muslim scholars such as Al-Kindi in the ninth century, CE., but it has been resurrected with gusto in recent years by William Lane Craig. See his book *The Kalam Cosmological Argument* (1979). This argument can become very sophisticated very quickly, but the heart of the argument is this premise: there cannot be an *actual infinite*, and therefore the world had to have a beginning. To say that there cannot be an actual infinite is to say, among other things, that a series of actual events cannot recede into the past infinitely, that is, forever. If that premise is true, that means that there cannot be an infinite number of events prior to the present moment in history, so the universe must have had a beginning, that is, there must have been a first moment of the universe. If that were not so then an infinite number of events would have to have been crossed to get to the present moment, but an infinite number of events cannot be crossed. The present moment is here, however, so only a finite number of events could have been crossed to get to the present moment, and therefore past time must be finite.

To be sure, there can be a *potential infinite* of events *going into the future* (the world might go on forever and ever), but that series is never *actually* infinite; we call it *potentially* infinite because it *could* go on forever, not because it ever is infinite. At any given moment time is always finite in length because (as Craig just argued) it had to have a beginning and it never reaches past the present. By analogy, if we start counting whole numbers from "1" and continue doing so forever, then that counting will be a potential infinite because the counting of whole numbers never reaches an end, but at any given moment the number of whole numbers that we have counted will always be finite because we started with "1" at a specific moment so that at any later moment the number of whole numbers counted from the first moment of counting to the present will always be finite. We can never reach infinity by adding one more number and one more number and one more number. No matter how long we do that, the total number of numbers counted from the first moment to the present will always be finite. Whatever unit of time is *actual*, Craig is arguing, is always finite, complete, and up to the present moment it is what it is forever without change.

In addition to the argument just presented, Craig presents points to show that belief in an actual infinite leads to absurd consequences (hence, he is trying to destroy the credibility of the idea of an eternally existing world by developing what we earlier called an "argumentum ad absurdum," i.e., an argument to absurdity). For example, if the past is an actual infinite, then if we start counting back the number of events from 100,000 BCE into the past, that number of events is equal to the number of events if we start counting back from 2000 CE because (on the assumption that the past is an actual infinity of events, that is, that the number of past events is infinite) each of those two sets of events will be infinite in number, and one infinite is not larger than another infinite (each unit in each infinite series can be matched one to one with a unit in the other series so that there are no left over units; they are equal in extension), but it is certainly odd to think that the number of events going backwards from 2000 CE is no larger than the number of events going back from 100,000 BCE, so something seems unacceptably odd about the idea of an actual infinity of past events. The more plausible assumption, which does not produce bizarre consequences, is that the number of past events or moments is finite – an assumption that is also supported by recent science. (Again, notice that this is a reductio ad absurdum argument.)

Now let me try an example of my own. If an analog clock with an hour hand, minute hand, and second hand has existed and run for an infinite amount of time, with the hour hand circling the face of the clock 1 time every 12 hours, the minute hand circling 12 times every 12 hours, and the second hand circling 720 times every 12 hours, then if the clock had been running an actually infinite amount of time, then the hour hand would have circled the face of the clock exactly the same number of times as the second hand because each would have circled the face of the clock an infinite number of times, and one infinite is no larger than another infinite. But that conclusion is obviously absurd; therefore the concept of an actual infinite must be flawed. (Note: in imagination we can suppose a clock that has, up to the present moment, run forever; the issue is whether it would make sense to suppose that an *actual* clock could have run for an infinite amount of time up to the present moment.

In order to do that, the hands would each have had to circle the face of the clock an infinite number of times in order to arrive at the present moment, but an infinite number of circlings cannot be achieved by adding one circling to another to another, etc.)

The significance for us of the preceding arguments is this, according to Craig: the world must have had a beginning; its existence cannot recede infinitely into the past or events would have never arrived at the present moment. Hence, the world must have had a beginning, and its cause must have been something outside the world. Obviously, something outside the world that caused the world would not be a total description of God, a supremely perfect being, but if the kalam argument succeeds, it certainly seems to establish that there is a being with at least two of the attributes of God: incomprehensibly great intelligence and power.

Hence, if the kalam cosmological argument succeeds, it does not by itself establish the existence of God, but, theists would say, it is a step in the right direction – a step that can be supplemented with other arguments that increase the probability that there is a being with other divine attributes, thereby developing *"a cumulative argument"* for the existence of God. For example, Aquinas's cosmological arguments might establish that the creator must be a necessary cause that has existed forever; the teleological argument might establish that God is an intelligent being and therefore a personal being; the moral argument might establish that the creator is a being concerned with fairness and justice; arguments from religious experience might establish that God is a loving, forgiving being; the argument from simplicity might establish that it is more plausible that all of these attributes are united in one being than that there are many divine beings each of which has one of these attributes. Hence, according to the cumulative argument, the overall case for the existence of God strengthens as more and more arguments accumulate in favor of the existence of God. (We will be looking at these other arguments soon.)

We must ask, however, does the kalam argument succeed in establishing a beginning to the world and a creator of it that exists outside the world? Here are two reasons that have been given for saying "no." *First*, we have no proof that God exists, so it may be that there is no God, but there must be something that exists necessarily (Craig would agree to that). Therefore it is possible, so far as we know, that *energy/ matter* is the necessary being, exists necessarily, is the "creator," the basis, the source of the world as we know it; perhaps energy/matter has always existed and is the "stuff" of which all things are made; perhaps there is only *one* thing that exists: energy/matter expressing itself in constantly changing forms and coagulations – forms and coagulations such as you and me, the Sun and the Earth! If that is true, then there would be an infinite regress of forms that matter/energy has been taking since forever, and we will simply have to figure out how to accommodate that fact philosophically (just as if it is a fact that *God* exists, there is much that we will have to learn to accommodate philosophically about God). As G.W.F. Hegel said, "The Owl of Minerva flies at dusk." That is, after facts are proven or probabilified, it is philosophy that must accommodate itself to the facts, not vice-versa. *Second*, Craig uses an *argumentum ad absurdum* to deny the possibility of an infinite regress of events into the past, but critics reply that the absurd consequences that *seem* to follow from assuming an actual infinite do not really follow because according to modern set theory in mathematics, the rules that apply to finite math (such as Craig employs) do not apply to infinite math (which is what critics say should be applied to the concept of the actual infinite). Infinite math, it is claimed by the critics, can explain away the absurdities that Craig derives by inappropriately applying finite math. To examine whether this criticism of Craig's argument is correct, would take us into deeper water than we should attempt to fathom now, but for the hearty it is a bracing, exciting debate.

Caveat ("caveat" is Latin for "warning"; a common phrase, "caveat emptor," means "buyer beware"):

Again we note that the cosmological arguments do not claim to be *proofs* of the existence of God. Taken together they do claim to be proof of the existence of a necessary being that is an unmoved mover, an uncaused cause, and the cause of the world. To be sure, those are necessary or essential characteristics of God in the classical sense, so if those arguments succeed, they cumulatively strengthen the case for belief in the existence of God. However, a supremely perfect being is much more than just a necessary being which is an unmoved mover, an uncaused cause, and the creator of the world. A supremely perfect being, a being than which none greater can be conceived, would also be, among other things, a personal being with knowledge, a free will, and the power to act and implement intentions, and who is wholly good. Consequently, let's now examine the teleological arguments, which are more relevant to the *personal* characteristics of God (characteristics such as intelligence, intention, free will, and a sense of justice and compassion); being an unmoved mover, an uncaused cause, a necessary being, etc., are generally considered to be *ontological* or *metaphysical* characteristics rather than personal characteristics of God.

For Reflection, Review, and Discussion

1. What are two aspects of the principle of sufficient reason?
2. Do you accept the principle of sufficient reason? If yes, why? If no, why not?
3. State Thomas Aquinas' argument from motion and his argument from contingent being.
4. Do you agree that *ex nihilo nihil fit*, that is, from nothing nothing can be created?
5. Make up a new example of the fallacy of division or the fallacy of composition.
6. State Paul Edwards' criticism of the cosmological argument from causation.
7. State a criticism of Edwards' criticism of the argument from causation.
8. State the oscillatory theory of the universe and one criticism of it.
9. The kalam cosmological argument says that there cannot be an actual infinite. What does that mean, and how, according to William Lane Craig, does it bear on Paul Edwards' critique of the cosmological argument from causation?
10. What is a cumulative argument? How does it bear on the question of the existence of God?

For Further Reading

Aquinas, Thomas, *Summa Theologiae* Part I, Question 2, Article 3.
Zagzebski, Linda, and Miller, Timothy, eds., *Readings in Philosophy of Religion: Ancient to Contemporary* (Wiley-Blackwell: 2009). Part II.B consists of selections presenting the cosmological argument by Plato, Aristotle, Aquinas, and others, plus an early statement of the kalam cosmological argument. For a contemporary presentation of the kalam argument see J.P. Moreland's article "The Kalam Cosmological Argument" in *Philosophy*

of Religion: Selected Readings, 2nd ed., edited by Michael Peterson (Oxford University: 2001), pp. 196–208.

Keller, James A., *Problems of Evil and the Power of God* (Ashgate: 2007), pp. 122–4, provides sophisticated criticisms of the kalam cosmological argument.

Rowe, William L., "Cosmological Arguments," in Taliaferro, Charles, Draper, Paul, et al., eds., *A Companion to Philosophy of Religion,* 2nd ed. (Wiley-Blackwell: 2010), An overview by an authority.

Edwards, Paul, "Objections to cosmological arguments," in Davies, Brian, ed., *Philosophy of Religion: A Guide and Anthology* (Oxford University: 2000).

Chapter 8

The Teleological or Design Arguments

A teleological argument is not an argument from the concept of God or from the mere existence of the world or from a simple property in the world, such as motion. Rather, a teleological argument presupposes the existence of the world plus motion and causation because it is based on what appear to be orderliness and purpose in the world. We will look at teleological arguments from Plato, Thomas Aquinas, William Paley, and F.R. Tennant. Then we will look at the fine-tuning argument and an argument from morality. The goal of these arguments is to demonstrate the probability of the existence of God, or at least the plausibility of the existence of God. (To say that something is *plausible* is to say there is enough evidence in its favor that it is not irrational to believe it, even though there may not be enough evidence to demonstrate that it is more likely true than not. If something is probably true, then of course it is also plausible that it is true; indeed, it is more than merely plausible that it is true.)

1. *Plato* (427–347 BCE), *Laws* X: Plato observed that in human affairs, order implies intelligence at work; neglect produces disorder. The universe is orderly (consider the changes of the seasons; the orbiting of the planets; the germination and growth of plants). Therefore, the universe is probably under the guidance of a supreme intelligence; otherwise we should expect the universe to be disorderly and chaotic. As a student told me, "Every big corporation has someone running it. The world is like a big corporation. Therefore there must be someone running it." As the ancient Greek philosopher Epictetus

Philosophy of Religion: The Basics, First Edition. Richard E. Creel.
© 2014 John Wiley & Sons, Inc. Published 2014 by John Wiley & Sons, Inc.

said, "What then, after all, is the world? Who governs it? Has it no governor? How is it possible, when neither a city nor a house can remain [orderly], ever so short a time, without someone to govern and take care of it, that this vast and beautiful system [of the universe] should be administered in a fortuitous and disorderly manner?" (*Great Traditions in Ethics*, 4th ed., eds., Albert, Ethel M., Denise, Theodore Cullom, et al. [D. Van Nostrand Pubs.:], p. 88.) Hence, the orderliness of the universe is a reason to think there is a God (and when there appears to be disorder in the universe, we discover order under the disorder when we examine it. Chaos always proves to be order that we just did not yet understand).

2. *Thomas Aquinas* (1225–1274): In his *Summa Theologiae* (Summary of Theology) Aquinas set forth five ways to demonstrate the existence of God. We have already examined the first three ways, which are cosmological. The fifth way is a teleological argument which Aquinas stated as follows:

    The fifth way is taken from the ordered tendencies of nature. A direction of actions to an end is detected in all bodies following natural laws even when they are without awareness, for their action scarcely ever varies and nearly always succeeds; this indicates that they do tend toward a goal, not merely succeeding by accident. Anything, however, without awareness, tends to a goal only under the guidance of someone who is aware and knows; the arrow, for instance, needs an archer. Everything in nature, consequently, is guided to its goal by someone with knowledge, and this one we call "God." (*Summa Theologiae* I, Question 2, Article 3, or see *An Aquinas Reader*, ed. Mary T. Clark [Image Books: 1972], p. 124.)

    In another work, *De Veritate* (On Truth), Aquinas set forth another statement of the teleological argument. Speaking of the regularities of nature and how things in nature are suited to one another's needs he said:

    > ...unless such suitabilities and aptnesses [of things in nature] were in some sense intended, they would come about by chance and so would not happen most of the time but only rarely, like other things which we say happen by chance. Hence we must say that all natural things are ordained and disposed to their well-adapted effects.
    >
    > There are two ways in which a thing may be ordained or directed to something else as its end: (1) by itself, as a man directs himself

to the place where he is going; and (2) by something else, as an arrow is aimed at a definite spot by the archer. Nothing can direct itself to an end unless it knows the end, for the one directing must have knowledge of that to which he directs. But even things which do not know the end can be directed to a definite end, as is evident from the arrow (*De Veritate*, Question 22, Article 1, Reply, paragraphs 1 and 2).

To summarize, in the human realm that which happens randomly or unintentionally does not happen for the most part. Accidents are rare, so the vast regularities of nature suggest a mind at work rather than chance. Moreover, to aim at a goal is a mark of intelligence and purpose. Nonintelligent things cannot envision goals and aim at them. Consequently, we should expect their behavior to be random and unpredictable, but it is not: fruit trees go through multistaged processes each year like clockwork; the fetuses of animals go through multiple stages of maturation with great predictability; moisture evaporates from the earth, gathers into clouds, disperses across vast stretches of terrain, condenses into rain and waters the vegetation of the earth, and then the cycle begins again. Yet in none of these cases can the cycle, or development, or behavior of the fruit tree, the foetus, or the weather be explained in terms of intentions on the part of the fruit tree, the foetus, or the weather. Those things behave as though they know what they are doing, yet they do not. They are not conscious beings. Therefore, the most plausible explanation of their behavior is that they are under the guidance of an intelligent being. Similarly, arrows do not fly to the bull's eye of a target because that's what they want to do. Rather, their behavior must be explained by means of the intentions of an archer who wants them to do so. In brief, the most plausible explanation for the fact that many things in nature behave as though they know what they are doing when they do not is that they are under the guidance of an intelligent being. Theophilus of Antioch, an ancient philosopher, illustrated this point as follows:

Just as the soul in man is not seen, as it is invisible, but is known through the movement of the body, so God cannot be seen with human eyes; but He is observed and known through providence and His works. Just as one, at the sight of a well-equipped ship which sweeps over the sea and steers towards a harbour, becomes aware that there is a helmsman on her, who directs her, so also one must be aware that God is the director of everything, even though He is not seen with bodily eyes, as He cannot be apprehended by them (Ludwig Ott, *Fundamentals of Catholic Dogma* [B. Herder Book Co.: 1958], p. 14).

3. *William Paley* (1743–1805): Now we turn to the most famous teleological argument – the one formulated by Englishman William Paley in his *Natural Theology*. Have you ever found a watch that was lost by accident? Many people have because many watches have been lost – including one of mine. (I put it on top of my car "for a moment," forgot about it, and drove off. Goodbye watch!) Now for another question: Have you ever found a watch that was *created by accident*? Whereas the first question seems ordinary enough, and a "yes" answer to it would not be surprising, the second question is amusing, and a "yes" answer to it would seem preposterous. Why? Because a watch is such a complicated mechanism that we would never expect one to come about by accident. As William Paley said, the mutual adaptation of diverse parts to one another for the production of a single end is a sign of intelligence at work. (I encourage you to reread the preceding sentence carefully.)

A watch of the kind that Paley had in mind in the eighteenth century was made of diverse parts and diverse materials. It had gears of various sizes made of brass so they would not rust, a spring made of steel because of steel's elasticity, a metal stem with which to wind the spring that turns the gears, metal hands turned by the gears, a face with numbers on it behind the hands, a metal case to protect all those parts, and a glass dome through which the hands could be seen – all fitted together in complex ways to enable a person to keep track of time. Of course, we would not expect to find such a complex mechanism created by accident, by, for example, the mindless churning of waves over the materials on a beach for even thousands of years. But if we would not expect something as simple as a watch to be created by the mindless churnings of natural forces, how much less should we expect something so complex as the human eye to be the product of the mindless churnings of nature.

The eye is enormously more complicated than anything that humans have yet invented. It consists of (among many other things) the sclera, which is opaque and white to keep light from coming into the eye from confusing directions; the cornea, which is clear to allow light to come through from the most useful direction; the pupil, which expands and contracts to adjust the amount of light that comes into the eye; the lens, which is clear and focuses the information that comes through the cornea; the muscles attached to the eye that allow us to move our focus up and down, right and left; and the retina – a black material at the back of the eye (the only naturally black material in the body) that absorbs incoming light and sends stimuli to the optic nerve, which transmits that stimuli to the brain, producing images that enable us to perceive and orient ourselves in the physical world. If we would not expect a watch to be produced by accident (not even if we started with all the parts, put them in a box, and shook them for a thousand years), how much less should we expect a human eye to come about by accident! To repeat the main point here: the mutual adaptation of diverse parts to one another for the production of a single end is a sign of intelligence at work.

4. *David Hume* (1711–1776): A Criticism of the Teleological Argument

   Dave Hume, an eighteenth-century Scot and one of the most influential modern philosophers, pointed out that if the universe consists of a finite number of self-moving particles, then over an infinite period of time all of the possible combinations of those particles will come about – just as if you roll dice long enough you will get all of the possible combinations, and if you roll them for a really long time, you should not be surprised to get a 1/1, 2/2, 3/3, 4/4, 5/5, and 6/6 in a row, one after the other. Sooner or later it is bound to happen. Similarly, Hume pointed out, it was almost inevitable that the combination of particles which constitutes the way the universe is right now would come about by sheer accident, due to the blind forces of nature churning those particles into various combinations. Hence, there is no need to postulate the existence of God in order to explain the occurrence of the eye or anything else. It was almost certain that the current state of the world would come about by accident sooner or later, and now it has.

Criticisms of Hume's Critique:
A. Hume simply assumed the existence of zillions of material particles, but so far as we know, they did not have to exist, so we

need an explanation for *why* they exist. If they were created by God, then we have an explanation. Otherwise, we do not have an explanation and the principle of sufficient reason is unsatisfied.

B.   Hume simply assumed that material entities are eternally self-moving. Our experience is that they are not. Energy diminishes over time, so we need an ultimate explanation for why things are moving rather than motionless, for why matter is dynamic rather than static.

C.   Hume assumed that there has been an infinite amount of time for the particles of nature to mix with one another, but there has not. The universe is only about 12 billion years old, which is infinitely less than an infinite amount of time. If you took all the sand from all the beaches, oceans, and deserts of the world and put it in one pile, and then took one grain from that pile, that one grain of sand would be far far greater in relation to the size of the pile from which it was taken than 12 billion years would be as compared to eternity. In the big scheme of things, 12 billion years is not that much time. Furthermore, given all the sequential, preparatory stages that had to arise in order for the current stage of the universe to be reached, 12 billion years was not that much time for it all to have happened by blind accident. Hence, the critic says, we should look for a better explanation than blind accident.

D.   Furthermore, for Hume's model to be plausible, the universe would have to be closed and static so that the atoms of the universe would neither drift too far apart from one another to be able to interact, nor get compressed too close to one another to be able to move, but, rather, would remain at the right distances from one another so that they would keep being thrown back into interaction with one another so that all combinations of them would take place. Unfortunately for Hume's argument, not only is the universe not eternal, it is also not closed. Rather, it is open. That is, there is no boundary or force in the universe which ensures that material particles will remain close enough to continue producing new combinations. Moreover, according to the latest research, material entities are racing away from one another at ever faster speeds, which means that the opportunities for particles to combine with one another are fewer and fewer as time passes and the material entities of the universe get farther and farther apart from one another. Since that is the natural inclination of the universe, according to the Second Law of Thermodynamics, the principle of entropy, and recent research, we need an explanation as to why complexity on the Earth, and perhaps beyond Earth, has been increasing steadily over 12 billion years rather than decreasing.

E.   Finally, *if* it is possible for life and consciousness to arise from atoms that are neither living nor conscious, why do such atoms exist? Why wasn't it rather the case that no atoms existed? Or only atoms from which it was not possible for higher properties, such as life and intelligence, to emerge?

In brief, Hume's critique of the teleological argument has serious problems of its own.

5.   *The Fine Tuning Argument, the Anthropic Principle, and the Multiverse*

The fine-tuning argument is an updated version of the design argument. Evidence for and against the fine-tuning argument becomes scientifically technical quickly, but we can grasp the outline of the argument without presuming to pass judgment on the technical data. The argument's basic point is that recent science has discovered many facts regarding the laws of physics and the initial conditions of the universe which if they had been only minutely different, life could not have emerged. To quote Robin Collins, "If the initial explosion of the big bang had differed in strength by as little as one part in 10^{60} (that's 10 followed by 60 zeros!), the universe would have either quickly collapsed back on itself, or expanded too rapidly for stars to form. In either case, life would be impossible." Collins points out in addition that if the strong force in the atom, or the strength of gravitational attraction, or the electromagnetic force had been even slightly stronger or weaker, or if the ratio of the mass of the neutron or the electron to the proton had been minutely larger or smaller, then life could not have emerged (*Readings in the Philosophy of Religion*, ed. Kelly James Clark, p. 55).

It is, then, as though these various natural elements are like thousands of tuning knobs on a life generating device, all of which had to be individually tuned within exceedingly small limits and coordinated with one another for life to emerge. Theists like Collins argue that it is far more plausible to think that such fine tuning and coordination resulted from intelligence at work than from a plethora of mindless accidents. It is certainly not our experience in science and engineering that sophisticated technological achievements, such as the Hubble Telescope or space station launches and operations, result from accident.

8.1   The Anthropic Principle

Some theists say that it is such an amazing thing that we are here to observe and marvel at the wonders of the universe that the fact of our astonishment counts as a reason to think that the universe was created by a God who wants us to marvel at it. It is, after all, a surprising and wonderful thing that we are here to observe and study the universe.

By contrast, *the anthropic principle* says we should not be surprised to find that the universe is adjusted to accommodate intelligent life. If it were not, we would not be here to observe it! Because we are here, of course, the fundamental constants and the evolution of the universe had to be consistent with the production of intelligent creatures who can observe it. Hence, we should not be "awed" by those facts, as though we arrived here with tremendous odds against us. It may just be the case that the universe is such that it *had* to produce intelligent life eventually, and therefore the existence of intelligent life tells us nothing about whether God exists; it just tells us something about the nature of the universe. As to those variables which if they had been only slightly different, intelligent life could not have existed, that is true – but that does not mean that those variables *could* have actually been different. The universe may be such that its constants, laws, basic properties, mass, etc., could not have varied significantly (or at all) and so of course, intelligent beings emerged and are observing the universe! The universe did produce us; but we may simply be an inevitable product of its components and processes. Consider an analogy. A billiard ball just sitting in the middle of a pool table has an infinite number of directions in which it can roll, but when it is hit by another ball there is only one direction in which it can go (because of the direction from which it is hit by the other ball), so we should not be surprised when it goes in that direction rather than in the infinite number of other directions in which it could have gone. Similarly, we should not be astonished that we are here to marvel at the universe; we should simply try to understand the natural processes whereby we came about.

That may be true, says the supporter of the fine tuning argument, but it seems questionable to claim that those constants could not have varied given some of the things we have learned in quantum physics, such as Heisenberg's principle of indeterminacy and the instability of microparticles, discoveries that undermine the thesis of strict determinism in the universe. It seems more plausible to assume that "the stars aligned" in a way that produced life because of intentional manipulation of the numerous, delicate, unstable variables involved than that it just happened by chance. But note: the fine tuning theist is not saying that it is impossible that our universe could have been "fine-tuned" for intelligent life by chance; ze is saying it is not as plausible to think that the universe came about by accident or "just happens" to be geared to produce intelligent life which marvels at its own existence and the wonders of the universe as that it was "engineered" to do so by a powerful, intelligent being who *wants* us to marvel and seek understanding.

8.2 The Multiverse

Some critics of the fine-tuning argument concede the force of the preceding criticism of the anthropic principle but add that there is another explanation as to why we should not be surprised that our universe is fit for intelligent life. These are people who believe in a *multiverse*, that is, a universe of universes. They believe that our universe is only one of very many simultaneously existing universes, perhaps an infinite number, that have been generated over time by *future-eternal fluctuations* or *vacuum fluctuations* of the universe. We will not go into the fascinating physics of these purported universe generators, but the point is that reality consists of virtually an infinite number of universes (each universe like an individual bubble in a surging sea of soapy water), so we should not be surprised that among those many universes there would be some that are conducive to intelligent life, and ours is one of them.

This "many-universes theory" is fascinating and is taken seriously by some astrophysicists, so it should not be dismissed as absurd. To be sure, to date there is little to no positive evidence for it. But stay tuned. Scientific research on the multiverse idea continues.

Finally, some critics say that the universe is not as orderly as has been claimed. Earth is the only pocket of the universe where we know life to have emerged. So far as we can tell, the rest of the universe is hostile to life, not supportive of it, so the claim of a fine-tuned *universe* that is favorable to life is greatly exaggerated.

6. *F.R. Tennant (1866–1957): The "Cosmic, Wider Teleology" (Evolution is Evidence for God)*

William Paley lived before Charles Darwin so his argument did not take Darwin's theory of evolution into account. Now that the Darwinian theory of evolution is almost universally accepted among scientists is there any longer any reason to think that an intelligent designer is at work in the universe? The British philosopher F.R. Tennant thought so. He was, with Darwin, a fellow Englishman and was very familiar with Darwin's theory of evolution by random mutations and natural selection. Tennant agreed that Paley's argument was not adequate after Darwin. Rare, isolated instances of order could be plausibly explained by accidental combinations. Consequently, if when we look at the universe we were to see chaos nearly everywhere with only occasional instances of order, then it would be plausible to explain such instances of order as a result of accident. But that, Tennant claimed, is not what we see. It is plausible that mindless processes could produce by accident a bit of complexity here and a bit of complexity there, but from random, mindless processes we should not expect the kind of steady progress in complexity that we see in the history of the cosmos.

If we consider what has happened over the 12 billion years of the existence of the universe, in spite of the principle of entropy – which says that disorder is gradually and inexorably increasing in the universe – we see a rather straightforward development of matter from less complex states to more complex states, from inorganic to organic, from inanimate to animate, from insentient to sentient, from nonconscious to conscious, from nonintelligent to intelligent, from non-self-conscious to self-conscious, from nonrational to rational, from nonaesthetically sensitive to aesthetically sensitive, from nonmoral to morally sensitive – each stage being prepared for by a preceding stage. For example, organizations of inorganic matter had to reach a high level of complexity before life could emerge in material entities. Then living entities had to reach a yet higher level of complexity before sentience could arise, and so on. In brief, Tennant said, there appears to be "directivity in the entire cosmic process." Goal-orientation in the universe is not merely an occasional, local occurrence; it cuts through the entire history of the universe. Indeed, very recent research in astrophysics, well after Tennant's time, indicates that there is probably life on numerous other planets beyond our solar system. Hence, an historical look at the universe does not give the impression of things happening according to blind chance. Rather, the history of the universe strongly suggests that its development from one level to another has been under the guidance of an intelligent being, from the Big Bang until now. Hence, evolution itself favors the hypothesis of a supreme director of the universe.

Some of the criticisms previously aimed at David Hume can also be aimed at Darwinian atheists: (i) they have no explanation for why the universe exists rather than not; (ii) they have no explanation for why the Big Bang occurred, injecting motion and causation in the universe rather than there being none; and (iii) they have no explanation for why mutations favorable to biological differentiation and progress occur so frequently rather than less frequently or not at all. About these things atheists simply say, "That's just the way things are. There is no explanation" – which is, of course, to abandon that principle which is so central to scientific research and progress: the principle of sufficient reason. Tennant thought it more plausible that the universe would be evolutionary if there is a God than if there is not.

Furthermore, we need an answer as to how it is that life can emerge from what is lifeless, that sentience can arise from what is insentient, that consciousness can arise from that which is not conscious, and so on. If there is no God, then the emergence of these radically different properties from particles which did not possess them in the first place is more astonishing than any miracle in the Bible. How, for example, can consciousness arise from that which is not conscious and never has been conscious? It seems more plausible and less mysterious that such properties would emerge if there is a God than if there is not. If there is a God, then God, who is supremely conscious and omnipotent, can confer consciousness on organisms that reach a certain level of complexity, or perhaps God can create a substance with the potentiality and the inner mechanisms for consciousness to emerge as in fact matter has developed over the history of the universe. But if there is no God, then it is an utter mystery as to how life can arise from the lifeless, or consciousness from that which is not conscious, or why matter which has these potentialities and tendencies should exist rather than not. As the eighteenth-century French philosopher Jean-Jacques Rousseau said, "combination and chance will never result in anything but products of the same nature as the elements that are combined." He added, "I do not have it within me to believe that passive and dead matter could have produced living and sensing beings, that a blind fatality could have produced intelligent beings, that what does not think could have produced thinking beings. I believe therefore that the world is governed by a powerful and wise will" (*Emile*, Basic Books, Inc.: 1979, p. 276). In other words, if you put a bunch of rocks in a box and shake them, all you're ever going to produce are different arrangements of a bunch of rocks – or mindless atoms. The great English philosopher John Locke published similar thoughts 73 years earlier in *An Essay Concerning Human Understanding* (1689). He said, "It is as impossible to conceive, that ever bare incogitative Matter should produce a thinking intelligent Being, as that nothing should of itself produce Matter." "And I appeal to everyone's own Thoughts, whether he cannot as easily conceive Matter produced by *nothing*, as Thought to be produced by pure Matter, when before there was no such thing as Thought, or an intelligent Being existing" (IV, X, Section 10).

The emergence of a completely new property in a system is either a mysterious brute fact or it requires the action of a higher being capable of (i) investing that property into that system or (ii) creating a substance which has those potentialities and inclinations in its very nature. To say, "There is no explanation for the emergence of these radically new properties," would be, again, to abandon the driving principle at the heart of science: the principle of sufficient reason. Hence, we should conclude that the best explanation for the emergence of radically new properties such as life, sentience, consciousness, self-consciousness, aesthetic sensitivity, moral sensitivity, and freedom of choice, is that there is a higher being who knows what they are and has the power to instill them into systems that are sufficiently complex to enable them to operate. This sentiment is expressed in Psalm 94:9 in the Bible by means of two questions: "He who planted the ear, does he not hear? He who formed the eye, does he not see?" In other words, doesn't it seem more plausible that the eye and the ear were created by someone who knows what it is to see and hear than by blind, deaf, mindless forces?

Two other features of the universe that Tennant believed favor the existence of a God who designed the universe have to do with the *fittedness* of certain things for one another. First, Tennant said, it is an amazing and wonderful thing that (i) we are intelligent enough to understand many things about the universe, and (ii) the universe is intelligible to us. It didn't have to be that way. It could have been the case that we were just as intelligent as we are now but that the universe was so different from the way it is now that it was unintelligible to us. Or, it could have been the case that the universe was just as it is now but that we were not intelligent enough to understand it very well or at all. Or, it could have been the case that the universe was unintelligible and that it contained no intelligent creatures. The last three arrangements would not be unlikely results to expect if the universe were the product of blind, mindless forces. Instead, the universe is intelligible and it contains intelligent creatures; indeed, the intelligibility of the universe and the level of human intelligence are wonderfully matched to one another. (Note: we just "ran out the permutations" in this paragraph. Some of you may be familiar with this concept from doing math or playing dice! To run out the permutations means to figure out all the basic possibilities of something. For example, the permutations of flipping a coin are heads and tails; there are no other alternatives. The permutations of rolling a normal six-sided die are 1, 2, 3, 4, 5, 6; there are no other possibilities. The permutations of rolling two dice are much greater, including 1/1, 1/2, 1/3, 1/4, 1/5, 1/6, 2/1, 2/2, 2/3, 2/4, etc., on through 6/1/6/2, 6/3, 6/4, 6/5, and 6/6. There are no other combinations. If you're shooting craps, don't bet on a double seven! We will return again and again to the concept of running out the permutations.)

In addition to the match of intelligence and intelligibility, we are capable of understanding far more about the universe than we need to know in order to survive as a species, and we crave such knowledge, whether it has any practical value or not. Those two facts – the way the intelligibility of the universe and the level of our intelligence are fitted to one another, and the generosity of that fit, which allows us to enjoy pursuing knowledge well beyond anything that is useful for the survival of our species – those two facts are better explained by the hypothesis that we and the universe are creatures of a divine being who wants us to be able to understand the universe and wants us to enjoy the pursuit of knowledge for its own sake, and not merely for its practical value, than they are explained by the hypothesis that we are the products of mindless, accidental, uncaring forces. It seems unlikely that the latter process would have produced so much more intelligence and curiosity on our part than is needed for mere survival.

Of the preceding four possibilities that could have existed, it is significant that the one which does exist is the only one that it is plausible to think a supreme being would create. Therefore, *its* actuality, rather than any of the other three possibilities, is a reason to think that the universe was created by a powerful, intelligent being who knows what knowledge is, treasures it, and wanted to create an intelligible universe plus creatures capable and desirous of understanding it. Finally, we are able not only to *understand* the universe as the creation of an intelligent being; we are also able to *contribute* to it. It is as though the creator of the universe has made us able not only to create things that have practical value but also to participate in the sheer joy of creation by creating things of beauty or fascination that have no importance for our survival or propagation.

Tennant's *second argument* from fittedness is parallel in structure to the preceding argument, but its focus is on beauty rather than knowledge. His beginning observations are that the universe is full of beauty and we are capable of appreciating and enjoying it. It could have been the case that our aesthetic sensitivities were exactly as they are now but that the universe was devoid of beauty, or it could have been the case that the universe contained all the beauty that it now contains but that we were incapable of appreciating it, or it could have been the case that there was no beauty in the universe and no one capable of enjoying beauty. Any of those last three arrangements would not be surprising in a universe created by blind, mindless forces, but what actually exists is the fourth possibility, which is the only one of the four that we would expect to be created by a supreme being who knows what beauty is, who treasures it, and who wanted to make it possible for others to enjoy and treasure it. Hence, the fact that the only one of these four permutations which it would be plausible for a supreme being to create is the one that exists is a good reason for thinking that God exists. Furthermore, in human culture, neglect (lack of mindful attention) usually produces things that are boring or ugly; it usually takes mindful attention to produce things that are aesthetically interesting or beautiful. Hence, the amount of beauty and aesthetic intrigue in the universe favors the hypothesis that the universe is the creation of a powerful, intelligent, aesthetically sensitive being, and not of mindless, insensitive forces.

Tennant's point about the feast of beauty that exists in the universe was expressed poetically by Robinson Jeffers in his poem "The Excesses of God" in his book *Be Angry at the Sun* (Random House: 1941), p. 104:

> Is it not by his high superfluousness we know
> Our God? For to equal a need
> Is natural, animal, mineral: but to fling
> Rainbows over the rain
> And beauty above the moon, and secret rainbows
> On the domes of deep sea-shells,
> And make the necessary embrace of breeding
> Beautiful also as fire,
> Not even the weeds to multiply without blossom
> Nor the birds without music:
> There is the great humaneness at the heart of things,
> The extravagant kindness, the fountain
> Humanity can understand, and would flow likewise
> If power and desire were perch-mates.

In criticism of the preceding theories see the work of Richard Dawkins, especially *The Blind Watchmaker* (1986) and *The God Delusion* (2006). Dawkins argues that "blind" production of natural complexity such as we see today can be explained by the painstakingly slow, *cumulative* organization of matter over eons of time. Such organization, Dawkins argues, is self-sustaining, self-perpetuating, and self-transcending, so together with accidental mutations that occasionally produce systems that are even more suited to survival than the previous systems, it should not be surprising that more and more complex systems gradually emerged until we are where we are today.

For Review, Reflection, and Discussion

1. The Goldilocks Principle says that this universe is "just right" for life – not too hot and not too cold! There are an infinite number of ways in which the universe could have been *in*compatible with life, so it is highly unlikely that it was not meant to be hospitable to life. If the universe weren't made to produce intelligent life, we would not be here to observe and marvel at it! What do you think about the force of the Goldilocks principle?
2. State Thomas Aquinas' teleological argument, the so-called "fifth way." Why is it called the fifth way?
3. How did William Paley use an analog watch to argue that God exists?
4. How did David Hume presume to undermine Paley's argument?
5. State a criticism of Hume's criticism of the teleological argument.
6. State the oscillatory theory of the universe and a criticism of it.
7. How does the fine-tuning argument appeal to recent science to make its case?
8. Some theists say that our being here to marvel at the universe should make us think that the universe was *purposely* designed for us to study and marvel at. How does the anthropic principle counter that claim?
9. What is the "multiverse" or "many universes" way of explaining why we should not be impressed that the universe has produced us?
10. How did F.R. Tennant argue that evolution is evidence for the existence of God?
11. Tennant thought that "emergent properties" were good evidence for a transcendent power being at work. What did he mean by that? Give an example of an emergent property.
12. What did Tennant mean by the "fittedness" of things to one another? Give an example and explain why he thought the fittedness of things favors the existence of a God.

13. How did Tennant run out the permutations on intelligence and the intelligibility of the universe? (Or beauty)
14. Do Tennant's arguments from fittedness undermine the anthropic principle or does the anthropic principle undermine Tennant's arguments from fittedness?
15. What is Richard Dawkins' argument against the kind of position that Tennant puts forth?
16. Do you think the teleological argument is stronger than the cosmological argument as an argument for the existence of God? If yes, why? If no, why not?

For Further Reading

Zagzebski, Linda, and Miller, Timothy, eds., *Readings in Philosophy of Religion: Ancient to Contemporary* (Wiley-Blackwell: 2009), Part II.A, "Teleological Arguments." Includes selections from Aquinas, Paley, Hume, Robin Collins, and others.
Craig, William Lane, "Theism and Physical Cosmology," in Taliaferro, Charles, Draper, Paul, et al., eds., *A Companion to Philosophy of Religion*, 2nd ed. (Wiley-Blackwell: 2010). The last section is on the fine-tuning argument, the anthropic principle, and the multiverse theory.
Tennant, Frederick R., *Philosophical Theology* (Cambridge University Press: 1969). 2 vols. Volume 1 originally published in 1928 and Volume 2 in 1930.
For sophisticated rebuttals of Richard Dawkins' Darwinian materialism see *Mind & Cosmos* (Oxford University Press: 2012) by Thomas Nagel, an atheistic naturalist who rejects materialism, and *Where the Conflict Really Lies* (Oxford University Press: 2011) by Alvin Plantinga, a theist and leading philosopher of religion.

Chapter 9

God and Morality

9.1 Two Arguments from Morality for Belief in the Existence of God

In closing the preceding section, I mentioned F.R. Tennant's observation that humans have consciences plus conceptions of moral and immoral, right and wrong, just and unjust. Tennant and other theists say that those phenomena would be strange things to emerge from a sea of energy consisting of nothing but mindless, lifeless atoms in a Godless universe. By contrast, the fact that we have consciences and concepts of morality and justice fits quite well with the hypothesis that we were created by an intelligent being who wants us to be moral and has given us the knowledge and encouragement to be so – whether by the influence of conscience, intellectual insight, revelation, or all of these. To be sure, we can to some extent explain conscience in terms of socially induced fear and guilt, but there is obviously more to morality than that. We can become critics of the behavior in other societies, and, more tellingly, we can become critics of the behavior, customs, and laws *in our own society*. When we do that we are obviously appealing to moral standards that are absolute and transcend social explanations. Such laws are best explained as coming from a transcendent source, so that is a reason to think there is a God.

Cardinal John Henry Newman makes a related point in his book *Grammar of Assent*. He says that the fact that we have consciences and sometimes feel ashamed or disturbed or frightened at having done what we believe is morally wrong is best explained by the hypothesis

Philosophy of Religion: The Basics, First Edition. Richard E. Creel.
© 2014 John Wiley & Sons, Inc. Published 2014 by John Wiley & Sons, Inc.

that there is Someone who has given us our consciences and to whom we feel responsible; that, of course, would be God. As pointed out earlier, some of what goes on in our consciences can be accounted for socially – some but not all, as sometimes we feel guilty for going along with what is socially approved, which implies that there is a higher moral authority than society of which we are aware. Therefore, the existence of conscience is more evidence in favor of the existence of God.

9.2 The Relation of Morality to God

Having spoken of God and morality, we should acknowledge that the concepts of God and morality have been intimately linked since at least the time of Moses, around 1250 BCE. Indeed, the story of Moses and the Ten Commandments is right at the heart of the first theory of God and morality at which we will look, so now let's ask *how* God and morality are related to one another. In total, we will look at three theories: the divine command theory, the theocentric theory, and the natural law theory. Note that these theories are not arguments for the existence of God. They are attempts to explain how we acquire moral knowledge from God.

9.2.1 The Divine Command Theory

The divine command theory assumes the existence of God, and further assumes that because God is our creator and sustainer, therefore we ought to obey God. But how can we know what it is that we ought to do? How can we know what is morally right and wrong? The divine command theory claims that God *determines* what is morally right and wrong and then *reveals* it to us. There is nothing morally right or wrong apart from a decision by God to make it such. Because God is perfectly independent, God is not constrained by anything, not even moral norms; indeed, there are no moral norms, no moral rights and wrongs, until God creates them. Hence, according to the divine command theorist, God did not reveal to Moses what was already right and wrong. Rather, God revealed to Moses what God *decided* would be morally right and wrong. Until God says that something is morally right or wrong it is not morally right or wrong. Hence, the only way for us to know what is morally right and wrong is for God to decide what it will be and to reveal zer decision to us – thus the relevance of the story of Moses and the revelation of the Ten Commandments on Mount Sinai (see the book of Exodus in the Bible, Chapters 19–20). This divine command theory is an effort to honor God's sovereignty and to recognize God's perfect freedom and independence.

There is, however, a problem with the divine command theory that was revealed long ago in a discussion that the Greek philosopher Socrates had with a man named Euthyphro. In Plato's dialogue named *Euthyphro*, Socrates asks Euthyphro whether something is morally right because God says it is or whether God says it is morally right because it is morally right. As much as those alternatives might sound alike, there is a big difference between them – a difference with serious implications. If something is morally right or wrong simply because God says it is, that means there are no moral principles independently of God *deciding* what they will be (just as the divine command theory says), and that seems to mean that God could make anything, including slavery, rape, infant cannibalism, and sadistic torture, morally right or wrong simply by declaring it to be so. Such an implication makes the divine command theory seem morally repugnant to many people.

On the other hand, if we say that God says that things are morally right or wrong because they are such independently of God's making them such, that implies that God has no freedom with regard to determining moral right and wrong. Right and wrong would be independent of God's decisions. God's only freedom would be to decide whether to tell us what is morally right and wrong. And if moral right and wrong are independent of the will of God, perhaps there is a way for us to find out what they are without having to get that information from God, as we will see when we examine the natural law theory. But before we examine that theory, let's consider the possibility that we should acquire our moral bearings from reflection on the concept of God.

9.2.2   Theocentric Ethics

"Theos" means "God" and "centric" means "centered" so theocentric ethics says we should try to figure out what is morally right and wrong by thinking about what a supremely perfect being, that is, God, would will that we do, would say about how we should live our lives, and treat one another and other living creatures. For those who believe in God, this approach seems unavoidable because even if someone, such as Moses, or some book, such as the Koran, declares that God has said that such and such is morally right or wrong, believers must ask themselves whether it seems reasonable that God, a supremely perfect being, would declare such a thing to be forbidden or required. Such an approach will require thought about the attributes of God and the implications of those attributes for our behavior. Of course, this approach does not rule out the possibility that God may have revealed to us what is morally right and wrong in order to make sure that we know it, but, again, that does not exonerate us from the responsibility of asking whether what is *declared* to be divine revelation is such that we can responsibly believe that it is divine revelation – or at least could be. Finally, note that theocentric ethics does not require belief in the existence of God. It claims only that the best way for us to gain our moral bearings is to reflect on what would be the will of a supremely perfect being for us.

9.2.3   Natural Law Ethics

Natural law ethics might be seen as an extension of theocentric ethics because it calls us to use our intellects to identify the goods that God would want us to pursue and the evils that God would want us to avoid. According to natural law ethics, however, such goods and ills are to be identified not by reflecting on the concept of God or by consulting the revealed will of God but by examining human nature. Natural law ethics is intriguing in part because it was pioneered by a great Christian philosopher and theologian, St. Thomas Aquinas, yet, as I will explain, it can be and has been adopted by secular as well as religious thinkers.

Natural law ethics begins with the observation, based on experience, that some things are good for all humans and some things are bad. These natural goods are such things as life, good food, comfortable shelter, health, supportive family, friendship, meaningful work, dignified treatment by others, justice, knowledge, leisure, recreation, the creation and enjoyment of beauty, freedom from undeserved, nonbeneficial pain, the freedom to pursue happiness in our own way, and so on. According to Aquinas, it is an objective observable fact that such things are natural, basic, universal human goods.

To say that they are natural goods is to say that it is not a matter of *convention* that they are called good; natural goods are not things that have been determined to be good by people, like which side of the road to drive on or whether to greet people by shaking hands or bowing. Because such things as we identified earlier are *natural* facts or truths about human beings, this theory is called the "natural" law theory. The significance here of "law" is not to signify that we have no alternative but to do what is morally right. Natural law theory holds that we have freedom of choice, even when our options are severely limited. Natural moral law is not like physical law, which forces itself on us whether we like it or not. The wit who said "Gravity is not just a good idea. It's the law!" was trading on the ambiguity between physical laws that "have to be obeyed" and social laws that do not have to be obeyed. But when we choose not to obey the natural moral laws that identify the goods that lead to the well-being and fulfillment of individual humans and communities, we do what is wrong – we act unreasonably; we act contrary to our knowledge that there are natural goods that we should honor, protect, and promote.

Note that natural law theory is not based on individual conscience (a personal *feeling* or *intuition* of right and wrong; a position called "subjectivism") or on social norms and practices (a position called "social or cultural relativism"). Natural moral right and wrong are based on the things that make for the well-being of individuals, communities, and societies. We do not discover what is morally right and wrong by looking into our hearts or consulting our consciences (subjectivism) or by observing the practices of the society around us (social relativism). We discover what is morally right and wrong by observing what is good for the development, maturation, and fulfillment of human beings and what is harmful to our development, maturation, and fulfillment. Moral right and wrong are grounded in human nature, and human nature is an objective reality that can be studied objectively, just as science is objective because it studies what is really there in the physical world. Hence, to do what is immoral is to act against reason; it is to act contrary to that which we believe is necessary for human well-being and fulfillment. (Note: I said "which we believe" because we can make mistakes in our moral thinking as well as in other areas of life, including science, but, according to Aquinas, that does not undermine the basic procedure by which we discover what is absolutely, objectively, universally morally right and wrong – "universal" not in the sense that everyone *does* agree with it but in the sense that everyone *ought* to agree with it because it is, by virtue of human nature, beneficial to everyone.)

I have said nothing about God in a while. Where does God come in here? The most influential spokesman for natural law ethics, Thomas Aquinas, believed that humans were created by God and were made by God such that some things *naturally* contribute to human well-being and other things naturally interfere with human development, maturation, and fulfillment. More generally, something is good for creatures of a certain kind because it contributes to the well-being and fulfillment of creatures of that kind, whether we are speaking of flowers, butterflies, fish, or humans. It was by creating humans as the kind of creature that we are that God determined what would be good and bad for us, and therefore what it would be morally right and wrong for us to do to ourselves and one another. That may sound a bit like the divine command theory since God decided what we would be like, but it is quite different. Yes, God decided our nature, according to Thomas, and because of the nature that God decided we would have, there are objective truths about what is good and bad for us, and it is on those truths that moral right and wrong are based. Those truths, according to natural law theory, can be discovered by experience and reason without the help of divine revelation and without reflection on the concept of God. To go at this another way, God didn't *decide* what would be morally right and wrong for humans, as though ze could have decided differently. Rather, God decided to create humans, and humans by virtue of the kind of creature they are have a nature such that some things are good for them and some are bad, and it is morally obligatory to avoid what is bad for us and do what is necessary for our fulfillment as humans.

According to Aquinas, then, because God wills that human nature be fulfilled in each of us, when we act according to the natural moral law we are acting according to the will of God – whether we believe in God or not; whether we've even heard of God or not. And since we do not have to believe in God in order to intellectually apprehend the goods that make for human flourishing, and thereby understand the moral rules by which we should live, atheists and agnostics can adopt a natural law theory of morality (and some do). It seems gracious in a sense that if there is a God, God made it the case that all humans can by means of reason and experience discover and understand what is morally right and wrong, and can thereby know what they ought to do and ought not to do without having to accept divine revelation or even believe in God (hence the moral law is "natural" not only because it is based on human nature but also because it does not depend on *super*natural revelation to be known). This means that all people can work together to figure out what is morally right and wrong. No one needs to be excluded from the conversation because of their religious beliefs or lack thereof. That does not, however, rule out the value of divine revelation if there is a God. Divine revelation could provide a valuable clarification and confirmation of what we know by reason about moral right and wrong, and it might reveal new moral truths that are later confirmed by reason.

There are of course theories of moral right and wrong that do not appeal to God in any way. Some of them claim that there are absolute ways to determine moral right and wrong; others claim there are not. It would be beyond the boundaries of an introduction to philosophy of religion to explore those theories, so we will not, but now that you are familiar with three forms of theistic ethics I urge you to take a course or read a book that introduces you to such nontheistic ethical theories as virtue ethics, care ethics, deontology, consequentialism, social relativism, subjectivism, and nihilism.

Let's conclude our examination of natural law ethics by considering three criticisms of it. First, natural law ethicists assume that it will be feasible, if not easy, to identify which things make for human well-being and fulfillment, but humans have notoriously different convictions as to what is good and evil, right and wrong. Hence, natural law ethics sounds good at first, but, the critic says, "the devil is in the details," that is, when we get down to trying to determine exactly what, for example, crime and justice, and fair labor conditions and payment are, the natural law theory bogs down in irresolvable disputes.

Second, natural law theory violates a rule that was articulated powerfully by Scottish philosopher Dave Hume. Hume said "ought cannot be derived from is." To paraphrase: "What is morally right and wrong cannot be figured out by examining what *is* the case in the world," which is what natural law theory tries to do. To say what is good is to *describe* something; it is to make a statement of fact: water is good for plants; pollen is good for bees; meaningful work is good for humans. But so what? That doesn't mean that anyone *ought* to do anything about those matters. It just tells us what to do *if* we want to achieve some end, such as keeping a bee hive healthy, but because something *is* the case does not mean that therefore it *ought* to be the case. Because it would be good for something to be the case does not mean that therefore someone has an obligation to make it the case and would be morally wrong not to do so. If moral right and wrong can be established at all, Humeans say, they have to be established on some basis that is independent of what *is* the case in the world.

The *third* and most fundamental criticism of natural law ethics comes from twentieth-century French philosopher and playwright Jean-Paul Sartre. Sartre argues in his magnum opus, *Being and Nothingness*, that there is no such thing as human nature. Hence, he believes, natural law ethics is completely baseless. Sartre believed there is no human nature because he was an atheist who agreed with the following statement by a character in Fyodor Dostoyevsky's novel *The Brothers Karamazov*: "If there is no God, then all things are permitted." Why? Because if there is no God there is no one with the authority or power to found absolute values; therefore, there are no objective moral rights or wrongs, and humans are radically free to do and be whatever they choose and to create their own values. So when it comes to moral issues there is no objectivity; there is only subjectivity.

Natural law theorists have replies to these criticisms, of course. In reply to the first criticism, that it is impossible for people to agree on moral right and wrong, they might point out that in 1948, when the world was profoundly divided shortly after World War II, the United Nations passed a Universal Declaration of Human Rights, an extensive, detailed statement of human rights for all people. Out of fifty nations which voted on that resolution there were only eight abstentions and no dissenting votes, so perhaps it is difficult but not impossible for people to identify what is good and bad for everyone, especially if they think about the nature and needs of human beings. Every nation condemns murder, rape, child abuse, and theft. Definitions of these concepts certainly differ to some extent among nations, but not so radically as to make agreements impossible.

Second, natural law theorists challenge Hume's claim that if something undermines human well-being, such as child abuse, then it is not necessarily wrong; it just is the case. This is such a deep disagreement that it is difficult to argue one way or the other; a decision here seems more intuitive, at least at this time, so for now I leave the issue to your consideration. Can moral right and wrong be derived from reflection on what is the case in the world? If not, how *can* morality be grounded? Or is morality groundless, as Sartre said?

Third, and finally, it is also difficult to imagine how people as far apart philosophically as a natural law theorist and a follower of Sartre might seek common ground, but it could be pointed out by the natural law ethicist that Sartre did seem to think that humans have an essential nature, and that nature is freedom – a value which Sartre believed should be protected and promoted. By nature we are free to choose among alternatives, and it is good that our freedom be maximized within limits determined by maximal freedom for all, so it seems that Sartre's position is compatible with a version of natural law ethics after all.

For Review, Reflection, and Discussion

1. F.R. Tennant and Cardinal Newman each presented an argument for the existence of God based on the existence of conscience. How do their arguments differ?
2. What is the natural highest goal of human beings? Happiness? Freedom? Something else? Is there no such thing as an ultimate goal toward which all humans naturally strive?
3. John Locke and Thomas Jefferson said that we have natural rights to life, liberty, property, and the pursuit of happiness. Do you agree? What would you add to or subtract from the preceding list? Why?
4. Civil rights are rights that are given by society and can be taken away by society, such as the right to vote or drive a car. Are all rights civil rights or do humans have some rights that are natural, not social, that cannot be taken away by society (though of course society can interfere with our exercise of them)?
5. It is said that some actions are *morally obligatory* (something we absolutely ought to do), some are *morally forbidden* (something we absolutely ought not to do), and some are *morally permissible* (something we may do or not as we wish). Name and defend at least one thing in each category (or defend a refusal to do so).
6. Are there some actions, attitudes, or customs that are wrong for everyone, everywhere, at every time? What are they? Why do you think those things are absolutely wrong? Is it because God says so or because we can see by reason that they are so?
7. Can moral right and wrong be derived from reflection on what *is* the case in the world? Or is David Hume right that "ought cannot be derived from is"?
8. Does theocentric ethics require belief in the existence of God? Does natural law ethics require belief in the existence of God?

For Further Reading

Zagzebski, Linda, and Miller, Timothy, eds., *Readings in Philosophy of Religion: Ancient to Contemporary* (Wiley-Blackwell: 2009). Part VI, "Religion and Morality," includes extensive selections from Aquinas (natural law ethics), Kant (the bearing of morality on life after death), Robert Adams (who defends a version of divine command ethics), and others.

Plato, *Euthyphro*. Is the good good because God says so, or does God say it is good because it is good?

Creel, Richard E., "Perfect Being Ethics," *THINK* (Spring 2008) (17/18), (A periodical of the Royal Institute of Philosophy, UK). This is a presentation and defense of theocentric ethics.

Idziak, Janine Marie, "Divine Command Ethics," in Taliaferro, Charles, Draper, Paul, et al., eds., *A Companion to Philosophy of Religion*, 2nd ed. (Wiley-Blackwell: 2010). See also Idziak's anthology *Divine Command Morality* (Edwin Mellen: 1979).

George, Robert P., "Natural Law Ethics," in Taliaferro, Charles, Draper, Paul, et al., eds., *A Companion to Philosophy of Religion*, 2nd ed. (Wiley-Blackwell: 2010).

Hume, David, *A Treatise of Human Nature*, Selby-Bigge, Lewis A., ed. (Oxford: 1960), Book III, Part I, Section I, pp. 469–470. In one paragraph Hume stirred up the "is-ought" controversy.

Sartre, Jean-Paul, *Existentialism and Human Emotions* (Philosophical Library: 1957). The easiest introduction to Sartre's important but difficult writings. His important but difficult magnum opus is *Being and Nothingness* (Washington Square Press: 1966).

For an introduction to a wide range of ethical theories see *Ethics: The Basics* by John Mizzoni (Basil-Blackwell: 2009).

Chapter 10

Religious Experience and Belief in God

10.1 The Principle of Credulity and the Rationality of Belief in God

N.B.: The phrase "religious experience" is used by different people to refer to very different kinds of experience, including naturalistic experiences of timelessness or a feeling of unity with Nature or the universe, as well as theistic experiences of a personal God. For our purposes here I will always mean an experience of or related to a personal God.

Some people believe in the existence of God because of a personal experience which seemed to be an experience of God. It is important to realize that such an experience does not usually serve as evidence from which the experiencer *infers* that God exists. A religious experience usually has such a compelling quality that during the experience the experiencer can no more doubt seriously that the experience is being caused by God than I can now doubt seriously that I am typing on a computer or than you can doubt seriously that you are reading words on a page. Here is how Simone Weil, a twentieth-century French thinker, put this point:

> When we are eating bread, and even when we have eaten it, we know it is real. We can nevertheless raise doubts about the reality of the bread. Philosophers raise doubts about the reality of the world of the senses. Such doubts are however purely verbal; they leave the certainty intact and actually serve to make it more obvious to a well-balanced mind. In the same way he to whom God has revealed his reality can raise doubts about this reality without any harm. They are purely verbal doubts, a

Philosophy of Religion: The Basics, First Edition. Richard E. Creel.
© 2014 John Wiley & Sons, Inc. Published 2014 by John Wiley & Sons, Inc.

form of exercise to keep his intelligence in good health (*Waiting for God* [Capricorn Books: 1951], p. 212).

As Weil points out, philosophers are notorious for raising doubts about everything, including things that seem obvious. "Perhaps," they say, "the world of physical objects, of trees and chairs, dogs and people, is just an illusion, like in a dream. Maybe what we call 'being awake' is an illusion just like dreaming. How can you prove it is not?" Upon adequate thought we discover that we cannot prove that what we call "being awake" is not also an illusion of some kind, and yet we remain supremely confident that it is not an illusion. Similarly, according to Weil, anyone who has had a clear and powerful experience of the reality of God can raise all the usual philosophical objections to the reality of God, yet ze can no more doubt God's reality than ze can doubt the reality of the food ze eats.

To appreciate how religious experiences cause belief in God, it is important to realize that there are two rather different types of religious experience. I will call them "interruptive" and "suffusive." Some people are convinced of the existence of God because of an interruptive, intense, and transient religious experience. Such an experience is *interruptive* in that it is not expected or under one's control. It breaks into one's life in a startling way. Such an experience is *intense* in the sense that it overwhelms one's attention, somewhat as a powerful noise or blinding light seizes one's attention. Such an experience is *transient* in that it normally does not last very long, usually minutes, in rare cases hours or a few days.

Consider, for example, Simone Weil's description of her first religious experience: "In a moment of intense physical suffering, when I was forcing myself to feel love, but without desiring to give a name to that love, I felt, without being in anyway prepared for it (for I had never read the mystical writers) a presence more personal, more certain, more real than that of a human being, though inaccessible to the senses and the imagination." (*Waiting for God*, p. 24) This was not an experience that caused Weil to begin to believe in God; she already believed. Her experience did, however, confirm and enrich her belief in God, and it is an excellent example of how sudden, powerful, and real such an experience can be. It was unexpected, overwhelming, and brief. During that experience, her sense of the reality of God was more intense than her everyday sense of the reality of people, so she could henceforth no more doubt the reality of God than she could doubt the reality of her friends and family.

When many of us think of religious experience, we think of the kind that Weil reported, but there is another kind. It is often overlooked because it does not involve the emotional fireworks of the interruptive religious experience. This second type of religious experience does not explode into one's life; rather, it is a gentle, *suffusive*, enduring way of seeing and feeling the world. It suffuses one's life (like a drop of dye in a gallon of water) in the sense that virtually all of one's life is experienced as being lived in the presence of God or in God's world. Some people who feel that way say they cannot remember ever beginning to feel that way; they just always have. Others can recall a beginning. Consider this story from Greg Tearney, a 10th degree Black Belt karate instructor who suffered a heart-attack which made him feel "like an elephant had stepped on my chest." Several years later he told a journalist that as he lay on a table in a hospital emergency room, he prayed to God: "Lord, if you're going to take me, that's OK. But if you let me get through this, all it will do is strengthen my faith in you." He continued, "Well, at that point, I felt this warmth. It was like a warm blanket immediately came down on me. Not in words, but God told me I was going to be OK. And I had this big smile on my face." For the most part, he added, that feeling and that smile haven't left him since. He experienced no words, no vision, no overwhelming religious experience like an elephant stepping on his chest, just a reassuring experience of warmth in response to a prayer – a warmth that has stayed with him. (*Syracuse Herald-American*, February 22, 1998, Section C, p. 1.)

This way of seeing and feeling the world is gentle in the sense that it is like hearing a continuous background whisper rather than being startled by an unexpected shout. To be sure, people who have this kind of relation to God are not always aware of it (just as one might not be aware of a soft breeze unless one focuses on it), but they find that it is almost always there when they search for it, and they say they often feel it without searching for it. (Hick, John, *Arguments for the Existence of God*, p. 112.)

Note that this suffusive way of experiencing the world, like the interruptive way, is not an argument for the existence of God. Rather, one simply feels that God is quietly present, or one experiences the world as God's creation, or both. This kind of conviction that there is a God is sometimes called "a basic belief" because it is not based on or inferred from any other belief; it is just the way things seem to an individual. Hence, the person who has a religious experience usually believes zer experience to be *veridical*, that is, revealing of the truth, rather than *delusory*. But basic beliefs are not necessarily rational. Someone might have a basic belief that his head is made of Swiss cheese! So we need to ask what makes a *properly basic* belief, that is, a basic belief that it is rational to hold. More specifically, is it *rational* to believe in the existence of God simply because of a religious experience which is not backed up by an argument?

An argument from religious experience to the rationality of belief in the existence of God can be developed on the basis of *the principle of credulity*. According to the principle of credulity it is rational for a person to believe that things are the way they seem to be as long as ze knows of no good reason why ze should doubt the veridicality of the experience (such as that ze was delirious because of drugs or fever). The justification for the principle of credulity is this: If we were to suspend judgment about, or reject the veridicality of, the experiences that seem true to us until we could prove that they were true, we would never be justified in believing anything about the world, and so we would perish in uncertainty. Why? Because every belief we have about the way the world is, is based on our experiences, and every belief we have about what the world seems to be like would have to be doubted, so no experience could justify any of our beliefs about the world. For example, if something *seemed* like a dangerous animal that was about to attack us, we would have to suspend judgment, and therefore action, until it was proven that the animal was dangerous and about to attack us, so if it was a dangerous animal about to attack us, we would be attacked, since any experience that seemed to confirm that the animal was dangerous and about to attack us (such as that it was baring its teeth) would itself have to be suspect until it was supported by another experience, which itself would have to be questioned, and so on. We would be trapped in an infinite regress of doubts and never be able to justify any single belief.

In brief, to reject the principle of credulity would be to reject the belief that we are usually justified in thinking that things are the way they seem to be. That means we would not be justified in thinking the world is the way it seems to be even after we take a closer look or find that several people agree with the way we see things, since these steps would only lead to further experiences, and those experiences, too, would have to be questioned. Hence, when the world seems to be a certain way, either we trust that it is that way or we do not; if we do not, we must seek another experience which will confirm that the first experience is true. But if we have rejected the principle of credulity, we cannot trust that second experience either (and so we cannot use it to justify the first experience), so we must seek a third experience to justify the second experience, and so on, without end. Hence, rejection of the principle of credulity is a recipe for paralysis or insanity. Because it would be irrational to reject a principle the rejection of which would lead to paralysis or insanity, it would be irrational to reject the principle of credulity (which is only common sense in fancy clothes).

Furthermore, we know from experience that the way things seem to be often turns out after further investigation to be the way they are, so by trusting our experiences we form a reliable understanding of the world. That understanding of the world enables us to distinguish illusory and delusory experiences from "the real thing," that is, from the way things usually are or are on closer inspection. If we did not assume that things are generally the way they seem to be, we could never form a background of normal experiences against which to identify which experiences are abnormal, such as dreams, hallucinations, and perceptual illusions. Consequently, we are justified in believing that things are the way they seem to be – unless there is a good reason to think otherwise. Hence, a person who has an experience which seems to be an experience of God, and who has no adequate reason for rejecting that experience or suspending judgment about it, is justified in accepting it as veridical, as revealing the truth, as being properly basic. Note, this means that the person who believes in God because of a religious experience does not have to justify zer belief by means of an argument in order to be rational in believing. Ze only has to be content in zer own mind that ze has no good reason for doubting the religious experience that ze had.

In summary, according to the principle of credulity it is rational for people who have what seems to them to be an experience of God to believe that God exists – unless or until they know something that undermines the credibility of their experience.

10.2   Religious Experience as Evidence for the Existence of God

It might seem that the use of the principle of credulity to defend the rationality of belief based on religious experience is of no relevance to people who have not had such an experience, but that is not true. Much of what we believe, including very important things, we believe on the testimony of other people: scientists, physicians, auto mechanics, journalists, family, friends, neighbors, and colleagues. Indeed, it is on the basis of testimony that we believe who our parents are, what our name is, what a country is like to which we have not traveled, and what someone else dreamed last night. If you sufficiently respect the intelligence, knowledge, and integrity of someone who claims to have had an experience of God, then their experience can serve as evidence for you to believe there is a God even if you have not had such an experience.

Note again that the issue here is not whether experiences that seem to be experiences of God *prove* the existence of God or show that God *probably* exists; the issue is whether it is *rational* for a person who has such an experience to *believe* that God is real (to say that a person is rational in holding a belief is to say that ze was intellectually responsible in arriving at the belief – even though it may be false, as people once were rational to think that the Sun revolved around the Earth). The conclusion was that it could be rational to believe in God without an argument to that effect, given the principle of credulity.

Religious experiences can also, as we saw in the preceding paragraph, be used as *evidence* for the existence of God on the basis of testimony from a trusted person. A second argument to that effect goes as follows: Much more often than not, when something seems real, further experience shows that it is real. Therefore, when something seems real, it probably is. What looks, feels, and smells like a banana probably is. What looks and behaves like a squirrel probably is, etc. One of the principles at work here is that the most plausible explanation of an experience is that it is being caused by what it seems to be being caused by. The most plausible explanation of my experience of seeming to see, feel, and smell a peach is that there is a peach causing my experiences. For the most part our experiences show that what looks, feels, and smells like a peach is a peach.

Our perceptual beliefs, that is, beliefs based on sensation, can, of course, be mistaken; that is why we must say that a perceptual experience is *evidence* that something is probably true, rather than that it proves it. Nonetheless, the fact that we *might* be wrong does not mean that we are *probably* wrong. Experience shows that when something appears to us to be the case, we are probably right; therefore, the appearance that something is the case is *evidence* that it probably is the case. However, that statement needs to be *disambiguated*, that is, it has two possible meanings that need to be distinguished. Sometimes an experience that something is the case is *by itself* (together with our usual commonsense assumptions) *sufficient evidence* that what seems to be true is probably true. If I hold my hand in front of my face in normal circumstances and see a thumb, then that is sufficient evidence for thinking that I have a thumb. If, however, an experience that something is the case is not by itself sufficient evidence that that something is probably true, nonetheless that experience is evidence that counts in favor of the truth of what seems to be true, according to the experience. That is, such an experience is evidence that *increases the probability* that what it seems to be an experience of is the case – even if by itself it is not strong enough to justify concluding that the experience is probably veridical. For example, if I seem to see a cylindrical tower but it is far off and the air is a bit foggy, I do not have sufficient evidence to conclude that the tower is cylindrical, but its appearance does increase the probability that it is cylindrical (though on closer examination it might prove to be octagonal).

Applying the preceding analysis to religious experiences we see that just as the most plausible explanation of my seeming to see a hand is that there is a hand that I am seeing, the most plausible explanation of people seeming to experience God is that there is a God whom they are experiencing. Furthermore, since most of our experiences of things seeming to be true turn out to be true, experiences that God exists are positive evidence that God exists.

Such experiences taken *as evidence* are not conclusive but they are evidence that *favors* the God hypothesis. In opposition, though, there are many naturalistic explanations for religious experiences in terms of social influences (such as being in an emotional worship service), mental states (such as being desperate for help "from on high"), etc. Hence, how strongly to count religious experience as evidence is very controversial.

10.3   Toward a Cumulative Argument for God

Before we leave these arguments for the existence of God we need to hear an important criticism that we have not dealt with yet. The criticism is that even if the cosmological, teleological, and moral arguments succeed, they don't show that *God* exists. The arguments from motion and causation may prove that there is a first mover and a first cause, but that is far from showing that a supremely perfect being exists! The first mover/first cause may be indifferent to human life, and looking at the universe there is certainly some reason to think that is true. Moreover, the necessary being on which all contingent things depend for their existence may be matter/energy rather than an intelligent being. If the teleological argument succeeds, it does not imply that the creator is omniperfect or even that the creator is only one being; perhaps the universe was created by a committee of gods!

The preceding are important points that indicate real limitations of what an individual argument for God can achieve even if it succeeds (except for the ontological argument, which if it succeeds is a proof of the existence of God). Nonetheless, a theist might agree but point out the following: if we put the results of the nonontological arguments together, we move impressively closer to establishing that there is a God, for if the arguments succeed individually and we put them together we will have shown that there is an extremely intelligent and powerful, morally aware and everlasting being who is the source of the existence of the universe and of the motion and causation in it. To be sure, that cumulative argument does not take us all the way to an omniperfect being, but it certainly moves in that direction and away from atheism. As to the claim that the creation of the universe may have been by committee, we cannot rule out that possibility, but it is Ockham's Razor which discredits it. The point of Ockham's Razor (to be explained more fully soon) is that we should not make things more complicated than they need to be. We should cut out unnecessary elements of an explanation. Why believe in polytheism if monotheism will do? Simplicity favors thinking that there is only one divine being unless there is a good reason to think otherwise – and at this point there is not a good reason to think otherwise.

For Review, Reflection, and Discussion

1. What is the difference between a veridical experience and a delusory experience?
2. How do interruptive and suffusive religious experiences differ from one another? Have you ever had either type of experience, or any other type of religious experience? Please explain.

3. Do you agree with Simone Weil that we simply cannot *seriously* doubt certain kinds of experiences?
4. What is the principle of credulity? Do you agree with it? If yes, why? If no, why not?
5. How does the principle of credulity support belief in the existence of God that arises from religious experience?
6. What is a basic belief? What is a properly basic belief? Can belief in God be properly basic?
7. What does it mean for a statement to be ambiguous? What does it mean to disambiguate a statement? Give an example of an ambiguous statement and disambiguate it.
8. As mentioned earlier, how strongly to count religious experience as *evidence* for the existence of God or as a basis for believing in God is very controversial. Some think it is strong evidence. Others think it is worthless. What do you think (and why)?
9. What is a cumulative argument? Does a cumulative argument for the existence of God increase the overall probability of the existence of God? Or is a cumulative argument like a chain that is no stronger than its weakest link?

For Further Reading

In addition to Simone Weil's account of interruptive religious experiences in *Waiting for God*, four other excellent examples, the first three in the Bible, are Moses' experience of God and the burning bush (Exodus 3), young Samuel being called by God (I Samuel 3), Saul on his way to Damascus (Acts 9), plus Blaise Pascal's transforming experience of spiritual fire; see his *Penseés*, trans., A.J. Krailsheimer (Penguin Books: 1966), pp. 309–10.

Draper, Paul, "Cumulative Cases," in Taliaferro, Charles, Draper, Paul, et al., eds., *A Companion to Philosophy of Religion*, 2nd ed., (Wiley-Blackwell: 2010). A sophisticated discussion of cumulative case arguments. See also Wainwright, William, *Philosophy of Religion*, 2nd ed. (Wadsworth: 1999), Chapter 7 for a brief overview of cumulative arguments and argument to the best explanation.

Chapter 11

Arguments against Belief in the Existence of God

Having explored four arguments for the existence of God and some criticisms of those arguments, now let's examine arguments *against* belief in the existence of God. Note, however, that a criticism of an argument for the existence of God is not necessarily an argument against the existence of God. Rather, it is usually just an argument against accepting that particular argument for the existence of God. There are, however, as we will now see, some arguments against the *rationality* of belief in the existence of God and others against the *existence* of God (there is a difference between arguing that it is not rational to believe that God exists and arguing that God does not exist).

11.1 Evidentialism and the Burden of Proof

The principle of *evidentialism*, stated by W.K. Clifford, says: "It is wrong always, everywhere, and for anyone, to believe anything upon insufficient evidence." Hence, according to the principle of evidentialism the burden of proof regarding belief in the existence of God rests on the believer to show that ze has sufficient evidence to believe that there is a God. This means that the nonbeliever, in order to justify zer position, does not have to prove that God does not exist. Ze only has to show that arguments *for* the existence of God do *not* succeed. Hence, according to the principle of evidentialism the time we have already spent looking at criticisms of arguments for the existence of God has also been time spent arguing against belief in the existence of God. Again, the burden

Philosophy of Religion: The Basics, First Edition. Richard E. Creel.
© 2014 John Wiley & Sons, Inc. Published 2014 by John Wiley & Sons, Inc.

of proof is on those who believe something, who claim something. The burden is not on those who do not believe.

In addition to criticism of arguments for the existence of God (which criticisms, according to the principle of evidentialism, are *indirect* arguments against belief in the existence of God), there are some *direct* arguments against the existence of God. We turn to two of those arguments now.

11.2   Conceptual Arguments: Analysis of the Concept of God

11.2.1   The Argument from Meaninglessness

This argument harkens back to points made by A.J. Ayer and Ludwig Wittgenstein. They said that the notion of a nonphysical thing is cognitively meaningless. Therefore, the word "God" is meaningless. It is just a word. Indeed, "God" is not even a word. By definition, a word has meaning, but "God" is just three letters joined together in a meaningless combination, like "Zom" or "Mog." The latter aren't words, either. They are just combinations of letters that can be spoken to make meaningless sounds. Hence, because the word "God" is meaningless, the question "Does God exist?" is also meaningless (as is the question, "Does zom exist?"). The appropriate response to the question "Does God exist?" is not "no." To say "no" would suggest that the concept of God makes sense. The appropriate response is simply to point out that the question doesn't make sense, and then to change the topic to something that does make sense. (This argument from meaninglessness succeeds unless one can make sense of the idea of a nonphysical being – assuming that God is or would be a nonphysical being.)

11.2.2   The Arguments from Incoherence and Self-Contradiction

The classical conception of God as formulated by Anselm and Descartes is not meaningless, say some critics, even atheists. The notion of a being who is pure spirit is not unintelligible, but the critics add that the concept of God is incoherent or self-contradictory in itself. It requires that God have qualities that are *incoherent in themselves*, such as omnipotence and unsurpassability, or it requires that God have properties that are *logically incompatible with one another* (remember the attribute dilemmas). Regarding omnipotence, for example, the critic says there can be no such property. No matter how powerful a being is, we can conceive another being that is even more powerful – just as the notion of an unsurpassably large whole number is incoherent. As to self-contradiction, in the section on divine attribute dilemmas we saw reasons to think that an actual being cannot be both omnipotent and omnibenevolent; omniscient and atemporal; immutable and an agent, yet the concept of a being than which none greater can be conceived requires that God have all of these properties simultaneously. (The argument from incoherence succeeds unless each of the necessary attributes of God is coherent, i.e., is intelligible, and the argument from self-contradiction succeeds unless all of the necessary attributes of God can be shown to be logically compatible with each other. This means, among other things, that each purported attribute dilemma must be solved in a way that leaves it possible for a being worthy of the name "God" to exist.)

11.3   Arguments from Science

11.3.1   The Natural Sciences: The Adequacy of Science

Ockham's Razor (formulated by the great medieval thinker William of Ockham) is a principle that says: do not multiply entities beyond necessity. That is, if a theory does a good job of explaining certain things, but the theory involves belief in something that doesn't do any of the explanatory work, then we should use Ockham's razor to cut away that useless part of the theory. To make this point in another way, consider that if two theories are alike in all respects except that one theory is less complicated than the other, then the less complicated theory is preferable. There is no point in hanging on to that extra element in the second theory. It doesn't earn its keep. It requires that we work to remember it, but it does not work for us, so we should use Ockham's razor to get rid of it.

Now let's apply Ockham's razor to belief in God. When we do that we discover that belief in the existence of God has become an unnecessary complication in our understanding of the world. This point was made in a dramatic way by Pierre Simon de LaPlace, a French mathematician and astronomer who authored a book titled *Exposition of the System of the World* (1796). Napoleon Bonaparte, the great emperor of France, read LaPlace's book and was startled by what it did *not* say. Napoleon summoned LaPlace to appear before him. He asked LaPlace (I paraphrase), "Why is there no mention of God in your explanation of the world? How could you possibly explain the universe without bringing God into the picture?" LaPlace replied, "Nous n'avons pas besoin de cette hypothese." That is, "We have no need for that hypothesis. We can explain why the moon does what it does, why the planets do what they do, why the weather does what it does, etc., without mentioning God, and so we should eliminate God from our understanding of how the universe works."

To be sure, one of the admirable things about us humans is that we have a powerful need to understand things. Hence, it is understandable that when our prescientific predecessors couldn't understand something, they would conclude, "It must have been an act of God." But as our knowledge of the world has progressed, and particularly since the relatively recent emergence of the scientific understanding of the world, we have come to see that everything about the world can be explained by science. For example, ancient people understood thunder and lightning in terms of fights between the gods, whom they thought lived in the heavens, but now we know better and explain thunder and lightning in terms of sudden rushes of massive amounts of electrons from one cloud to another, or from the earth to a cloud.

Also, there is the biblical story of the Israelites escaping across the Red Sea while God parted the waters for them, whereas when the Egyptians in pursuit of the Israelites tried to do the same thing, the miracle ceased, the waters closed, and the Egyptians were drowned. There is, however, another explanation which is more plausible and which fits with our scientific understanding of the world. The end of the Red Sea over which the Israelites fled is rather shallow. Furthermore, there are strong winds that periodically blow north from the shallow end of the Red Sea and thereby push the water toward the middle of the sea, temporarily uncovering parts of the bottom of the southern end of the Red Sea. Moses, who led the Israelites in their escape from Egypt, had lived in that area of the Middle East all his life. He would have known about the preceding phenomenon. He was also a clever man, so he led the Israelites out of Egypt when he knew that the wind was blowing hard and the water would be gone or very shallow where they would cross the Red Sea. He also knew when the winds would die down and the water would return. Hence, he timed the flight of the Israelites so that when they reached the Red Sea the water was low or gone, and the Sea was easy to cross on foot, whereas by the time the Egyptians reached the Sea, the wind had died down, the water was getting deeper, and the narrow iron wheels of the heavy Egyptian chariots got stuck in the soft bottom of the Sea, so the Israelites escaped, and the Egyptians drowned. Hence, the escape of the Israelites from slavery in Egypt should be attributed to the brilliant strategy of Moses, not to the miraculous intervention of God.

In brief, the view of naturalism (sometimes called "scientism") is that there are only two kinds of things in history: (i) those that can be explained by science and (ii) those that are *brute facts* and therefore have no explanation (it's not just that they have no explanation *now*; it's that they have no explanation, period).

11.3.2   Criticisms of Naturalism

Critics of naturalism make the following kinds of objections:

1. Naturalism doesn't explain why there is a universe rather than none. So far as we know, nothing could have existed. So why is there something rather than nothing? (Or as Martin Heidegger put it in German, "Warum gibt es seiendes und nicht viel mehr nichts?")
2. Naturalism doesn't explain why the laws of nature are as they are rather than different. For example, why is there a law of gravity? Why does it have the strength it has rather than some other strength?
3. Naturalism doesn't explain how intelligent, aesthetically sensitive, morally sensitive life could emerge from mindless, lifeless matter. It is strange verging on bizarre, say critics, that from a sea of lifeless particles life would emerge, and not only life but creatures with a sensitivity to and compulsion to create beauty, and a sense of moral right and wrong and a compulsion to do what is right and oppose what is wrong. We don't want to rule out the possibility that science can explain these things, but it is certainly nowhere near being able to do so now – or perhaps ever. In brief, the burden of proof is on naturalism.
4. Naturalism doesn't explain the progressive emergence of so many levels of existence in such a short period of time: from nonliving to

living to conscious to self-conscious to morally sensitive to aesthetically sensitive.

5.   Naturalism rejects the principle of sufficient reason by saying, when it cannot come up with an explanation, that some things are just brute facts. That is a criticism that naturalists aim at theists when theists explain something in terms of God, but naturalists have their own problem with "brute facts," that is, things that have no natural or scientific explanation.

Naturalists have replies to the preceding points, of course, but lest I spend too much time on this topic I will leave those replies to your imagination except for one. That one reply concedes that at least some of the preceding points have merit, but it adds that ultimately there must be some *brute facts*, that is, facts that have no explanation – whether those facts have to do with the existence and nature of God or whether they have to do with the existence and nature of the universe. Moreover, say the naturalists, it only makes things more mystifying to appeal to God (the so-called "god of the gaps") to explain these difficulties rather than stopping with the brute facts of nature. Just because there is a gap or dead end in our understanding of things does not mean that appealing to God will fill the gap or extend the dead end in a helpful way. We should stop with nature, say the naturalists.

11.3.3   The Social Sciences: Religion and Emotion

The social sciences, as developed by people like Karl Marx and Sigmund Freud, have helped us see that religious belief is based on emotion, not reason. People believe in God because they want to, and they want to because of many different motives. Some people are averse to death; they don't want death to be the end of their existence, so they allow themselves to believe there is a God who can extend their lives beyond death. Some people feel profoundly guilty for things they have done or failed to do, so they allow themselves to believe there is a God who is merciful and will forgive them. Some people are painfully shy and lonely, so they allow themselves to believe in a God who is an ever present, caring companion. Some people are lazy and want God to solve their personal problems or the problems of the world, so they allow themselves to believe in God so they can pray to God to solve their problems and the problems of the world rather than exerting themselves to solve them. Some people are desperate, such as parents with a dying child; they want to believe there is a God who can do the impossible for them, so they allow themselves to believe in a God who can save their child. Some people want an excuse for their behavior, so they can say, "Don't blame me. It was the will of God," so they allow themselves to believe in God.

Notice, however, that none of these motives for wanting there to be a God is *evidence* for thinking that God exists. In addition, many of these motives are unworthy of a self-respecting human being. We should not believe in God because belief in God can be an effective escape mechanism, crutch, or excuse. We should believe a proposition only if we have sufficient evidence that it is true (remember the principle of evidentialism), and there is not sufficient evidence for belief in the existence of God. Moreover, we should be realistic about the evils and limitations of life, and we should accept responsibility for our decisions and actions. Then even though life will not be all we would like it to be, at least we can live it with integrity and dignity.

Criticisms of the Arguments from Social Science:

1. The Social Science Argument and the Genetic Fallacy

    Even if emotions are the only causes of people believing that there is a God that does not mean there is no God. The social science argument, as presented earlier, is a form of *the genetic fallacy*. The genetic fallacy consists of rejecting a claim as false because of the source (genesis) from which it came. This is considered a fallacy because the source from which a belief comes can be totally irrelevant to whether or not the belief is true. If a man rejects an idea just because a woman said it, or if a woman rejects an idea just because a man said it, ze has committed a genetic fallacy. The social science argument, as presented earlier, says that because belief in God is generated by people's emotions, it is false. But even if all believers believe in God because of emotion, not evidence, that does not prove that there is no God. It might prove that it is irrational to believe that God exists, but it does not prove that God does not exist.

2. An argument from emotion against atheism

    It is true that there are emotions that cause some people to want there to be a God. It is *also* true that there are emotions that cause people to want there to be *no* God. Hence, the argument from emotion is *a two-edged sword* that cuts against atheists as well as theists. Some people dislike the idea that there is a being who is infinitely superior to themselves, and so they allow themselves to believe there is no God. Some people don't like to feel indebted to anyone, or that they should feel gratitude to anyone; they dislike the idea that there is a God to whom they owe their lives and their most important blessings, so they allow themselves to believe there is no God. Some people don't want there to be moral standards which they ought to obey; they want to feel completely free to live any way they wish; they dislike the idea that there might be a God who sets rules for how we ought and ought not to live, and for how we ought and ought not to treat one another and other sentient creatures, so they allow themselves to believe there is no God. Some people don't want to be held responsible after death for how they live this life; they want to feel free to live this life as they wish without regard for possible consequences after death, so they allow themselves to believe there is no God who will hold us responsible for how we live this life. Obviously, none of those emotions is evidence for believing that there is no God, so a self-respecting person should not allow such emotions to cause mer to believe that there is no God. Just as obviously, even if those are the real causes of all atheists being atheists, theists would commit a genetic fallacy if they were to conclude that there *is* a God because atheism is based on emotion rather than reason.

In conclusion, if the arguments from emotion by both the atheists and the theists are sound, then the beliefs of all theists and atheists alike are discredited as irrational. Presumably, we should therefore all be agnostics until we can come up with sufficient evidence for believing that God does or does not exist. Note, however, that the arguments from emotion have not shown that it is impossible to believe or disbelieve in God on the basis of evidence, or that there is no significant evidence for or against the existence of God, so perhaps what should result from our consideration of the arguments from emotion is that we examine our own theism or atheism, and that of others, to see whether and to what extent our belief is based on emotion rather than evidence, and henceforth be careful to base our beliefs on evidence rather than emotion. (Of course belief in God might not be based on evidence but, rather, as we saw earlier, be properly basic – but so might atheism be properly basic;

consequently the appeal to properly basic beliefs makes no head-
way in either direction if we are looking for *arguments* regarding
the existence of God.)

11.4   The Problem of Divine Hiddenness

In the Bible, the Psalmist frequently laments that God is absent; silent;
nowhere to be found. For example, "My God, my God, why hast thou
forsaken me? Why art thou so far from helping me, from the words of
my groaning? O my God, I cry by day, but thou dost not answer; and by
night, but find no rest" (Psalm 22:1–2). Obviously the psalmist did not
doubt God's existence. After all, God could not be hidden if ze did not
exist. Rather, the psalmist yearned for God to come out of hiding, to
make zer presence felt and perhaps provide some kind of help. But
rather than raising a question in the believer's mind as to why God is
silent, the failure of God to respond to a prayer or a longing can be
taken as evidence that God does not exist. We have seen that religious
experiences are a powerful cause of religious belief for those who have
such experiences; by parallel, the failure to have a religious experience,
the failure of God to respond, can be taken as a reason to think that God
does not exist – and there are many who have no such experience, so
let's explore three arguments from divine hiddenness against the
existence of God:

1. Hiddenness is incompatible with the purported nature of God;
2. Hiddenness allows immorality and injustice to flourish;
3. Hiddenness is cruel to seekers.

The first argument is a simple argument from the incompatibility of
scarce, ambiguous evidence with the concept of God. If God exists, God
certainly has the power to convince all humans of zer existence, and if
God is loving, as is claimed by the Bible and many philosophers, then
God would want to establish a personal relationship with all of us, so
the fact that billions of people over the centuries have never had a
personal experience of the presence of God is evidence that disconfirms
the hypothesis that God exists. Some say, "People do report experiences
of the reality of God, so it's not that there is no experiential evidence;
rather, the evidence is ambiguous, that is, it can be taken in either of

two ways, pro or con." The critic replies that God should want the reality of zer presence to be clear and decisive, not ambiguous. Because the evidence is uncertain and ambiguous, that counts against the existence of God. (A corollary to the preceding argument is that the *distribution* of religious experiences of a personal God does not seem to be rational and fair, as one would expect from God. People in the Middle East have had much more of such experiences than people in Asia – which suggests that culture, psychology, and circumstance, rather than God, are the primary determining factors in whether one has a religious experience of a personal God.)

The second argument points out that if it were obvious to all that God exists, there would be a lot less injustice, immorality, and unkindness in the world because people would know that they were watched by God at all times and were certain to be held responsible for their actions. We put policemen on streets and patrolmen on highways to deter people from behaving harmfully and driving dangerously. Surely a perfectly good God would want to do the same thing on a grander scale by making zer existence obvious. But it is not obvious that God exists, so there is much crime and cruelty, therefore God probably does not exist. The sun makes its existence obvious, and God is infinitely greater than the sun, so if God exists, the existence of God should be far more obvious than that of the sun in order to deter immorality, injustice, and unkindness, but it is not; therefore, God probably does not exist.

Like the preceding argument, the third argument can be considered to be part of the problem of evil (which we will examine next at length). The relevant fact here is that people who dearly want to experience the reality of God, who want to have a personal relationship with God, but do not, consequently suffer from anguish, distress, and doubt. Again, it seems obvious that if there were a God, God would want to have a personal relationship with everyone, and certainly with people who sincerely, deeply desire such a relation, yet there are many such people for whom the "hiddenness" of God is a cause of suffering. Therefore, it seems unreasonable to think that there is a good and loving God. (Nor can it be argued, at least on the basis of the Bible, that God provides a sense of zer presence only to the virtuous and not to sinners: King David, one of God's darlings, was an adulterer and a murderer; St. Peter was a braggart and a coward; St. Paul persecuted the church and abetted the murder of Christians, yet they all purportedly had religious experiences of a personal God.)

What might be said in objection to the preceding arguments? Let's look at two responses. First, *indifference*, *sin*, and *aversion* might cause us to be oblivious to the presence of God, especially if that presence is subtle rather than overwhelming. If we are *indifferent* to something, we are less likely to see it (before I got a fireplace, I did not see firewood along rural roads; after I got a fireplace I saw firewood all over!). Some people are indifferent to the question of the existence of God; they don't care if there is a God, so of course they are not sensitive to the gentle presence of God. Second, if we do things that harm our hearing, we consequently do not hear things that otherwise we would hear. Similarly, sins of various kinds – cruelty, injustice, selfishness, unkindness – can *damage our sensitivity* to the presence of God. If we had not damaged our souls by means of sins, we might otherwise be aware of the presence of God. Third, if we *don't want* to see something we are less likely to see it. Some people want there to be no God; they don't want to believe that God exists; they want to feel completely free to live their lives as they wish, so they do not allow anything to count as a token of the presence of God.

A second response is that God does not want us to believe in mer and follow zer will because ze has *forced* on us an awareness of zer reality. In this life, God wants to discover whether we truly love mer because we hope, even without proof or presence, that ze is real and want to have a personal relationship with mer, and that we follow what we believe is zer will because we believe it is right and good (as the theocentric ethicist would say), not because we fear punishment if we don't obey. Consequently, in most cases God's presence is subtle if felt at all. (But of course if God has a special role for someone to play in history, someone such as David or Peter or Saul, then ze might overwhelm mer with zer presence rather than take the gentle approach.)

11.5 The Problem of Many Religions

There are many religions in the world – Judaism, Christianity, Islam, Hinduism, Buddhism, Confucianism, Taoism, Shinto, and more, and there are many factions within each religion. But if there is only one Supreme Being, why are there so many religions? The skeptic's reply is that there are so many religions because there is no Supreme Being. If there were, there would only be one religion. Perhaps we could account for some religious differences, such as styles of worship, due to different cultures and histories, but not such radical differences as we see. The so-called "great religions" differ radically on what the Ultimate Being is like, how it or ze is related to the world, what a human being is, what the meaning of life is, what the destiny of humans is, and more. Hence, it is most plausible to conclude that such radical differences as we see between the religions of the world are because religions are *not* revelations from a Supreme Being; they are human products of different historical, cultural, psychological, and environmental circumstances under the influence of gifted individuals such as Moses, Jesus, Buddha, Confucius, Lao Tzu, Mohammed, Bahá'u'lláh, and so on.

There are several reactions by believers to the skeptic. These are well summarized by three categories employed by such influential philosophers of religion as John Hick and William Rowe: *exclusivism*, *inclusivism*, and *pluralism*. The *exclusivist* agrees with the skeptic that most religions are mere human creations. However, contrary to the skeptic, the exclusivist insists that there is one – and only one – true religion, revealed by God. That true religion is, of course, the exclusivist's religion. Only those who accept its truths and live according to its teachings can achieve or receive salvation. All others are excluded. Conservative Protestant Christians (but not liberals) often hold this point of view.

The *inclusivist* also believes that zer religion is the only completely true religion, but ze also believes that God, in zer mercy, has influenced aspects of other cultures and religions that were not originally exposed to the true religion, so there are some truths in other religions. Consequently, people who do not know of the true religion, or have not had enough exposure to it to accept it, may still achieve or receive salvation if they sincerely strive to know the truth and live a good life. Hence, those people may be included among the saved. Inclusivism is the position of the Roman Catholic Church and most Hindus.

Finally there is pluralism. The *pluralist* believes there is no one-true-religion; all the great religions have been founded by the Ultimate Being and are equally efficacious for the development of good character and the achievement or receipt of eternal salvation. No religion is superior to the others in terms of its power to transform lives for the good and orient them to the divine. The fact that religion is a *universal, enduring* phenomenon is reason to believe that there is a divine being at work in the world. The fact that religions are so different can be explained because each was instilled by the Ultimate Being into a radically different historical and cultural situation. What was needed and would be efficacious in ancient Egypt was not what would have worked and been helpful in ancient Japan. This is not to say that there have not been unnecessary, even harmful human inputs to religions; it is to say that the Ultimate Being's contribution to the great world religions was wisely tailored to what was needed by and would be understood by people in their particular historical, cultural, and environmental situations. The great world religions developed originally in utter isolation from one another; people in radically different cultures had to strive to understand the divine in terms of their particular experiences and ways of thought. Now that the world has "grown smaller," however, people in the different religions are beginning to talk with one another and discover commonalities; some even wonder whether a new religion might develop that incorporates two or more of the older religions and rises above them. (Read for example about the relatively new religion, Bahá'í, which emphasizes not only the unity of God and the unity of humankind but also the unity of religions.)

To repeat the skeptic's most basic response to these defenses of religion by believers, if there were one Supreme Being ze would have made zer message to humans more clear and more widely and fairly distributed so that in spite of geographical, etc., differences it would have been obvious to members of the different religions when they came into contact with one another that their religions were gifts from the same God. Instead, there are widespread conflicts and incomprehension.

We are not through, however, with arguments against the existence of God. Next we will examine what many consider to be the most powerful evidence against the existence of God: the existence of evil.

For Review, Reflection, and Discussion

1. What is the principle of evidentialism? Do you agree with it?
2. The arguments from meaninglessness, incoherence, and self-contradiction presume to prove that God does not exist. Do you think they succeed?
3. Explain Ockham's Razor. State how a naturalist might use it against theism.

4. State two criticisms of naturalism.
5. What is a brute fact? Do you believe there is such a thing? If yes, give an example.
6. What is the argument from emotion against belief in the existence of God?
7. What is a genetic fallacy? How can it be applied to the argument from emotion against belief in the existence of God?
8. Why can it be said that the argument from emotion is a two-edged sword?
9. What are some of the problems that are generated by the fact that there are many religions instead of just one?
10. Because religions contradict one another, obviously not all of them can be true, but one of them could be the truth about God and humans. Are exclusivists arrogant to hold that they and they alone are right? What if they are right? Is it wrong to believe something with absolute confidence? If yes, why?
11. Why is "divine hiddenness" a problem? Does it have a solution that is satisfactory to you? If yes, what is it? If no, why not?
12. Which do you think is the most plausible of the following positions regarding the fact of many religions: skepticism, exclusivism, inclusivism, or pluralism? Why?

For Further Reading

Zagzebski, Linda, and Miller, Timothy, eds., *Readings in Philosophy of Religion: Ancient to Contemporary* (Wiley-Blackwell: 2009). Part XI.B, "Science, Religion, and Naturalism," includes six articles on these topics, including selections from Galileo, William Dembski, and Daniel Dennett

Zagzebski, Linda, and Miller, Timothy, eds., *Readings in Philosophy of Religion: Ancient to Contemporary* (Wiley-Blackwell: 2009). Part IX consists of four selections on the diversity of religions, including a brief interview with the Dalai Lama, leader of Tibetan Buddhism.

Freud, Sigmund, *The Future of an Illusion* (Anchor Books: 1964). (short, easy, classic). See also *Civilization and its Discontents* (W.W. Norton & Co.: 1961). A social science attempt to discredit religious beliefs and practices.

Marx, Karl, and Engels, Friedrich, *Marx and Engels on Religion* (Schocken Books: 1964). See especially the opening to Marx's "Contribution to the Critique of Hegel's Philosophy of Right" and his "Ludwig Feuerbach and the End of Classical German Philosophy."

For a sophisticated exploration of the problem of divine hiddenness plus an extensive bibliography see: Schellenberg, John L., "Divine Hiddenness," in Taliaferro, Charles, Draper, Paul, et al., eds., *A Companion to Philosophy of Religion*, 2nd ed. (Wiley-Blackwell: 2010).Hick, John, "Religious Pluralism," in Taliaferro, Charles, Draper, Paul, et al., eds., *A Companion to Philosophy of Religion*, 2nd ed. (Wiley-Blackwell: 2010). Hick's magnum opus on this topic is *An Interpretation of Religion* (Yale University Press: 1989), Part IV: "Religious Pluralism." In Part V he develops criteria for evaluating religions. See also his *Philosophy of Religion*, 4th ed.

Rowe, William, "Many Religions" in *Philosophy of Religion*, 2nd ed. (Wadsworth: 1993), chapter 13.

Wainwright, William, *Philosophy of Religion*, 2nd ed. (Wadsworth: 1999). In Chapter 8 Wainwright discusses the diversity of religions; in Chapter 7 he, like Hick, develops criteria for evaluating religions.

van Inwagen, Peter, "Non Est Hick," in Clark, Kelly James, ed., *Readings in the Philosophy of Religion* (Broadview: 2000), pp. 336–44. A critique of pluralism; a defense of exclusivism.

Flew, Antony, "The Presumption of Atheism," in Taliaferro, Charles, Draper, Paul, et al., eds., *A Companion to Philosophy of Religion*, 2nd ed. (Wiley-Blackwell: 2010).

Martin, Michael, "The Verificationist Challenge," in Taliaferro, Charles, Draper, Paul, et al., eds., *A Companion to Philosophy of Religion*, 2nd ed. (Wiley-Blackwell: 2010).

Martin, Michael, "Theism and Incoherence," in Taliaferro, Charles, Draper, Paul, et al., eds., *A Companion to Philosophy of Religion*, 2nd ed. (Wiley-Blackwell: 2010).

Nielsen, Kai, "Naturalistic Explanations of Theistic Belief," in Taliaferro, Charles, Draper, Paul, et al., eds., *A Companion to Philosophy of Religion*, 2nd ed. (Wiley-Blackwell: 2010).

Chapter 12

The Problem of Evil

It is the existence of evil that prevents some people from ever becoming believers in God, and it is the existence of evil that causes some believers to stop believing. When I speak of evil here, I do not mean minor things like an annoying itch or a mild headache. I mean horrendous evils like gut-wrenching migraine headaches, various forms of cancer, muscular dystrophy, cerebral palsy, Alzheimer's disease, hurricanes, earthquakes, tsunamis, forest fires, tragic accidents, torture, murders, genocide, etc.

What is evil? That of course is a difficult question to answer. Any answer will be controversial, but for our purposes let's work with the following definition (a definition that can be modified to apply to creatures other than humans, but for our purposes let's focus on humans): Evil is anything that destroys or diminishes the natural capacities of a human or interferes with the exercise of those capacities. Birth defects or accidents, for example, can destroy or diminish one's eyesight or one's ability to work. Pain or depression can interfere with one's ability to perform well athletically, artistically, or in everyday life.

Arguments from the existence of evil against traditional beliefs about God began early in western civilization. Speaking of God, an ancient Greek named Epicurus (342–270 BC) asked: "Is he willing to prevent evil, but not able? Then he is impotent. Is he able but not willing? Then he is malevolent. Is he both able and willing? Whence then is evil?" (Notice that Epicurus has constructed a dilemma with two horns.)

Philosophy of Religion: The Basics, First Edition. Richard E. Creel.
© 2014 John Wiley & Sons, Inc. Published 2014 by John Wiley & Sons, Inc.

12.1 G.W. Leibniz (1646–1716)

An even more powerful version of the argument from evil was formulated by G.W. Leibniz. It goes as follows:

> Because God is *all-powerful*, God has the power to prevent any and all evil from existing in the world.
> Because God is *all-knowing*, God knows how to prevent any and all evil from existing in the world.
> Because God is *all-good*, God wants there to be no evil in the world.
> Therefore, if there is a God, then there is no evil in the world.
> There is evil in the world.
> Therefore, there is no God.

12.2 The Logical Argument from Evil: Arthur Schopenhauer (1788–1860)

From the aforementioned argument, the German philosopher Arthur Schopenhauer concluded that if in the world there is *any* evil, no matter how small, then that fact, together with the preceding argument, *proves* conclusively that there is no God. The existence of God and the existence of any evil are incompatible with one another. If one exists, the other doesn't. It is obvious that evil exists; therefore it is just as obvious that God does not exist. QED, that is, *quod erat demonstrandum*, which in Latin means, "That which was to be demonstrated has been demonstrated." That which was to be demonstrated was that God does not exist. The logical argument claims to have proved that.

12.3 The Evidential Argument from Evil: Edward Madden, Peter Hare, William Rowe

Contemporary American philosophers Madden, Hare, Rowe, and others, think that Schopenhauer's conclusion was too strong. God might have a good reason for allowing *some* evil in the world. For example, God might allow us to suffer some evils in order that we might, by contrast, be able to appreciate the good things in life more than we could without that contrast, or God might allow us to suffer a little pain as a warning not to do things that can cause harm to our bodies. However, if there is *too much* evil in the world, or evil of the wrong kind, then there probably is no God.

Madden, et al., point out that there is a great deal of evil in the world. Moreover, much of it is intense (even excruciating), nonbeneficial (no one benefits by it), and is sometimes inflicted on innocent humans and animals who do not deserve it. These seem like states of affairs that a supreme being would not allow. Therefore, there probably is no God. Note: Schopenhauer thought his argument was a proof that God does not exist; Madden, Hare, and Rowe's do not claim to have a proof; they claim that the extent and nature of evil in the world show that there *probably* is no God.

12.3.1   Criticisms of Arguments from Evil against the Existence of God

N.B.: Although G.W. Leibniz formulated the powerful version of the argument from evil given at the beginning of this chapter, he was not persuaded by it. In spite of evil, he believed that a supremely perfect God exists. See his *Theodicy* (a theodicy is an attempt to justify God's allowing of evil).

Numerous criticisms of the arguments from evil against belief in God have been made, including the following.

1.   God Cannot Be Responsible for Evil

Only a person can be held responsible for evil. God is not a person (remember Ludwig Feuerbach's and H.N. Wieman's definitions of God):

Feuerbach: God is just an idea of ideal human potentialities (but a very important idea!).
Wieman: God is an impersonal natural force, like electricity or magnetism, which promotes and sustains human good.

Therefore, God cannot be held accountable for evil. Therefore, the existence of evil is not incompatible with the existence of God in these senses.

2. **There is no evil**

The seeming existence of evil is an illusion. Therefore, evil is not a reason for thinking that God does not exist or for thinking that God does exist but is not perfect in all respects:

Mary Baker Eddy, founder of Christian Science: Eddy reasons as follows in her *Science and Health with Key to the Scriptures* (Allison V. Stewart: 1916, pp. 330, 339–40): "Since God is All, there is no room for His unlikeness. God, Spirit alone created all, and called it good. Therefore evil, being contrary to good, is unreal." Moreover, "Divine Love is infinite. Therefore all that really exists is in and of God, and manifests his love." "Evil is nothing, no thing, mind, nor power." Obviously Eddy was a pantheist of sorts who reasoned that since God is all and because God is perfectly good and is the creator of all, therefore all is good and there is no evil. Evil is an illusion. In this same spirit, Edward Lyttelton said we need to "see sin and all evil as a good disguised by our own wrong thinking" (*Hibbert Journal*, xix, 53–60).

Advaita Vedanta Hinduism is a far eastern version of pantheism which reasons that if evil existed, it could only exist in the world, but the world is an illusion. Therefore so is evil. Brahman, the Absolute, is all that exists, and Brahman is beyond good and evil.

3. **There is no problem of evil**

This criticism holds that evil is real but says there is no *problem* of evil because evil suffered is always deserved, and evil performed is always punished. Hence, there is no unjustified evil.

Hinduism and the Law of Karma. Hinduism holds that there are spiritual laws as well as physical laws. Physical laws apply only to our bodies in this life. Spiritual laws apply to us in this life and beyond. Our souls are reincarnated over and over, sometimes into lower forms such as animals or reptiles. Our basic situation in each incarnation is a result of how well or badly we lived our previous lives. There is no escaping the law of karma (the law of spiritual consequences), but there is good karma and bad karma. We can escape from *bad* karma only by living in ways that produce *good* karma. By such living, we eventually escape the cycle of reincarnation and become reunited with Brahman, thereby entering eternal bliss. Hence, in the ultimate scheme of things, justice prevails. Because of past offenses we *deserve* the evils we suffer in this life, and in a *future* reincarnation we will suffer for any evils that we *inflict* in this life. Hence, there is no problem of evil. Justice always prevails.

This outlook was expressed exquisitely by a blind Hindu whom a European tourist encountered in India. Speaking of the blind Hindu, the tourist reported, "Not knowing that he had been blind from birth, I sympathized with him and asked by what unfortunate accident the loss of sight had come upon him. Immediately and without showing any sign of bitterness, the answer was ready to his lips, 'By some crime committed in a former birth.'" In other words, he sincerely believed that he deserved his blindness, and so he was at peace with it; it was not an evil. (See Charles Taliaferro, *Contemporary Philosophy of Religion*, 1998, p. 180.) Notice that neither God nor Brahman plays any role in this account of evil. Just as the laws of nature ensure that the total amount of matter/energy in the universe is always the same, the law of karma ensures that evil is always cancelled out. Evil suffered is always punishment for evil done, so there is no "problem" of evil.

4.   **God cannot prevent evil**

12.4   Charles Hartshorne's Panentheist or Process Theodicy

As we saw in the chapter on diverse conceptions of God, panentheist process philosophers such as Charles Hartshorne think there are excellent reasons for believing there is a divine being who is guiding the development of the world. They also think that the only way to account adequately for all the evil in the world is to concede that although God is perfectly good, God does not have the power to forcibly prevent evil. Zer only powers are the powers of influence by way of inspiration, persuasion, and companionship, and those are not coercive powers. Hence, God cannot make us be good or make the laws of nature benign.

Note that Hartshorne reconciled God and evil by giving up the traditional conception of divine omnipotence. A similar strategy (running out the permutations) could be followed with either omniscience or omnibenevolence. For example, one could say, "God is omnipotent and omnibenevolent, but ze is not omniscient. Therefore ze does not *know* how to prevent all evil." That is why Leibniz's formulation of the argument from evil is more powerful than that of Epicurus. Epicurus did not say or imply that God is omniscient. Hence, in answer to his question, "If God is able and willing to prevent evil, whence then is evil?," one could say, "Evil occurs because God does not know how to stop it." One could also say, "God is omnipotent and omniscient but is not omnibenevolent." That is, God has the power and knowledge to stop evil but does not care to stop it. Each of the preceding strategies saves the existence of God, but some theists think the price of denying the reality of evil or giving up divine omnipotence (as did Hartshorne) or omniscience or omnibenevolence or God's personhood (as did Feuerbach and Wieman) is too high a price to pay, so now let's look at how theists who refuse to deny the reality of evil or to give up divine omnipotence or omniscience or omnibenevolence or God's personhood have responded to the problem of evil.

5. We will be recompensed for evil that we suffer

The Greater Goods Theodicy: St. Paul, in his letters in the New Testament, provides an example of what is called "The Greater Goods Theodicy" (remember: a "theodicy" is a justification as to why God permits evil). He says, "I consider that the sufferings of this present time are not worth comparing with the glory that is to be revealed to us" (Romans 8:18). St. Paul said this even though he personally knew great suffering. He had severe physical illnesses, was shipwrecked, bitten by a snake, chased out of towns that were hostile to Christianity, arrested and jailed more than once, and finally executed by crucifixion. St. Paul's point was that if we choose the Kingdom of God over its opposite, then God will ensure that no matter how much we suffer in this life, one day we will enter such magnificent, eternal joy that all our past sufferings will seem a very small price to have paid.

That is reassuring, but it does not answer a very important question: Why do we have to suffer at all? If a wealthy sadist intentionally burns one of your arms painfully with a cigarette, without you having agreed to it or having known that it was going to happen, and then gives you a million dollars to recompense you for your suffering, you might say, "Hey, how about another million for the other arm?" Nonetheless, what that person did in the first place was wrong, and the fact that ze recompensed you in an acceptable way did not make it right or okay; it didn't justify what ze did (and you might henceforth be rather nervous around that person!). Similarly, the critic of the greater goods theodicy says: just because God gives us eternal happiness later does not make it okay for God to first afflict us with all sorts of involuntary sufferings (see the book of Job in the Bible for an example of divinely inflicted, undeserved suffering). To torment someone and then "buy them off" sounds like the behavior of a sadistic person, not of a divine person. Hence, in addition to assurances that someday we will receive such blessings that we won't mind the sufferings we had to go through to get them, we need an explanation as to why our sufferings are justified in the first place.

6. Evil and moral choices

The Irenaean Theodicy: Building on the theology of Irenaeus, an early Christian thinker who flourished around 180 AD, John Hick has proposed in his book *Evil and the God of Love* that God's purpose in creating rational creatures, such as humans, is to give them an opportunity to choose for or against citizenship in the Kingdom of God. One makes that choice when one chooses between good and evil. Why doesn't God just make us good and place us in zer kingdom? Because God doesn't want puppets in zer kingdom. God wants zer kingdom to be populated by people who want to be there, who have freely chosen to be there, and who have, by their choices, shared with God the work of transforming themselves into people fit for citizenship in the kingdom of God. Our earthly life, then, is a realm or "vale" of *moral decision-making* and *character development*. When we choose for or against truth, beauty, goodness, compassion, loyalty, integrity, honesty, courage, and kindred things, we are expressing the kind of person we are and creating the kind of person we will become, and we are expressing our desire for, or our hostility or indifference to, citizenship in the kingdom of God.

Evil results from people choosing to actualize evil possibilities instead of good ones. Hence, evil in the world is our fault, not God's. In order to give us an opportunity to freely choose for or against citizenship in God's kingdom, God had to make it possible for us to choose evil as well as good. Hence, given that God's purpose in creating the world was to give us opportunities to choose between good and evil, and to participate in creating our own moral character, the existence of evil, when we choose evil rather than good, is compatible with the existence of a God who is all-powerful, all-knowing, and all-good.

Two objections to Hick's Irenaean theodicy are as follows. First, allowing that it was good for God to give us the freedom to choose between good and evil, rather than making us into moral robots, couldn't God have given us moral freedom without giving us the power to hurt one another so viciously as we can? Couldn't God have made us so that we could hurt but not kill one another? So that we could cause a little pain, like a slap to the face, but not enormous pain, as in torture?

Second, in addition to what is called "moral evil" (evil inflicted by humans on one another and other creatures), there is an enormous amount of "natural evil," that is, evil that has *not* resulted from human actions, for example, the suffering and deaths caused by diseases, birth defects, tornadoes, hurricanes, earthquakes, blizzards, droughts, floods, forest fires, and volcano eruptions. According to theists it is God who created the world and made nature like it is, so God seems directly responsible for these afflictions. If a human inflicted such devastation on other humans and animals, we would think ze was evil. To be consistent, we should conclude, on the basis of all this natural evil, that if God exists, then God is evil. If we think God cannot be evil, then we should conclude that God does not exist.

7.   There are reasons for natural evil

Richard Swinburne, in *The Existence of God*, shares John Hick's biblical notion of God's reason for creating rational creatures and giving them freedom of choice. Swinburne adds that in order for God to make it possible for humans to make moral choices, God had to create a lawful world in which we can know what the consequences of our actions will be. We can choose meaningfully between holding someone's head under the water for five minutes or not doing so only if we know we are in a world in which the consequences of our actions are predictable and dependable. If sometimes when we held someone's head under the water for five minutes they died, other times they didn't die, other times they died if we *didn't* hold their head under the water, and yet other times if we held someone's head under the water for five minutes, they would not die but we would, if that's how things were we could never make a meaningful choice to drown or not drown someone because we would never know what was going to result from our action of holding them under the water. Hence, in order to make meaningful moral choices possible, God had to create a world in which the consequences of our actions are dependable and knowable. That means, however, it will be possible that people can be hurt as well as helped by the phenomena of nature: the same water that can slake our thirst or cleanse our bodies can drown us accidentally or enable us to drown someone intentionally. Hence, natural evil is an unavoidable possibility in a world in which significant moral choices are possible.

Moreover, in a world which is adequate to God's purpose for creation, natural evil must be not only a possibility but an actuality. God doesn't want us to be able to sit on the sidelines and avoid making moral decisions until we die a natural death. Hence, it is important that natural evils, such as birth defects and monsoons, reach out and afflict at least some of us, thereby forcing us to choose between, for example, being compassionate or indifferent, being courageous or cowardly. In brief, Swinburne argues, because it is good that we exist and that we have moral freedom, and because it is God's intention that we participate in deciding and creating the kind of a person we will be, the existence of natural and moral evils is compatible with the omnipotence, omniscience, and omnibenevolence of God.

Still, we might ask, why didn't God make the laws of nature less able to hurt us so seriously, and why didn't God give us moral freedom but less of it, so that we could not hurt one another so badly? Swinburne suggests that God created a world in which the laws of nature and human choices can inflict such serious evils on us in order to make it clear that the life we are living and the choices we are making are neither meaningless nor trivial. This life is serious business. Our choices can lead to great goods or great evils, both in this life and beyond. Swinburne argues that God has shown great respect for us by giving us the ability to accomplish great things in this life and by inviting and challenging us to do so through the pursuit of truth, the institutionalization of justice, the protection and promotion of the well-being of other creatures, the creation of beauty, the practice of compassion, and the building of friendship among all peoples. God has also given us the ability to neglect or oppose these things, but whatever we do, we are choosing for or against the kingdom of God, and we are choosing for or against becoming a kind of person who will feel at home in that kingdom – both here and hereafter.

8.   The Free Will Defense, Alvin Plantinga

Alvin Plantinga, in *God, Freedom and Evil*, adds another dimension to the theist attempt to reconcile the existence of God with the existence of natural evil. Speaking along Biblical lines, and Genesis and Job in particular, Plantinga states that God may not be directly responsible for natural evil. Maybe there are supernatural beings, for example, Satan, who are responsible for the natural evil in the world. Even if the Garden of Eden story is not literally true, maybe the deep and important truth in it is that God made the world perfect and zer creatures fouled it up. It would be presumptuous of us to assume that humans are the highest or even second highest creatures in the universe in terms of power and intelligence. Perhaps God has created other creatures as invisible to us as we are to microbes, but who are enormously superior to us, have the same moral freedom that we do, and have, with our cooperation, made a mess of the world. The existence of such beings would also help explain the seductive and powerful attraction of evil in our lives, and why humans sometimes become demonically possessed. Why would God create such powerful beings? For the same reason that ze created us – to give them the opportunity to choose for or against the kingdom of God. Unfortunately, Plantinga says, it appears that some of them have chosen against the kingdom of God, and we are the worse for it – just as our children and wards and innocent animals are the worse for it when we neglect or oppose what is good.

Finally, I mention that some people think it would be a very great evil if there is no life after death in which the innocent and virtuous are rewarded with happiness – especially those who have suffered innocently or have suffered because of their kindness or their courage on behalf of justice. How sad and unfair if there is no life after death! So next let's examine the possibility of life after death.

For Review, Reflection, and Discussion

1.   What is a theodicy?
2.   What do you think are some examples of evil? What do you think is the essence of evil?
3.   Recite Leibniz's argument from evil to the nonexistence of God. Why is his argument more powerful than that of Epicurus?

4. What is the difference between the logical argument from evil and the evidential argument from evil in terms of what they are trying to show regarding the existence of God?
5. Many Hindus do not deny that there is evil, but they claim that there is no "problem" of evil. Explain how they justify that claim.
6. How does Charles Hartshorne justify his belief that God cannot directly prevent evil in the world?
7. Many people agree with "the greater goods" theodicy. What is that theodicy? Do you agree with it?
8. What is the difference between natural evil and moral evil?
9. How do John Hick and Richard Swinburne justify God's allowance and even causation of evil in the world?
10. Alvin Plantinga suggests that some evil in the world may be caused by beings far superior and invisible to ourselves. What do you think of that possibility?
11. In his novel *The Brothers Karamazov*, Book V, Part IV, "Rebellion," Fyodor Dostoyevsky presents an example of a horrendous evil. The fictional character Alyosha is then challenged by his brother Ivan as to whether he would allow such horrendous evils to occur if he were God. Would you?

For Further Reading

Zagzebski, Linda, and Miller, Timothy, eds., *Readings in Philosophy of Religion: Ancient to Contemporary* (Wiley-Blackwell: 2009). Part VII, "The Problem of Evil," includes numerous selections from Leibniz, Hick, Plantinga, J.L. Mackie, Wm. Rowe, and others.

Hick, John, *Evil and the God of Love* (Fontana Library: 1968).

Plantinga, Alvin, *God, Freedom, and Evil* (Eerdmans: 1977). Plantinga raises the possibility that some evil is a result of intelligent beings beyond our ken.

Swinburne, Richard, *The Existence of God* (Clarendon Press: 1979).

Adams, Marilyn McCord, *Horrendous Evils and the Goodness of God* (Cornell University: 1999).

Peterson, Michael L., "The Logical Problem of Evil," in Taliaferro, Charles, Draper, Paul, et al., eds., *A Companion to Philosophy of Religion*, 2nd ed. (Wiley-Blackwell: 2010).

Oppy, Graham, "The Evidential Problem of Evil," in Taliaferro, Charles, Draper, Paul, et al., eds., *A Companion to Philosophy of Religion*, 2nd ed. (Wiley-Blackwell: 2010).

Madden, Edward, and Hare, Peter, *Evil and the Concept of God* (Charles C. Thomas: 1968). A classic example of an evidentialist argument from evil against belief in God.

Keller, James A., *Problems of Evil and the Power of God* (Ashgate: 2007). A sophisticated analysis written from the point of view of process theism. See especially Chapter 8.

Chapter 13

God and Life after Death

We have solid evidence that humans have believed in life after death or have been profoundly interested in its possibility for many thousands of years. That interest has not vanished in our age of science and technology. Most of us love life. We want to be happy and we want it to last forever – not just for a few decades. And if we aren't happy in this life, we want there to be another life in which we can be happy. We don't want to cease to exist. Perhaps death need not mean the end of our existence. Are there reasons to think that death is not the end of personal existence? Let's begin a systematic examination of answers to that question by running out some permutations. When exploring philosophical problems, it can be helpful to run out the permutations, or at least *try* to figure out all the possible positions, because doing so forces us to be more objective about certain possibilities than we might otherwise be. And even though it is sometimes impossible to figure out *all* the possibilities, trying to do that sometimes leads us to discover possibilities that we otherwise would not have thought of (one of which, I suspect, is coming up for you in the next paragraph!).

How can running out the permutations be useful to us in thinking about life after death? The most basic permutations about life after death are two in number, like flipping a coin: either there is life after death or there is not. If there is not, then that is the end of the story, but if there is life after death we need to flip the coin again: either life after death is everlasting or it is not. The traditional idea is that if there is life after death, it lasts forever, but we cannot rule out the

Philosophy of Religion: The Basics, First Edition. Richard E. Creel.
© 2014 John Wiley & Sons, Inc. Published 2014 by John Wiley & Sons, Inc.

possibility – and *possibilities* are all we are considering here – we cannot rule out the possibility that we survive death, live for a limited amount of time (whether one year or a thousand years) and eventually pass into oblivion forever. (Sorry if that permutation upsets you! To explore this possibility, see the writings of process philosopher David Griffin.)

Now let's look at three positions regarding what happens to us at death (cessationism, immortalism, and resurrectionism), and three world views that are associated with these positions (naturalism, transcendentalism, and classical theism). With regard to each of the three world views – naturalism, transcendentalism, and classical theism – I will (i) set forth its position regarding life after death, (ii) explain the *metaphysical* position that undergirds it, (iii) give some reasons for thinking it is true, and (iv) give some reasons for thinking it is not true. (A *metaphysical* position is a position about reality that cannot be investigated or settled by sensation or science alone. It is a position that "goes beyond" the physical. For example, whether God or Brahman *exists* is a metaphysical question, not a physical question. Scientific questions can, at least theoretically, be answered by sensation and physical experimentation.) Now for our three positions regarding what happens to the mind or soul at death.

13.1 Cessationism

According to cessationism the self, mind, soul, spirit (whatever you want to call it) ceases to exist at death. According to the world view of naturalism, there is a simple reason for thinking that cessationism is true. The reason is that there is nothing more to reality than nature, so a human is a physical body and nothing more. Death means that the body ceases to function, so the self and consciousness cease to exist. Consciousness is generated by the body as light in a light bulb is produced by a generator. When the generator stops, the light doesn't go anywhere. It just ceases to exist. Similarly, when the brain permanently ceases to function, consciousness doesn't go anywhere; it just ceases, permanently. But that is not a reason to be upset. As the great ancient Greek philosopher, Epicurus, said: "Where I am, death is not. Where death is, I am not." Therefore, death is not to be feared any more than a dreamless sleep is to be feared.

Moreover, according to naturalism, there is no God to prevent the event of death or reverse it or punish us after death! (Death is to be feared if there is life after death and a God to punish us!) For reasons to think that naturalism is true, go back to arguments against the existence of God in Chapters 11 and 12 and to the criticisms of arguments for the existence of God in Chapters 6–10. Consider also that we cannot sense the reality of anything beyond physical objects, their properties and relations (such as color and distance), so it seems unlikely that there is any more to reality than physical objects and their properties and relations. The objects of nature are accessible, vivid, and dependable in ways that purported supernatural objects are not, so why think the latter exist? When we do think they exist we have simply misunderstood nature or have not understood it deeply enough.

As to "the soul" or "the mind," it is an illusion to think it exists as a thing or entity. The consciousness that is generated by the brain is like the picture of a horse prancing around on a television screen. It looks like the horse is a real thing, an independently existing object, but that is only an illusion generated by thousands of flashing pixels. Similarly, the belief that there is an independently existing mind is an illusion created by thousands of mental events occurring in rapid succession. When the television turns off, the horse on the screen immediately ceases to exist; when the brain ceases to function, "the mind" immediately ceases to exist. (This "bundle theory of the mind" was pioneered by David Hume, an eighteenth-century Scottish philosopher. See his *A Treatise of Human Nature*.) In support of this position, note how medical anesthesiologists can control the *degree* to which patients lose consciousness, whether they lose consciousness altogether and when and how quickly they are brought back to consciousness – and of course excessive administration of anesthesia can cause permanent loss of consciousness, that is, death. Consciousness is also dependent on nutrition and hydration and can be affected by a blow to the head, a stroke, or a disease such as Alzheimer's. All of the preceding seem to show that the existence and clarity of consciousness and the functioning of the mind are functions of neural activity in the brain. (For reasons *against* cessationism see the reasons *for* the next two positions: immortalism and resurrectionism.)

(Parenthetically, process theists are theists rather than naturalists, but most are also cessationists. A few, however, such as David

Griffin, argue for an afterlife of *limited* duration. See "Further Readings" at the end of this chapter.)

13.2 Immortalism

Immortalists believe that at the core of every human is an immortal soul, a spiritual entity, "a transcendental ego," which has existed forever, will exist forever, and separates from the body at death. (Don't confuse "immortalist" with "immoralist." The extra "t" makes a big difference!) Transcendentalists, such as Hindus, Socrates, and Plato, go beyond the fundamental position of immortalism to hold that death is good because our body is a burden that distracts us, afflicts us, burdens us, seduces us, prevents us from seeing the beauty and wonder of the spiritual world, and deceives us into thinking that the body is what we are and that physical pleasures are what are most important. But the truth is quite the opposite. The body is just temporary housing. It is like an inhibiting container to be escaped from (a container we usually do not even realize we are in!). Happiness comes from realizing these facts about the self and the body and breaking free from the snares and delusions of the body, entering into life on another plane, or in another, a spiritual, dimension. (That dimension, as with the biblical heaven or kingdom of God, has no spatial location relative to this universe, no direction or distance from it. That might sound problematic, but it is the same thing that some respected physicists believe today, namely, that there are multiple universes that have no spatial relations to one another. If reputable physicists think that makes sense for multiple universes, it should be considered intelligible also for the relation of the spiritual realm to the physical realm.)

By contrast to naturalists, the world view of transcendentalism holds that a person is an uncreated, immortal, nonphysical soul. After all, the mind is not a physical thing like the brain. The brain can be located, measured, and weighed, but the mind cannot be; it is not physically accessible; the brain and its contents are physically accessible; the contents of the mind are private in a radical sense. Mental events such as thoughts, memories, and intentions are nonphysical; they have no shape, weight, color, or other physical properties. Therefore, the physical world is not all there is to reality. Moreover, as just mentioned, transcendentalists believe the physical world is an inferior realm (or an illusion) in which the soul is temporarily trapped and from which it must escape in order to achieve deep, enduring happiness.

Transcendentalism is typically connected with a doctrine of *karma* according to which there are inescapable *moral laws* as well as inescapable *physical laws*, so that just as our intentional and unintentional physical actions have inevitable consequences, so our moral and immoral behaviors have consequences from which we cannot escape – and if it appears that some people escape by death, that is an illusion because the law of karma ensures that each of those people is reincarnated into a new body and a new situation in such a way as to suffer the consequences of their immorality in a previous life or lives. Happily, karma also *rewards* people in this life for their moral behavior in this and past lives. Hence, the doctrine of karma explains why there is such disparity between the lives of individuals at birth and during their lives: the condition of each birth and life is a consequence of how the individual lived previous lives. In this way, the law of karma ensures that over the long haul there is justice in the universe. (Many transcendentalists believe that eventually, after many lives of being purified by suffering and learning, everyone will enter into the blessed state of nirvana, unity with Brahman.)

Seven reasons for believing that a person survives the death of the body and perhaps lived before this life are these. (i) Some people, especially in the Hindu tradition, claim to have memories of previous lives of their own – memories that are correct and do not seem to involve things that the person could have learned in this life (beware of frauds, but don't rule out the possibility of the real thing). (ii) People have déjà vu experiences in which they visit a place where they seem to have been before but where they've never been in this life, or they meet someone whom they seem to have met before but could not have met in this life, or they seem to know something they did not learn in this life (see the dialogues of Plato – especially *Meno* and *Phaedo* – for reasons to believe that we know things in this life that we must have learned in a previous life). (iii) The soul or mind, as we have seen, seems to be a nonphysical thing that would not be subject to creation or destruction, and so would precede and postcede this life. Physical things are *created* by putting physical particles together; they are *destroyed* by being separated into their parts, but the soul is not made of parts. Like God the soul is a simple substance and therefore does not have parts from which it can be created or into which it can be broken and thereby destroyed, so there is reason to think the soul has always existed and always will. (iv) Many perfectly sane people attest to having experiences with a dead friend or relative. (I had one such startling experience of a deceased person, my mother. I both saw and heard her. Was the experience veridical? Or was it a visual and auditory hallucination? I don't know, but it was very realistic and I was wide awake!) Moreover, *mediums* conduct séances in which there sometimes appears to be startling communication from the dead (yes, there are fakers in this field, but also a few astonishing "communications" that appear to be real). (v) Some people have had "near death experiences" in which they were clinically dead, encountered friends and relatives who had predeceased them, and then were revived and reported their experiences. (vi) Some people have a deep intuition or feeling that the soul survives (deep intuitions that are wide-spread should not simply be dismissed; they may be telling us something). (vii) Finally, I mention that if one accepts the teachings of a religion, one can appeal to the authority of its sacred texts to confirm that the soul survives death (and perhaps even preceded birth), texts such as the Torah for Jews, the New Testament for Christians, the Koran for Muslims, and the Bhagavad-Gita for Hindus.

Several *criticisms* of transcendentalism are these. *First*, Hinduism claims that the soul has always existed, but, as we have seen, the kalam cosmological argument argues that time had to have a beginning, and therefore anything that exists in time, such as the soul, had to have a beginning. Nothing other than God can have existed forever without a beginning.

Second, Immanuel Kant, an eighteenth-century German philosopher, argued that even if the soul is simple and cannot be destroyed by being broken apart, that does not rule out the possibility that God, if there is a God, could simply annihilate the soul all at once – like turning out a light. *Third*, Kant added, even if the soul cannot be destroyed by *annihilation*, it might be destroyed by *diminution*. That is, the powers of the soul, such as awareness, imagination, will, and reason, might be diminished to the point that the soul would be a meaningless thing, like an eye the power of which is diminished to the point of blindness. The eye still exists, but it may as well not; functionally speaking, it is no longer an eye. *Fourth* and finally, any appeal to scripture is always problematic because of the multiplicity of conflicting scriptures and the difficulty of verifying scriptural claims, which are usually ancient or scientifically unverifiable.

13.3   Resurrectionism

Classical theists in the Jewish, Christian, and Muslim traditions believe in *resurrection* rather than permanent annihilation or immortality. ("Re-surrection" literally means "re-creation.") The doctrine of resurrection does not denigrate the body. It holds that the body is good, and a body is necessary for a full and rich life after death. There are two basic conceptions of resurrection. The *first* conception holds that a human is a physical entity that has no immortal soul, so at death the person perishes completely. Lights out. Eventually, however, God will resurrect, that is, recreate, the physical individual for life after death. The *second* conception holds that a human is a *combination* of a body and a soul (this is a dualist conception of a human; the first conception is a monist conception – "mon" meaning "one," here signifying that a human consists of one substance, matter). According to dualists, the soul survives the death of the body, but without the body the soul lives an impoverished life; for a rough analogy consider losing all or most of your ability to see, hear, touch, taste, and smell while still being conscious. You would still exist, but you wouldn't have much of a life. (The Homeric conception of death in ancient Greece – see Homer's *Iliad* and *Odyssey* – held that life after death for many is lived in a joyless shadow world.) Obviously, if dualism is true, then in order to live a rich and full life after death we need a body, so eventually, it is said, God will rejoin the soul with a body. (To be the same person does it have to be the same body? Or just an appropriate body with the same soul? We will return to such questions soon.)

According to classical theism, biblical and philosophical, each human has a soul and it has not always existed; it was created by a benevolent God. In the words of a prayer in "The Holy Eucharist: Rite Two" of the Episcopal Church, "Holy and gracious Father: In your infinite love you made us for yourself." If that is true, then it is reasonable to think that God would want not only to create us but also to preserve us for eternal fellowship in the Kingdom of God. But how to do that? As we have seen, the classical idea is that the body perishes at death, whether or not there is a soul that survives it. If there is a soul that survives the death of the body it is not immortal of its own nature, according to classical theism. Rather, it was created by God and depends on God for its continued existence after the death of the body.

Things get complicated at this point. Some theists (the monists) believe there is no soul that survives the death of the body, but there will be a time when God resurrects (recreates) the body, and thereby the soul of the person will reemerge due to the renewed activity of the brain, like someone turning on a light bulb that was turned off earlier. God may rejoin the very atoms that constituted a person at death, or, by contrast, as we now understand in this computer age, God may use any old atoms to reconstitute the person but ensure that it is him or her by programming the brain to have the identical character, personality, and memories of the person who died. (But will the resurrected person have a gender? Genitals?)

In the case of dualists who believe that humans have a soul that survives the death of the body, a person's memories, character, and personality remain in existence in the soul that survives the body, but, as already mentioned, in order to live a full and rich life again each person needs for God to create a new body for mer so that ze can again have a full range of experiences – perhaps it will be a perfected version of the kind of body we each have now, or perhaps, as St. Paul said, it will be "a spiritual body." In brief, if the transcendentalist idea that souls are uncreated and indestructible is rejected, as it is by classical theism, then life after death seems to require a power that can create souls and resurrect the dead. Obviously, say classical theists, God would have such power, so all the arguments given earlier for the existence of God are reasons for thinking that resurrection is the truth about life after death, and arguments for resurrection are arguments for God.

Now allow me to present two unusual reasons to *hope* that there is life after death. Immanuel Kant claimed that philosophy takes away *knowledge* about philosophical issues but gives them back to us in the mode of *hope*. When we come to realize that we don't *know* that something is true, we can nonetheless *hope* that it is true. Consequently, Kant gave two unusual reasons for hoping there is a God and a life after death. First, he said, good people deserve to be happy; people who live kind, moral lives deserve happiness, but obviously there is no close correlation between morality and happiness in this life. Therefore, we should hope that there is a God who can reward virtue with happiness, and a life after death in which ze can do that. Second, we have a deep ethical obligation to become morally perfect. Few, if any of us, achieve such perfection in this life, so we should hope there is a life after death in which we can continue to strive toward moral perfection, leaving our weaknesses, vices, and flaws behind. As we achieve greater progress toward moral perfection, we should also enjoy greater happiness, but, Kant said, greater happiness should not be our objective in pursuing moral perfection; greater happiness should simply be a happy by-product of our pursuit of perfection. Virtue should be pursued above all and for its own sake.

Before we move to a final issue in this chapter, let me summarize what we have covered so far. We have looked at three basic conclusions regarding the question of life after death: Cessation, Immortality, and Resurrection. Atheists who are naturalists and many process theists believe that death is followed by oblivion. Hindus and Platonists typically believe in two-way immortality: the soul has always existed, never began to exist, and will never cease to exist. Many immortalists also believe that the soul becomes reincarnate many times until it achieves liberation from the tormenting cycle of reincarnation. Most Christians, Muslims, and many Jews believe in resurrection, with or without a soul that survives the death of the body. The soul or mind, whether or not it can exist independently of the body, was created by God and so had a beginning of existence. It lives only one life in this world and then is either recreated wholly, or the postmortem soul is recombined with a resurrection body.

Earlier, I said that atheists, Christians, Hindus, etc., "usually" or "typically" believe something or "most" of them do because it is important to realize that there are almost always exceptions to any dominant position in philosophy or religion. For example, not all atheists are naturalists; some Hindus, such as Samkhyas, are atheist transcendentalists, and, as I've mentioned, not all process theists are cessationists – some believe in a temporary afterlife. Once again it is important to consider all the permutations (and to realize that there are conflicting opinions in fields in addition to philosophy, fields such as history, politics, economics, art, and even physics).

13.4   Personal Identity and Continuity

Before we leave this chapter, we need to touch on two of the most controversial topics in contemporary philosophy – topics that have an important bearing on the issue of life after death: (i) the nature of *personal identity*, and (ii) the necessary and sufficient conditions for *personal continuity* over time. We have been going along merrily as though the only question is *whether* there is life after death, as though the *idea* of life after death is not problematic – but many find it very problematic. First, there is the issue of *personal identity*: what makes something to be a person rather than not, and what makes a person to be the person that ze is rather than some other person? Is it the body? Same body, same person? If that is the case, as seems reasonable to surmise, at least initially, then a person would be the same person even if all of zer memories and personality were wiped out by disease (such as Alzheimer's or by accident (such as a severe blow to the head) – but would that body be the same person after such a loss? It's the same *human*, but is it the same *person*? It hardly seems so, but the matter is controversial. What do you think? (N.B.: A *necessary* condition is one that *has* to be the case in order for something to exist. For example, having three straight sides is a necessary condition of something being a triangle. However, having three straight sides is not a sufficient condition of being a triangle because those three straight sides may not all intersect each other. *Sufficient* conditions are conditions that by themselves are adequate to make something be the case (having three, straight, closed sides is sufficient for something being a triangle). However, a sufficient condition may not be necessary. Kindling can be set on fire by a match, but that is not a necessary condition for setting kindling on fire as it can also be done by rubbing sticks together or focusing the rays of the sun through a magnifying glass onto the kindling. So remember: "necessary" means "has to be the case"; "sufficient" means "adequate to cause the effect" but may or may not be necessary.)

By contrast to the idea that a person is zer body, if a person is zer mind (zer memories, character, personality, ambitions, and such), as also seems reasonable, rather than zer body, then such a mind could be programmed into *more* than one body after the death of the original body. Then which embodied mind would be identical with the person who lived before death? To use an analogy, is a person like *a memory chip* or like *a program on a memory chip*? If the person (let's say "Kelly") is the memory chip (zer body), then Kelly continues to exist though the program is wiped out (such as with Alzheimer's disease). If Kelly is the program (zer mind), then Kelly can exist though the chip is destroyed, and the program can be embedded in any number of chips so that there could be many Kellys at one time! Which one would be identical with the original chip/program/person? (There is a similar issue with amoebas. When an amoeba mitoses, that is, self-divides into two amoebas, does the original amoeba still exist? If yes, which of the two new amoebas is identical with the original amoeba? The one on the right? The one on the left? Both? Neither?)

An obvious third alternative is that a body and a nonphysical soul are both necessary for something to be a person who continues to live after death (to return to our earlier analogy, a program on a chip would be required – not just one or the other). If that is true, it would seem that naturalism and transcendentalism are both false if there is life after death because naturalism says that our minds perish permanently with the death of our bodies, and transcendentalism says that we are spiritual beings who will eventually exist apart from our bodies and are best off that way.

A related set of puzzles has to do with *personal continuity*, and especially personal continuity as it pertains to life after death. Specifically, what would it take for *you* to survive the death of your body? More generally, what are the *necessary and sufficient conditions* for a person who lives after death to be the same person as a person who lived before death? If all the atoms of the premortem person are reassembled so that the postmortem body is the same as the premortem body in appearance and structure, but the memories, character, and personality are not the same, would that be the same person? If the same atoms are reassembled and the memories, etc., are also the same, would that be the same person or would it just be a person who was *indiscernible* from but not *identical* with the premortem person? (Two things are *indiscernible* but *not identical* if they are *numerically different* (can be counted separately) but cannot be distinguished from one another on the basis of their properties, such as two number eight black billiard balls produced on the same assembly line. Two things are *identical* if they are not two things but are the same thing, like the Morning Star and the Evening Star (people once thought they were two different stars, one appearing at dawn and the other at dusk, but not only are they not two things, they are not even a star; "they" are the planet Venus!) So, to return to our topic, could a reassembled person after death be *identical* to a person before death or could ze at best be only *indiscernible* from the premortem person but *not identical* to mer?

Also, as stated earlier, if a person can be completely recreated after death, then that person's body could be duplicated multiple times simultaneously. If that were so, which postmortem duplicate would be identical, that is, personally continuous, with the premortem person? One suggestion is that if there is only one postmortem duplicate that is indiscernible from the premortem person, then, that duplicate will be the same person as the premortem person, but if there is more than one postmortem duplicate, then none of them will be continuous with the premortem person – indiscernible from the premortem person though each be.

Then there are puzzles as to what the resurrected body must be like if the resurrected life is to be better than this life, as most theists believe it will be, at least for some. If one dies of old age and has deteriorated greatly due to aging, must one's resurrected body be from an earlier age of that very individual? If so, what age? 16? 21? Or does it just need to be a younger and healthier body? Does it need to be constituted of the very same atoms as the earlier body or can they be different? A little? A lot? If one dies from a terrible disease or accident that greatly disfigures one's body, must those disfigurements be corrected in the resurrected body? To what extent? Must one be resurrected with the body of an Apollo or a Venus? Or with the features of one's own body at an earlier stage – skinny or porky, pigeon-toed or splay-footed, tall or short, hirsute or not, etc.? Then there are issues of birth defects that one has always had. It seems that some people wouldn't be themselves without those characteristics. What, if anything, needs to be done about them?

Some people think the preceding complications and others are so extensive and the questions so mind-boggling that they cast serious doubt on the plausibility of life after death. Others concede the difficulty of the questions but are confident that God can answer them.

It is important to notice that we are dealing here with metaphysical issues, not epistemological issues. *Metaphysics* deals with questions about the nature of *reality*. *Epistemology* deals with questions about the nature of *knowledge*. I have not been asking how we could *know or tell* that a later person was the same as an earlier person. I have been asking what would *make* a later person to be the same as an earlier person. What are the necessary and sufficient conditions for a later person to *be* the same person as an earlier person? Related but different questions must be asked to determine how we could *tell* that a later person is or probably is identical to an earlier person. Obviously, the epistemological issue is critical when we try to determine whether someone is responsible for a crime. So the distinction between metaphysical and epistemic questions is very important to keep in mind.

It is not obvious what the solutions to the brainteasers in this section are. The philosophical pot is still boiling furiously with issues of personal identity and continuity, so we will not attempt to solve them here, but it is important to be aware of them. In philosophy, life is never as simple as it seems – and that is because life is never as simple as it seems.

For Review, Reflection, and Discussion

1. What does it mean to "run out the permutations" of something? Can you think of an example not given earlier?
2. Distinguish cessationism, immortalism, and resurrectionism from one another. With regard to the possibility and nature of life after death, distinguish naturalism, transcendentalism, and classical theism from one another and relate them to cessationism, immortalism, and resurrectionism.
3. What is the basic difference between the kinds of questions that metaphysics and epistemology ask? Which kind of question is, "What is the difference between knowledge and belief?" Which kind of question is, "Does God exist?"
4. Recite Epicurus' famous statement that was intended to take away our fear of death. Do you agree with his statement? Does it reconcile you peacefully to death? Why? Why not?
5. What is the difference between the monistic theory of resurrection and the dualistic theory of resurrection?
6. Explain the difference between necessary and sufficient conditions.
7. What do you think are the necessary and sufficient conditions for something to be a person?

8. What are the necessary and sufficient conditions for someone who lives after death to be the same person as someone who lived before death?

9. Are all humans persons? I had a relative who lived from birth to 21 years of age in a coma. She lay in bed and never opened her eyes or responded meaningfully to anyone. Was she a person or only a human? Or is there no difference? Is it the case that to be a human is to be a person? Is it the case that to be a person is to be a human? Could there be persons who are not human?

10. If resurrection of a deteriorated body is possible, it appears that more than one postmortem indiscernible body could be created unless the very same atoms are used again, but attempting to use the same atoms leads to serious problems in cases of cannibalism and when animals have eaten human flesh and we eat the animals. Also, if someone dies with a body that age and/or disease has ravaged, must the ravaged body be resurrected? At what age or in what condition must a person be resurrected to be the same person?

11. What were Immanuel Kant's arguments against the claim that the soul could not be destroyed because it is simple?

12. Kant said we cannot know that there is life after death. What did he say is an appropriate attitude toward the *possibility* of life after death? Why did he encourage that attitude?

For Further Reading

Zagzebski, Linda, and Miller, Timothy, eds., *Readings in Philosophy of Religion: Ancient to Contemporary* (Wiley-Blackwell: 2009). Part VIII includes selections from Epicurus, Plato, Averroes (a Muslim), Thomas Nagel, Bertrand Russell, Paul Badham (on near death experiences), and others.

Hick, John, *Philosophy of Religion*, 4th ed. (Prentice-Hall, Inc.: 1990) . In Chapter 10 Hick provides an intriguing series of examples to help make personal continuity and the possibility of life after death intelligible. In Chapter 11 he discusses karma and reincarnation. His book length treatment of these topics is his *Death and Eternal Life*.

Griffin, David Ray, *Reenchantment Without Supernaturalism: A Process Philosophy of Religion* (Cornell University: 2001), pp. 236–46. A leading process theist provides an argument for life after death that has a fulfilling quality but only *temporary* duration.

Perry, John, *A Dialogue on Personal Identity and Immortality*: (Hackett Publishing Company: 1978). A short, illuminating introduction to the issues by a leading thinker.

Dennett, Daniel C., "Where am I?" in *Brainstorms: Philosophical Essays on Mind and Psychology* (Bradford Books: 1978). A fascinating excursion, in story form, through issues of personal identity.

Chapter 14

Miracles, Revelation, and Prayer

We spoke earlier of the omnipotence or all-powerfulness of God. The power of God is associated most frequently with the creation of the universe and with miracles. We have already spoken a bit about God and creation, so now let's think about miracles and two things that are closely associated with them: revelation and prayer. I will turn to the Bible for examples of miracles, since those are the miracles with which most readers will be familiar or be able to look up most easily. To make things read more smoothly, I will write as though the miracles in the Bible all took place as reported, but eventually there will be criticism of miracles as well as support for them.

14.1 Miracles

What is a miracle? (Note again that philosophers usually approach a topic by first asking for a definition of the concept under consideration. How to formulate a satisfactory definition of anything, is in itself a fascinating philosophical subject.) People use the word "miracle" in at least three different ways. I will label those ways (i) astounding good luck, (ii) wonder, and (iii) anomaly.

Astounding Good Luck: Sometimes we call an event a miracle because it is highly contrary to what would normally be expected. Say someone was in a terrible automobile accident in which there was every reason to think that she should have been killed – yet she walked away! We

Philosophy of Religion: The Basics, First Edition. Richard E. Creel.
© 2014 John Wiley & Sons, Inc. Published 2014 by John Wiley & Sons, Inc.

say "It was a miracle she wasn't killed!," and it *was* terribly fortunate that she wasn't killed, but that is not the kind of miracle we are interested in here.

Wonder: Sometimes we call an event a miracle because it evokes a sense of astonishment and wonder, and especially a sense of the greatness and goodness of God. I recently heard an art historian exclaim that the Pieta and David statues by Michelangelo were "miraculous." Some see the grandeur of snow-capped mountains for the first time and feel as though they are in the presence of a miracle. Some see the birth of a baby and say it was a miracle; it was deeply touching, emotionally overwhelming, and made one profoundly grateful – but neither is that the kind of miracle that we in philosophy are most interested in, though it is closer because it usually involves a sense of the reality and greatness of God.

Anomaly: The previous "miracles" can be explained in terms of the laws of biology (the birth) and the laws of physics (in the case of the car wreck the car went off the cliff at just the right point and in just the right way as to minimize injuries to the occupant while totaling the car), but some purported events (such as Jesus changing water to wine or the resurrection of Jesus from the dead) cannot be explained by any laws of nature that we know; they seem to be exceptions to or violations of the laws of nature, thereby requiring something beyond nature to account for them. (Because *a miracle is an exception to the laws of nature* it is beyond the power of a mere human to cause a miracle; for us to accomplish anything we must act within the laws of nature.) For an example of a miracle to analyze, let's focus on the biblical report that Moses saw a bush that was burning but was not consumed (Exodus 3:1–6). If that happened, it was contrary to all the laws of nature with which we are familiar. Consequently, if you already believe in an omnipotent God, it makes sense to assume that that anomalous event was caused by God – and if you are not sure whether there is a God, then you could take that event to be some evidence that there is a God because you have no other way of accounting for it.

Or so it would seem, but rather than turning to God for an explanation one can always insist that there is a natural explanation that we just do not yet know. After all, there is no reason to think that we already know all the laws of nature, or that we might not have to modify and improve our understanding of the laws that we do know. So when we encounter an anomalous event we have a choice to make between considering it to be a divine miracle that cannot be explained scientifically or a natural event that we just cannot explain yet.

Regarding that choice, consider this famous criticism of miracles by David Hume. First, Hume pointed out that nature consists of what happens over and over the same way, millions of times as witnessed by millions of people without exception. Consequently, he argued, whenever it seems like there is an exception to a law of nature, that is, a miracle, it is always much more likely that the witness or witnesses have *misperceived* what they saw, or *misunderstood* it, or that *fraud* was involved, than that a miracle occurred. People misperceive things often. Witnesses to an accident give sincere but conflicting reports; they can't all be right about what happened. An octagonal tower at a distance looks round. It looks like the sun moves around the earth, not like the earth is rotating on its axis relative to the sun. People also misunderstand things. For thousands of years, humans thought that disease was caused by evil spirits and that the moon was a self-luminous object like the sun. In brief, we can never have enough good evidence to be justified in believing that a miracle occurred. We can never gather enough evidence to overturn the centuries of evidence that such things just don't happen! The probability verges on zero. It is always more probable that the witnesses misperceived or misunderstood or were fraudulent than that a miracle occurred, so we are never justified in believing that one did. (Note: Hume's criticism does not rule out the *possibility* that a miracle might occur; it only rules out the possibility that we might ever be *justified* in thinking that a miracle occurred.)

Before turning to the topic of revelation, let me provide a working definition of "miracle" that you might find helpful to use or improve on: *A miracle is an exception to the laws of nature that is performed by God for some good purpose* and is usually witnessed by someone other than God. I say "usually witnessed" because we don't want to rule out the possibility that God could perform a miracle that no one witnessed. For example, God might heal someone who would have died otherwise, though no one realized what God did for the person. God might do such a thing because the person has some important role to play in the future. By contrast, miracles that are witnessed have religious significance because the miracle brings the power or goodness or mercy or judgment of God to bear on the minds and hearts of the witnesses. (But of course a miracle might be perceived as a *natural* anomaly by someone who is unaccustomed or disinclined to perceive things in a religious way.)

14.2   Revelation

In spite of David Hume, there is more that might be said in justification of belief in miracles. Miracles always *reveal* something, such as the grandeur, goodness, or judgment of God, but there are different kinds of revelation. I chose the burning bush example for us to explore because Moses didn't merely see a burning bush that was not consumed; he also heard a voice. From the bush God called Moses by name, revealed that the Israelites, who were in slavery in Egypt, were miserable, and that God wanted Moses to go to Egypt and lead the Israelites out of slavery. A revelation plus a miracle to authenticate it should be a powerful combination that makes it more likely to a witness that a seeming miracle really is a miracle and that a seeming revelation really is a revelation (though of course we don't want to give up appropriate skepticism about such things; remember the "wizard" behind the curtain in "The Wizard of Oz" – but don't rule out the possibility that not every case is fraudulent!).

The kind of revelation we are most interested in here is what is called *"propositional revelation."* Sometimes God or an angel might reveal merself in a vision without using words – perhaps a vision of compassion to convey deep sympathy, or a vision of disapproval to convey judgment, but in *propositional* revelation words are always used (a proposition is simply a statement, whether a statement of fact, a prediction, or a command). The Koran is an instance of propositional revelation (the entire Koran is said to have been dictated to Mohammed by the angel Gabriel), and of course the Bible is full of propositional revelations from God and angels.

The main point here is that if an anomalous event is accompanied by a religiously significant propositional revelation, then that is all the more reason to think that the event is a miracle and the revelation is authentic; the miracle and the revelation help confirm one another (as in the burning bush and the voice of God). Moreover, if an anomalous event occurs subsequent to a prayer for that very event and it is accompanied by a propositional revelation which supports it, that would make a powerful threefold combination in favor of belief that there is a God and that God has responded to that prayer. More often than not, it seems, an "answered prayer" is *not* also accompanied by revelation or a miracle, and many, perhaps most, answered prayers can be accounted for by natural processes which do not point to a clear violation of a law of nature, but nonetheless an answered prayer might be explained by God nudging rather than violating the processes of nature to render an outcome favorable to the prayer.

14.3 Prayer

Having raised the topic of prayer, let's examine it a bit more systematically. Prayer consists of talking to God, whether out loud or just in our minds and hearts (prayer might also of course include listening to God, and especially if we have asked God for something such as guidance or forgiveness). There are at least four kinds of prayer (not listed in order of importance). *First*, there are prayers of *praise*, such as when we acknowledge and laud the greatness, the wisdom, and the goodness of God. *Second*, there are prayers of *thanksgiving*, such as when we thank God for our blessings. One may thank God for the general blessings of one's life (friends, family, meaningful work, etc.), or one may thank God for something special that has happened, such as a terribly injured or sick person getting well. *Third*, there are prayers of *confession*, in which we confess our sins of commission and omission (things we ought not to have done but did, and things we ought to have done but did not do). *Fourth*, there are prayers of *petition* in which we *ask* God for something, whether it be forgiveness for our sins, strength to resist a temptation, guidance with a difficult decision, solace in the midst of sorrow, success at getting a job, or for our sibling to come home safe from war. Of course, these different kinds of prayer can be and usually are joined with one another.

Not all miracles are preceded by prayer. Jesus' disciples were utterly devastated and left hopeless by his death; there is no evidence that they prayed for or expected him to be resurrected from the dead, but, according to the New Testament, it happened. When we do pray for a miracle, however, that is a petitionary prayer, and when a prayer is answered, that is some reason to think that there is a God who cares for us.

When prayers are not answered, that can be taken as evidence that God does not exist or that God is wiser than to grant our request.

For Review, Reflection, and Discussion

1. How was "miracle" defined in this chapter for philosophical purposes? What are two other kinds of things that people call "miracles?"
2. How did David Hume argue that it is never rational to believe that a miracle occurred?
3. What is meant by propositional revelation? Can you think of an example that is not included in this chapter?
4. What are four different kinds of prayer that were identified in this chapter? Don't just name them; please explain them.
5. If a petitionary prayer is answered, is that evidence that God exists? If a petitionary prayer is not answered, is that evidence that God does not exist?

For Further Reading

Zagzebski, Linda, and Miller, Timothy, eds., *Readings in Philosophy of Religion: Ancient to Contemporary* (Wiley-Blackwell: 2009). Part XI, Section A is on miracles and includes selections from Aquinas, John Locke, David Hume, and George Mavrodes.

Schlesinger, George N., "Miracles," in Taliaferro, Charles, Draper, Paul, et al., eds., *A Companion to Philosophy of Religion*, 2nd ed. (Wiley-Blackwell: 2010).

Peterson, Michael, Hasker, William, et al, eds., *Philosophy of Religion: Selected Readings*, 2nd ed. (Oxford University: 2000). Part XIII includes an article on revelation by George Mavrodes and an article on petitionary prayer by Eleonore Stump.

For David Hume's criticism of belief in miracles see Section X of his *An Enquiry Concerning Human Understanding* (Hackett Publishing Company: 1977). For a sophisticated criticism of Hume's position on miracles see the writings of Richard Swinburne, such as *The Concept of Miracle* (Macmillan and Co., Ltd. and St. Martin's Press: 1970).

Chapter 15

Rationality without Evidence

Hard agnostics think that the question of the existence of a supremely perfect being can never be settled by human reason. Soft agnostics think that perhaps the issue can be settled by evidence eventually, but for now they see the evidence as too vague or ambiguous or incomplete or weak or equally balanced for both sides to warrant a confident conclusion as to whether God exists or not. If the agnostics are correct, does that mean we should suspend belief about the existence of God and refrain from living a religious life? Some people think not. Consider, for example, "Pascal's Wager."

15.1 Pascal's Wager

Blaise Pascal (1623–1662) argues in his *Pensées* (which is French for "thoughts") that if you do not think you have enough evidence to believe in God that does not mean that you should remain neutral as to whether God exists. The smart thing to do is to assume there is a God and live accordingly. His argument (which is an attempt to run out the permutations on the rationality of believing in God) is as follows.

If we believe and live as though there is not a God and there is not a God, we gain little or nothing by not believing. Perhaps we enjoy a few pleasures that we would not have had if we had been religious, but at death we simply cease to exist and there is no memory of those pleasures.

Philosophy of Religion: The Basics, First Edition. Richard E. Creel.
© 2014 John Wiley & Sons, Inc. Published 2014 by John Wiley & Sons, Inc.

If we believe and live as though there is a God and there is not, we lose little or nothing by believing. Perhaps we pass up a few pleasures that we would have enjoyed otherwise, but there are also pleasures that come from living a religious life. Nonetheless, if there is no God there will be no memories or regrets beyond death.

If we believe and live as though there is not a God and there is, we lose an infinite good, eternal life in the Kingdom of God.

If we believe and live as though there is a God and there is, we gain an infinite good: eternal life in the Kingdom of God.

Pascal concludes that the smart thing to do (the smart bet or wager to make) is to believe and live as though God exists even if we are not convinced of that by evidence. Indeed, taking Pascal's argument to an extreme, even if we think the evidence is *against* the existence of God, but also think it is at all *possible* that God exists, we should bet on God. What we bet, our life in this world, is a finite good. What we gain or lose is an infinite good.

Two criticisms of Pascal's Wager are these. *First*, one cannot *make* oneself believe anything. Beliefs happen to us as a result of experience, reasoning, socialization, etc., so we cannot *choose* to believe that God exists. Pascal could respond to that criticism by saying he agrees and is using the word "belief" not in the sense of sincerely thinking that something is the case but in the sense of *acting as though* one believes something (as when we act on an hypothesis to see if it is true) – and he does say that by acting as though we believe something we sometimes do come to believe it sincerely. A *second* criticism is that the motivation for the wager is unworthy and inappropriate. It is a self-centered way of life; not a God-centered way. To be sure, it seems the prudent way to live, but won't God see through that motivation? Will God honor people who are being religious just to get into heaven?

If we reject Pascal's argument (not all do) and continue to assume that agnosticism is true, does that mean that therefore we should suspend judgment as to whether God exists, and refrain from living a God-oriented life? Thinkers such as Soren Kierkegaard, William James, and Paul Tillich say there are things other than evidence and wagers that can make it rational to live a life devoted to God. Indeed, some theists think that God does not want us to believe in mer on the basis of evidence or wagers. A merely intellectual belief in God would be unemotional. It would be belief *that* God exists, but it would not be belief *in* God. To believe *in* a person is much more than to simply believe ze exists! A mere unemotional belief *that* God exists would be the result of a failure to understand the greatness and goodness of God. To believe *in* God is not merely to think that God exists; it is to feel the awesome, even terrifying greatness of God; it is to feel the uncanny, eerie otherness of God; it is to feel the humbling contrast of God's purity to our impurity; it is to feel one's utter dependence on God; it is to feel deeply and appreciate profoundly the unmerited mercy and love of God. Hence, mere intellectual belief that God exists would be like a one-dimensional apprehension of a four dimensional object. An appropriate understanding of God, together with the belief that God exists, cannot help but be emotional and not merely intellectual. Consequently, religious existentialists claim that to prevent us from satisfying ourselves with a merely intellectual belief that God exists, God has put epistemic distance between merself and us; that is, *God* has made sure that we do *not* have the ability or resources to resolve the question of zer existence on the basis of evidence. Hence, if we are going to believe in God, it will have to be on some basis other than evidence, a basis such as faith or hope or love.

15.2   Evidentialism vs. the Right to Believe

W.K. Clifford (1845–1879) first formulated the *principle of evidentialism.* He said there is no acceptable basis for belief other than adequate evidence. He wrote, "It is wrong always, everywhere, and for anyone to believe anything upon insufficient evidence." That is a powerful statement worth memorizing and reflecting on.

William James, a late nineteenth-century American philosopher, disagreed with Clifford (see James' essay "The Will to Believe" in his book by the same title). James said that if the truth or falsity of an hypothesis can be settled by evidence, then it should be. However, if it cannot be settled by available evidence, and if the issue is important to an individual, and if not to make a decision on the issue would be equivalent to deciding negatively, then as long as that individual is willing to accept the risks that would come from being mistaken, ze has a right to believe, that is, ze has a right to decide to live as though that hypothesis is true. James added that the truth of *some* hypotheses can *only* be discovered by acting as though they are true, so it would be folly to always suspend judgment in the absence of adequate evidence.

If, for example, someone who is visiting Hawaii for two weeks offers free housing to you if you visit mer, you can find out if zer offer is true only if you act as though it is true, that is, only if you go visit mer. And if for those two weeks you cannot make up your mind as to whether to go, you will lose the opportunity just as surely as you would have if you had said "no" before the two weeks began.

James' principle also holds true in science (and James was a medical scientist as well as a philosopher). Nearly every experimentally interesting idea begins as an hypothesis. "hypo" means "low," so an hypothesis is a "thesis" or idea that has low evidence for it so far; one must act on it as though it is true in order to find out if it is true (hence, James' approach to the worthiness of ideas was pragmatic). Scientists risk time, money, and reputation by conducting experiments to discover whether an hypothesis is true or false, but there is no alternative if we are going to discover the truth. Similarly, people take risks by choosing to believe a religious hypothesis, but there is no other way to find out whether a certain way of thinking and living holds up in the laboratory of life.

15.3   Fideism

Fideism says that faith (a nonevidential conviction, a belief not based on evidence, a basic belief, i.e., a belief not based on other beliefs) can be rational and even virtuous, but we need to distinguish two very different meanings of "faith" – faith as action and faith as passion.

15.3.1   Faith as Action or Leap

We have all heard the expression "a leap of faith." Faith conceived as a leap is understood as an action on our part, just as a leap across a chasm is an action on our part. That is what William James meant by a person choosing to act on an hypothesis, whether scientific or religious.

According to Paul Tillich, the act of faith is an act of courage (see Tillich's *The Courage to Be*). Faith, he says, does something which reason cannot do but which must be done in order for us to live a full life. Reason cannot give us all that we need to live life fully. Faith, says Tillich, goes beyond reason in order to *complete* reason. At some point we must leap beyond what reason can assure us of if we are to live in terms of a full world view, and, as James said, it is only by *living* in terms of a world view that we can discover its truth or worthiness. Keep in mind that atheism, too, according to fideism, is a world-view that requires a leap of faith. Reason, according to fideists, falls as short of establishing atheism as it does of establishing theism. To deny that there is a God or anything supernatural requires a leap of faith just as surely as does the affirmation that there is a God or a supernatural dimension of reality. Reason does not dictate either of those conclusions or any other world-view.

A student once asked me, "How can a believer doubt?" Many think that if you have *faith* then you have no doubt, but a fideist would say that because the evidence for religion is not conclusive one can have *intellectual* doubts about one's religion even if one has no *emotional* doubt (recall what Simone Weil said in Chapter 10 about religious experience). A mature faith does not deny doubt or escape doubt or destroy doubt. And remember, it is also possible for an atheist to doubt zer atheism. An honest faith acknowledges grounds for doubt but goes beyond doubt for the sake of life.

A leap of faith is a declaration as to what one *believes* would be good and *hopes* is true. The act of faith on the part of a theist is a declaration that one hopes that God exists because one believes it would be supremely good if God, a supremely perfect being, exists. Hence, a leap of faith is an expression of love and of hope that God exists. It is a declaration that if God exists, one wants to know God personally and to live in fellowship with God eternally. It is a declaration of devotion to God, and of hope that, if God exists, God will accept that devotion and enter into a personal relationship with oneself.

15.3.2 Faith as Passion or Gift

An action, such as a leap of faith, is what we *do*. A passion is what happens to us. The usual meaning of "passion" in English suggests that passion is something active, indeed, very active, but the Latin meaning from which the philosophical meaning comes is more closely related to the word "passive." Consider that we speak of being overwhelmed by passion – rage or lust or greed, for example – as though we are its victim. Faith in this sense is a conviction that is not based on evidence. It is a conviction that happens to us independently of evidential considerations. There may *be* evidence that favors what one has faith in, and one may even be aware of it, but the evidence is not the cause of one's faith. The more common word for *a conviction generated by evidence* is "belief." (I *believe* that the moon is illuminated by the sun.)

Theists and naturalists can agree that faith is a passion, but they have very different explanations as to why faith occurs. The naturalist believes that religious faith is the result of natural factors, such as the influence of one's parents or one's religious environment or one's emotions, such as hope and fear. Theists believe that the kind of faith that is most worth having is a gift from God. This belief is expressed exquisitely in the New Testament in Hebrews 11:1, which says, "Faith is the assurance of things hoped for, the conviction of things not seen." Note the word "assurance" in the preceding quotation. Faith is a nonevidential conviction or feeling that things that one hopes are true are true – things that one cannot see for certain to be true but which one feels to be true. (Faith is similar to intuition but perhaps not identical.) I think Blaise Pascal was speaking of faith as a passion when he said, "Faith is God felt by the heart, not by reason" (Pensée #424). That is, faith is a felt conviction of the reality of God – not a conviction arrived at by intellectually gathering and evaluating evidence. And according to the principle of credulity, a person who has faith (a nonevidential conviction) that God exists does not have an intellectual obligation to justify zer faith to merself or to others as long as ze knows of no good reason why ze should doubt it.

15.4   Agathism, Agatheism, and Religious Hope

Agathism is the belief that a good life is a life lived in devotion to the good ("aga" in Greek means "good"). From the agathist point of view, religion at its best is self-conscious, disciplined pursuit of knowledge of the good plus devotion to it. Such a life may or may not involve belief in a personal, transcendent God. Recall the positions of Feuerbach, Dewey, and Wieman.

How should we be religious, according to agathism? We should be *unconditionally* committed to (i) *finding* out what is the highest good and (ii) *living* according to it, but because we are *fallible*, we should be only *conditionally* committed to what seems to us at any time to be the highest good. We should always be open to the possibility that the good than which none greater can be conceived is different from or greater than we have so far conceived it. Hence, our unconditional commitment should be to what the highest good *is*, and not to what we *think* it is. (Charles Peirce, 1839–1914, one of the great American pragmatists, taught a doctrine of "fallibilism" according to which we can be profoundly mistaken in what we believe, as even the history of science shows, so we should be humble in what we claim to know.)

Agatheism (note the "e") is that species of agathism which holds that the ultimate good is God, the supremely perfect being. The agatheist, as distinguished from the naturalistic agathist, believes that the highest good would be a personal being who is all-powerful, all-knowing, everlasting, perfectly just and perfectly good. For the agatheist, to be religious means to be devoted to God, who is conceived as that good than which none greater can be conceived.

But why be religious in a theistic way? Because, according to agatheism, the best way to live, the most noble way to live a human life, is in devotion to the highest good, and the highest good is God. Hence, a good life is a life lived in devotion to God. Furthermore, from devotion to God come many important goods: anger at injustice, compassion for innocent suffering, loyalty to friendship, reverence for Nature, the craving for knowledge, love of beauty, the urge to create, and more. To be sure, these things come not only from conscious devotion to God, but, according to agatheism, love of God points to these things, and love of these things points to God.

Love of the idea of God and *hope* that God is real are more central in agatheism than are *belief* and *faith*. The agatheist says, "How wonderful if God exists! How sad if God does not exist!" Therefore, says the agatheist, hope and live as though there is a God! But always exercise epistemic responsibility and humility, remembering Thomas Aquinas's saying: "We must love them both, those whose opinions we share, and those whose opinions we reject. For both have labored in the search for truth, and both have helped us in finding it."

In conclusion, as Titus 1:8 says in the New Testament, each of us should above all be a "philagathist," literally, a lover of goodness. We should live in devotion to the good and in hope that the highest good we can conceive of is the ultimate truth about reality. That, I submit, is the maturest form of religion, whether it is naturalistic, transcendentalistic, or theistic.

For Review, Reflection, and Discussion

1. State W.K. Clifford's principle of evidentialism. Do you agree with it? If yes, why? If no, why not?
2. What is William James' argument against the principle of evidentialism? Do you agree with James or Clifford? Why?
3. What is the difference between believing *that* God exists and believing *in* God? (See Kierkegaard, Soren, *The Sickness Unto Death*, Hong and Hong, eds. [Princeton: 1980], pp. 103–4.)
4. What is the difference between faith as action and faith as passion?
5. What is the position of agathism? How is agatheism different from agathism?
6. Has this book changed or enriched the way you think about philosophy? If yes, how?
7. What do you now understand philosophy to be?
8. Has this book changed or enriched the way you think about religion? If yes, how?
9. What do you now understand religion to be?
10. What is philosophy of religion? How is it different from what you thought it would be?
11. What is fallibilism?
12. Write a paper expressing your current understanding of religion, explain how some philosophical issue that you find particularly interesting grows out of the nature of religion, discuss the philosophical pros and cons of that issue, and state your own position as a conclusion.

For Further Reading

Zagzebski, Linda, and Miller, Timothy, eds., *Readings in Philosophy of Religion: Ancient to Contemporary* (Wiley-Blackwell: 2009). Part X. A includes many selections on "Faith and Reason." Part X. B contains selections on "Pragmatism and the Ethics of Belief."

Taliaferro, Charles, Draper, Paul, et al., eds., *A Companion to Philosophy of Religion*, 2nd ed. (Wiley-Blackwell: 2010). Chapter 50 is by Jeffrey Jordan on *pragmatic* arguments. Chapter 52 is by Terence Penelhum on *fideism*. Chapter 79 is by Alvin Plantinga on reformed epistemology, which defends the rationality of *"properly basic beliefs."* Chapter 80 is by Richard Swinburne on *evidentialism*.

Pascal, Blaise, *Pensées* (Penguin Books: 1966), 149–55. There are many editions of the *Pensées*, but the *pensées* (thoughts) are arranged differently in different editions so in other editions you will have to hunt around for the location of the wager argument.

James, William, "The Will to Believe," in *The Will to Believe* (Dover: 1956). Perhaps would more appropriately be titled "the right to believe."

Tillich, Paul, *Dynamics of Faith* (Harper: 1957). This little book is a classic and one of the easier ways to begin to understand the most influential philosophical theologian of the twentieth century.

Muyskens, James, *The Sufficiency of Hope* (Temple University: 1979). Muyskens argues that hope, as distinguished from belief, is an adequate foundation for religious life.

Holley, David, *Meaning and Mystery: What It Means To Believe in God* (Wiley-Blackwell: 2010). Religions, according to Holley, are "life orienting stories" that help us understand and live our lives in meaningful, uplifting ways, so our choices among them, for or against them, should be made with that understanding.

Creel, Richard E., "Propositional Faith as a Mode of Belief and a Gift of God," *The Journal of Philosophical Research* (1994), 19, 243–56.

Creel, Richard E., "Faith as Imperfect Knowledge" in *Faith in Theory and Practice*, Radcliffe, Elizabeth S., and White, Carol J., eds. (Open Court Publishing Company: 1993), 67–73.

Creel, Richard E., "Faith, Hope, and Faithfulness," *Faith and Philosophy* (1993), 10(3), 330–44.

Creel, Richard E., "Agatheism: A Justification of the Rationality of Devotion to God," *Faith and Philosophy*, (1993), 10(1), 33–48.

Glossary

Agatheism the good life is a life lived in devotion to God, the supreme good

Agathism the good life is a life lived in devotion to the highest good

Agnosticism the position that one does not know whether there is a personal supreme being; hard agnostics say there are reasons to think we can never know whether there is such a being; soft agnostics say perhaps we can know eventually (these positions can be softened by being expressed in terms of whether or not one is *justified* in believing, rather than in terms of *knowing*)

Analogical use of a word the same word is used to mean two things that are meaningfully related but different in kind, such as when we speak of the birth of a nation and the birth of a child; a mere difference in degree (my dog is fast; my horse is fast) is univocal usage not analogical (see "equivocal" and "univocal")

Anthropic principle just because we are astonished to exist and be aware of the universe is no evidence that the universe was *intentionally* made to produce us; the universe may simply be such that it had to produce us or accidentally produced us, so we should not be surprised that it did

A posteriori an *a posteriori* argument is based on some simple fact about the world, such as that it exists, or things exist contingently, or there is motion, or every event has a cause

A priori an *a priori* argument is based solely on logical analysis of the implications of a concept, such as when we infer that the internal

Philosophy of Religion: The Basics, First Edition. Richard E. Creel.
© 2014 John Wiley & Sons, Inc. Published 2014 by John Wiley & Sons, Inc.

angles of any Euclidean triangle must add up to 180 degrees; there is no appeal to experience

Argument   one or more reasons given in support of a conclusion, for example, "All humans are mortal. I am human. Therefore I am mortal." An argument may be a good argument or not depending on whether the reasons given are true and whether the reasoning is valid. For example, "That swan is white. Therefore all swans are white" is invalid reasoning, and "The Evening Star is a star. Therefore the Evening Star is self-illuminating" has a false premise (if the Evening Star were a star it would be self-illuminating; however, the Evening Star is a planet that people once thought was a star).

Argumentum ad absurdum   an argument that attempts to discredit a claim by showing that it has an implication that is absurd (obviously false or highly questionable). Gaunilo's criticism of the ontological argument is a valuable example of an argumentum ad absurdum that did not succeed; see also "Kalam cosmological argument"

Atheism   the belief that there is no personal supreme being

Basic belief   a belief that is not held on the basis of other beliefs that serve as evidence for it; a basic belief just seems to the person to be true, for example, "I had toast and eggs for breakfast three days ago." Belief that there is a God or that there is not a God can also be a basic belief. But can it be rational to have a basic belief? (See "properly basic belief")

Code   the moral and behavioral rules of a religion

Cognitively meaningful   intelligible, understandable, comprehensible, not nonsensical or self-contradictory

Community   the social and organizational aspect of a religion

Composition, fallacy of   the invalid reasoning that because part of something has a certain property that therefore the whole thing must have that property, such as concluding that because the inside of a coconut is edible that therefore the whole thing must be edible, or, perhaps, reasoning that because each object in the universe is destructible that therefore the whole universe must be destructible

Concept, word, thing   a *concept* is an abstract idea of a *thing*, such as the concept of a circle or a helicopter; a *word* refers to the concept of a thing (as when we speak of the *idea* of a helicopter) or to the thing itself (as when we refer to an actual helicopter)

Contingent   dependent on something other than itself for its existence or some property; the existence of a sculpture is dependent on a sculptor; the shape of a piece of pottery is dependent on a potter

Cosmological argument   an *a posteriori* argument based on some simple property of the universe, such as its mere existence, or the existence of motion or causation or contingent objects in it

Credulity principle of   we have a right to believe what seems true to us as long as we have no good reason to think otherwise (this puts the burden of refutation on anyone who challenges what seems true to us, rather than the burden of proof being on us)

Creed   the aspect of a religion that states in words its core beliefs about reality, life, and destiny

Cult aspect of religion   the external aspects and practices of a religion that are intended to identify the religion and cultivate understanding and loyalty among its members; this includes symbols, rituals, celebrations, and more

Cumulative argument   two or more arguments which together constitute a more powerful argument for a conclusion than does any of the arguments by itself

Debate   two (or more) people each of whom presents an argument to the opposite of what the other person is claiming; the objective of each debater is to persuade the other person(s) to agree with mer

Deism   the belief that there is a personal God who created the universe but is not involved in it, so ze does not cause miracles, answer prayers, etc.

Dilemma   a situation in which there are two or more alternatives between which we must choose or suffer something more undesirable than what will happen if we choose (if it is a happy dilemma we may lose all the good alternatives if we don't make a choice; if it is an unhappy dilemma we may be afflicted by all the bad alternatives if we do not choose)

Divine command theory   there is nothing moral or immoral until God decides what it is to be, and God is free to make anything moral or immoral; what is morally right and wrong is such because God wills it to be so; God does not will it because it is already morally right or wrong

Division, fallacy of   the invalid argument that because the whole of something has a certain property that therefore its parts must have that same property, such as reasoning that because a coconut is hard and brown that therefore all of its contents must be hard and brown

Empiricism   the belief that the nature of reality can be discovered only by experience; reason may be helpful in analyzing and speculating about the results of experience, but nothing about reality can be discovered by reason alone (see "rationalism")

Epistemology   the study of the nature of knowledge and related concepts, such as belief, faith, rationality, and probability

Equivocal use of a word   a word is used equivocally when it is used to mean two completely different things, as when the word "pen" is used to mean an implement with which to write and when it is used to mean a structure in which to confine pigs

Evidentialism   the principle that it is wrong and irresponsible to believe anything except on the basis of sufficient evidence (hence, according to evidentialism there are no properly basic beliefs, and the principle of credulity is unsound)

Ex nihilo nihil fit   (see *nihilo*)

Fallacy of   (see "composition" and "division")

Fine-tuning argument   the physical constants and variables of the universe could have been inconsistent with life in almost an infinite number of ways; those constants and variables had to be so exact for intelligent life to be created that it is more plausible that they were adjusted by intention rather than happened by accident;

Genetic fallacy   the mistake of thinking that the truth or falsity of a claim is determined by its source so that if it came from the "wrong" kind of source, for example, a man or a woman or a child, a black person or a white person, a Catholic or a Protestant, etc., it can be dismissed and not taken seriously

God   the supremely perfect being; that being than which none greater can be conceived

Goldilocks principle   states that the universe had to be "just right" for intelligent life to emerge (see "fine-tuning argument")

Identical   two things are identical when they are not two things but are one thing mistakenly thought to be two things, such as the ancient thinker Cicero and Tully (thought by some to be two people but really was one person) (see "indiscernible")

Immanent   inside of or involved in (Is God immanent in the world or aloof?)

Immortality   the idea that the human soul is uncreated and everlasting by its very nature; it may be incarnate in a body, even reincarnated many times, but true happiness comes when the soul becomes wise and pure enough to be forever separated from the afflictions and limitations of the body

Immutable   does not and cannot change in any or a certain respect (see "mutable")

Impassible   is not and cannot be affected by anything or in a certain respect (see "passible")

Indiscernible   two things are perfectly indiscernible when they cannot be differentiated except that they are two things rather than one; indiscernibility depends to some extent on the powers of perception of the perceiver; objects that are indiscernible to one person may be discernible to another because of better vision or hearing, smell or touch

Interruptive religious experience   a religious experience that breaks in on one's awareness suddenly and is overwhelming and short-lived (see "suffusive religious experience")

Kalam cosmological argument   argues that the notion of an infinite regress of events into the past leads to absurdities that discredit the credibility of such a regress; any regress must be finite; therefore, the universe must have had a beginning; moreover, any series of events into the future can only be potentially infinite in number and never actually infinite

Logical positivism   the position that talk about real or imaginary things makes sense only if those things can be understood and described in physical terms, such as shape, weight, color, motion, size, location, etc.; therefore, talk about God and other supernatural things is nonsense

Logically impossible   self-contradictory and therefore cannot exist, for example a married bachelor or a square circle

Logically possible   cognitively meaningful and not self-contradictory so therefore might exist; something that is logically possible can be necessary or contingent, probable, plausible, or merely possible

Metaphysics   the study of reality insofar as reality goes beyond what we can physically sense or construct physical models of; *science* is the study of reality insofar as it is physical (obviously logical positivism rejects the legitimacy of metaphysics) (see "science")

Monotheism   belief in one and only one God. Dualism and polytheism are belief in more than one divine being.

Multiverse Theory   the position that reality consists of a plethora of infinitely diverse universes that are inaccessible to one another

Mutable   capable of change (see "immutable")

Natural law ethics   the position that moral right and wrong are rooted in what humans naturally need to develop, mature, and flourish; hence, we can figure out what is morally right and wrong by studying those needs

Naturalism   the position that reality consists of Nature and nothing more; there is no being or dimension that transcends Nature

Necessary condition   that which is necessary is that which must be the case; a necessary condition is a condition that is required for something to be the case; the presence of oxygen is a necessary condition of fire (also see sufficient condition)

Nihilo   *ex nihilo nihil fit* is Latin for "nothing comes from nothing"; the idea is that nothing has no potentiality from which anything could come; because of this principle some claim that God could not have created the universe *ex nihilo;* the universe has always existed

Non-contradiction, law of   a statement that is self-contradictory cannot be true because it would have to be true and false at the same time but nothing can be true and false at the same time, for example, "The bachelor kissed his wife on the cheek."

Obligatory, forbidden, permissible   an action is obligatory if it ought to be done, that is, if we have a moral duty to do it; it is forbidden if it ought not to be done; it is permissible if it may be done or not done at one's own discretion without violating what is morally right

Ockham's razor   "Do not multiply entities beyond necessity"; remove any unnecessary complexity from a theory; every part of a theory should earn its keep or be eliminated

Omnibenevolence   the attribute of being supremely and perfectly good

Omnipotence   the attribute of being all-powerful; able to do anything that can be done

Omnipresence   (ubiquity) the attribute of being present everywhere, absent nowhere; alternatively, everything is present to one

Omniscience   the attribute of being all-knowing, of knowing everything that can be known

Ontological argument   an *a priori* argument to the existence of God from sheer logical analysis of the concept of a being than which none greater can be conceived

Oscillatory theory   the theory that the universe has existed and will exist forever as an unending sequence of explosions and contractions

Panentheism   the position that God and the world depend on one another for their existence; neither can exist apart from the other; each is intimately and profoundly involved in the other; God is mutable and passible (see "transcendent" and "deism")

Pantheism   the position that reality consists of God and God alone; individuals are either illusions or are temporary forms that God is taking

Pascal's wager   an attempt to run out the permutations in order to show that it is wiser to bet on the existence of God than on the nonexistence of God

Passible   subject to influence; can be affected by others (see "impassible")

Permutations, running out the   a systematic effort to identify all the variations that something might take in order not to overlook a possibility; see, for example, how Pascal develops his wager argument

Petitionary prayer   prayer in which one petitions (asks) God for something (see "prayer")

Philosophy   a passionate, systematic pursuit of knowledge of the real and the good

Philosophy of religion   the philosophical study of concepts and issues in religion, especially the nature of religion, the nature of God, the relation of God to the world, the existence of God, and science and religion

Plausible   an assertion is plausible if there is some evidence to believe it is true but perhaps not enough evidence to indicate that it is probable (something that is merely possible might be implausible; something that is probable would of course also be plausible)

Possible   might be the case; this is the weakest epistemic case, but of course it is more powerful than impossibility

Prayer   talking to God by way of praise, confession, petition, or thanksgiving (see "petitionary prayer")

Probable   an assertion is probable when evidence indicates it is more likely to be true than false (however, there can be degrees of probability from 99% to 1%, the latter meaning improbable; to say that something is "probable" is to say that it is more than "50%" likely)

Process theism   see "panentheism"

Proof   an argument the premises and logic of which show for certain that the conclusion is true; this is what philosophers call a "sound" argument – the premises are true and the reasoning is valid, therefore the conclusion must be true

Properly basic belief   a basic belief for which one has no good reason to think otherwise; combined with the principle of credulity this means, for example, that a person to whom it just seems that there is a God does not have to defend zer belief to be rational in holding it; similarly for someone for whom atheism is a basic belief (see "basic belief")

Proposition a statement that can be true or false; an assertion that something is the case, for example, "The sun is larger than the moon" and "It is wrong to abuse a child."

Rationalism the belief that some truths about reality – supernatural, transcendent, or metaphysical truths – can be discovered by reason and reason alone (see "empiricism")

Reductionism the position that talk about God is meaningful but is not talk about a supernatural being

Regress, infinite Paul Edwards claimed that up to the present moment there has been an infinite series of events in the history of the universe; by contrast, the kalam cosmological argument concludes that an infinite regress of events is impossible, therefore the regress of events must be finite, which implies that the universe must have had a beginning

Religion a way of thinking and living which involves devotion to a supreme being or value

Resurrection the position that the body and the soul are both created by God; the soul may be a separate entity from the body or it may be generated by the body; at death the body perishes – and with it perhaps the soul; eventually God recreates the body; there may or may not be a soul that separates from the body at death; if there is, then the soul and the body are reunited at resurrection; if there is not, then the soul is regenerated when the body is reconstituted

Revelation a self-disclosure of the divine to a human; perhaps through a vision, the hearing of a voice, a feeling, writing, or a combination of these (see "verbal revelation")

Science the study of reality insofar as it is accessible to *physical* experience, methods of investigation, and speculations (see "metaphysics")

Sufficient condition a sufficient condition is adequate to make something be the case but it may not be a necessary condition for that thing to be the case; a fire and a flashlight are each sufficient to illuminate a tree at night, but neither is necessary – the moon might do a good job; oxygen is a necessary condition of fire, but it is not a sufficient condition (a source of ignition is also necessary) (see "necessary condition")

Sufficient reason, principle of   for everything that exists and event that occurs there is an explanation that is satisfactory to reason – or would be if we knew it

Suffusive religious experience   religious experience that is gentle, relatively long-lived, and pervades one's experience, even during normal activities (see "interruptive religious experience")

Teleological argument   an argument from the great complexity and goal-oriented nature of things in the universe to the existence of a great designer or intender

Theism   the belief that there is a supreme being who is personal in nature; beliefs differ as to whether God is finite or infinite, mutable or immutable, passible or impassible, etc.

Theocentric ethics   the position that the best way to figure out what is morally right and wrong is to reflect on what would be the will of a supremely perfect being for the behavior of humans toward one another and nature

Transcendent   does not depend on the world for existence; could exist with or without the world (for contrast see "panentheism")

Univocal use of a word   univocal usage of a word consists of using the word more than once to mean the very same thing, for example, "My oldest brother is tall" and "My youngest brother is tall" (a mere difference in degree, if one brother is taller than the other, does not constitute a different meaning of "tall")

Verbal revelation   a revelation from God that takes the form of spoken or written language, for example, "Hear O Israel, the Lord is One!" and "Thou shalt not kill" (also called "propositional revelation")

Via analogia   the position that human language when used about God can be literally true if it is used in an appropriately analogical way (see "Analogical use of a word")

Via negativa   the position that human statements about the way God is cannot be true because God is too different from everything that we experience, know, or can possibly understand

Ze, zer, mer   personal pronouns with no gender; to be used generically for males and females in general and for nongendered beings such as perhaps God, angels, extra-terrestrial beings, robots, and science-fiction creatures

Biographical Notes

Anselm, Saint (1033–1109): born in Burgundy in Europe; become archbishop of Canterbury in England. Most famous for his version of the ontological argument, but also wrote brilliantly about the divine nature, human freedom, sin, and redemption. See his *Proslogion* and *Monologion*.

Aquinas, Saint Thomas (1225–1274, Italy and Paris): until Aquinas, Christian thought had been influenced primarily by the works of Plato – in part because most of the works of Aristotle had been lost to the West. In Aquinas' time those works were rediscovered and Aquinas made brilliant use of them, shifting the primary orientation of western Christian thought from Plato to Aristotle.

Ayer, A.J. (1920–1989): the foremost British exponent of logical positivism, which attacked the credibility of supernatural metaphysics and absolutist ethics. See his *Language, Logic, and Truth*.

Clifford, W.K. (1845–1879): Clifford was most important and influential as a mathematician and geometer, but his principle of evidentialism is still influential on the topic of the ethics of belief. See his essay "The Ethics of Belief," available in many books of readings on philosophy of religion.

Dawkins, Richard (1941–): an English evolutionary biologist who is an outspoken atheist and critic of religion, and especially of creationism. He argues, contrary to people like Paley and Tennant, that naturalistic evolution can account for the emergence of intelligent life in a relatively short time. See *The Blind Watchmaker* and *The God Delusion*.

Descartes, René (1596–1650, France): "the father of modern philosophy" shifted the primary focus of philosophy from theological issues to the mind/body problem and a mechanistic understanding of nature. Most famous for inventing analytic geometry and attacking skepticism by

Philosophy of Religion: The Basics, First Edition. Richard E. Creel.
© 2014 John Wiley & Sons, Inc. Published 2014 by John Wiley & Sons, Inc.

saying, "I think, therefore I am." See his *Discourse on Method* and his *Meditations on First Philosophy*.

Dewey, John (1859–1952): one of the great American pragmatist philosophers, along with Charles Peirce and William James. Dewey was an eloquent naturalist and an extremely influential philosopher of education, emphasizing the importance of hands-on, experiential education that tries to take advantage of what students themselves are interested in. See *A Common Faith* and *Human Nature and Conduct*.

Dostoyevsky, Fyodor (1821–1881): a Russian novelist who in his novels wrestles profoundly with philosophical problems, and especially the problems of evil, justice, morality, the nature of sanity, and the value of reason. See *The Brothers Karamazov, Crime and Punishment, The Idiot,* and *Notes from Underground*.

Edwards, Paul (1923–2004): born in Austria, educated in Australia, employed in the United States, zealously antireligious, Edwards' most enduring critique has been his critique of the cosmological argument. He was the editor-in-chief of the eight volume *Encyclopedia of Philosophy* and was a signer of the *Humanist Manifesto*.

Epicurus (341–270): this eloquent Greek philosopher was deeply concerned with the nature of happiness and how to achieve it, as a consequence of which he was concerned to help people overcome their fear of death and the gods. He taught that the gods are aloof and death is painless oblivion. Happiness consists of physical and mental pleasures and the absence of pain; we must use reason, not impulse, to achieve stable, enduring happiness.

Feuerbach, Ludwig (1804–1872): an important German philosopher who rebelled against the church and the spiritual philosophy of G.W.F. Hegel. He totally reinterpreted religion and the idea of God as subconscious endeavors on the part of humans to express their own ideal capabilities. See *The Essence of Christianity* (an abridgment of which is available through Frederick Ungar Publishing).

Freud, Sigmund (1856–1939): virtually obsessed with religion the founder of psychoanalytic psychiatry wrote several books discrediting religion as a hopeful illusion unworthy of rational human beings. See his *Future of An Illusion, Civilization and Its Discontents,* and *Totem and Taboo*.

Hartshorne, Charles (1897–2000): second in importance only to Whitehead in the development of process philosophy, but even more important in the development of process theism. See his *Man's Vision of God, The Divine Relativity,* and *A Natural Theology for Our Time*. For an introduction to process theism see *Process Theology* by John B. Cobb, Jr. and David Ray Griffin (Westminster: 1976).

Hegel, G.W.F. (1770–1831): one of the three great figures in German idealism, along with Johann Gottlieb Fichte and Friedrich Schelling. Famous for interpreting everything as an expression of an absolute spirit, including the whole development of history. His most famous work is *Phenomenology of Mind (or Phenomenology of Spirit)*. An easier introduction is his *Lectures on the Philosophy of History* (published under the title of *Reason in History* by the Library of Liberal Arts).

Hick, John (1922–2012): a British philosopher of religion who, unlike most philosophers of religion, thought and wrote as much about religion as he did about the existence and attributes of God. See, for example *An Interpretation of Religion: human responses to the transcendent*, *Evil and the God of Love*, and *Death and Eternal Life*. An excellent introduction to his positions can be found in his introductory text *Philosophy of Religion* (4th ed.).

Hume, David (1711–1776): a Scottish philosopher, historian, and diplomat who helped shift philosophy from its rationalist orientation in the seventeenth century to empiricism. He raised difficulties for theism, ethics, and philosophy of mind that continue to this day. See his *Dialogues Concerning Natural Religion* and *An Enquiry Concerning Human Understanding*.

James, William (1842–1910, United States): a teacher of medical science at Harvard University and a philosophical pragmatist who believed that the critical test of the truth or falsity of an idea is whether it works. Most famous in philosophy of religion for arguing that when evidence is insufficient to justify the probability of a belief and the belief is important, people have a right to believe that proposition at their own risk. See *The Will to Believe* and *Varieties of Religious Experience*.

Lane, William Craig (1949–): an American analytic philosopher and Christian theologian who is best known for reviving the kalam cosmological argument. See his book *The Kalam Cosmological Argument*.

Leibniz, G.W. (1646–1716, Germany): Leibniz was a universal genius who made important contributions in mathematics, jurisprudence, and more, as well as philosophy. He is best, and most controversially, known for arguing that there is a God and therefore this is the best possible world. He pioneered the metaphysical notion of "possible worlds" that has been utilized so well by Alvin Plantinga. See Leibniz's *Theodicy*.

Locke, John (1632–1704): an English philosopher and physician whose political writings were very influential on the founding fathers of the United States (see *A Letter Concerning Toleration* and *Two Treatises of Government*), and whose magnum opus, *An Essay Concerning Human Understanding*, helped move philosophy from a rationalist to an empiricist orientation in epistemology and philosophy of language.

Marx, Karl (1818–1883, Germany and London): Marx studied philosophy, became a naturalist, and concluded that history is driven by economic arrangements, not ideas. From a naturalist point of view he critiqued the origin and functions of religion in society. See his *Communist Manifesto* and his *Contribution to the Critique of Hegel's Philosophy of Right*. An excellent anthology is *Marx & Engels on Religion* (Schocken Books).

Nietzsche, Friedrich (1844–1900, Germany): a prolific writer and critic who sought to turn traditional religion and morality upside down. Perhaps most famous for declaring "God is dead, and we have killed him" and for exalting "master morality" over "slave morality." See *Thus Spake Zarathustra, The Anti-Christ*, and *Twilight of the Idols*.

Ockham, William (circa 1287–1347): one of the three most influential philosophers in the high Middle Ages, along with Aquinas and Scotus. Propounded metaphysical nominalism versus Aquinas's metaphysical realism. Most well-known for formulating what is known as "Ockham's Razor": Do not multiply entities beyond necessity.

Paley, William (1743–1805): an English philosopher who is best known for his teleological argument for the existence of God using a watchmaker analogy. See his *Natural Theology*. See Richard Dawkins' *The Blind Watchmaker* for a critical response.

Pascal, Blaise (1623–1662): a brilliant French mathematician and scientist whose philosophical thoughts anticipated religious existentialism and were published as a collection of brief reflections titled *Pensées*.

Plantinga, Alvin (1932–): an American analytic philosopher who is very sympathetic to a conservative Christian view of the world. He has used modal logic to advance the authority of the ontological argument, and has more recently argued against naturalism and atheistic versions of the theory of evolution. See *God, Freedom, and Evil* and *Where the Conflict Really Lies: Science, Religion, and Naturalism*.

Plato (427–347 BCE): one of the greatest and most influential of ancient Greek philosophers, along with Socrates and Aristotle. Plato was a rationalist who believed that in addition to this world there is another realm of reality in which our true happiness lies; that realm is accessible by the mind in this life and by the soul after death – although the soul may have to be reincarnated many times before it becomes wise and pure enough to escape the cycle of reincarnation.

Rousseau, Jean-Jacques (1712–1778): born in Switzerland, moved around Europe. Trusted feeling more than reason. Taught that humans are by nature good. Major contributions to political philosophy, moral psychology, and philosophy of education. See *Emile* and *The Social Contract*.

Rowe, William (1931–): an American analytic philosopher of religion who has made important contributions regarding the attributes of God, the cosmological argument, and the problem of evil. Rowe describes himself as "a friendly atheist," that is, an atheist who allows that a theist might be rational in believing even if ze is mistaken. See his *Philosophy of Religion*, 2nd ed., *The Cosmological Argument*, and *Can God Be Free?*

Sartre, Jean-Paul (1905–1980): a French existentialist philosopher and playwright who echoed Nietzsche's cry, "God is dead!" A major part of his philosophizing consisted of trying to figure out all the implications of atheism, from which he concluded that there is no such thing as human nature or absolute values.

Scotus, Duns (circa 1265–1308): one of the three most influential philosopher-theologians in the high medieval period, along with Aquinas and Ockham. Called "the Subtle Doctor" because of his keen conceptual analyses. See Wolter, Allan B., ed., *Duns Scotus: Philosophical Writings* (Hackett Publishing Company, 1987).

Socrates (469–399 BCE): perhaps the greatest of ancient Greek philosophers. Socrates earned the nickname of "the gadfly of Athens" because of the relentless way in which he questioned people who claimed to know things they did not know. He wrote nothing, but his dear and brilliant student Plato wrote many dialogues in which he set forth Socrates' personality, philosophical style, and thoughts. See especially Plato's dialogues *Euthyphro, Apology, and Phaedo.*

Spinoza, Benedict (1632–1677, Holland): one of the three great seventeenth-century rationalists, along with Descartes and Leibniz. Spinoza was a pantheist who rejected the idea of a transcendent, personal God but promoted the idea of the universe as God. In his magnum opus, *Ethics,* he tried to capture and explain the world by means of geometrical reasoning from axioms. He was also a brilliant political theorist. See his *Theological-Political Treatise.*

Swinburne, Richard (1934–): a British born Oxford philosopher who has used the tools of conceptual analysis and probability theory to argue for the probability of the existence of God. He has also written in defense of theological doctrines such as miracles and revelation. See his trilogy *The Coherence of Theism, The Existence of God,* and *Faith and Reason.*

Tennant, F.R. (1866–1957): a British philosophical theologian who emphasized the importance of *arguments* for the existence of God, as distinguished from faith, and endeavored to reconcile the growing influence of Charles Darwin's theory of evolution with Christian thought. See his *Philosophical Theology* (2 vols.).

Tillich, Paul (1886–1965): an existentialist philosophical theologian who had enormous influence on psychology as well as theology in the twentieth century. His magnum opus is his *Systematic Theology.* More immediately accessible are his *Dynamics of Faith* and *The Courage to Be.*

Whitehead, Alfred North (1861–1947): first a brilliant English mathematician; then a brilliant philosopher at Harvard University, where he gave process philosophy a scientific framework. His magnum opus is *Process and Reality.* On religion see *Religion in the Making* and *Science and the Modern World.*

Wieman, Henry Nelson (1884–1975): an American naturalist philosopher who used the word "God" to stand for that force in nature that transforms us for the good in ways in which we cannot transform ourselves. See his books *The Source of Human Good* and *Man's Ultimate Commitment*.

Wittgenstein, Ludwig (1889–1951): an Austrian philosopher who later lived in England and visited the United States. His influence was transformative, first by way of logical positivism and then by way of ordinary language analysis. See his *Tractatus* and his *Philosophical Investigations*.

Index

agathism, agatheism, 190–191
analogy, 67–70
anomaly, miracle as, 180
Anselm, St., 31–2
anthropic principle, 108–9
a posteriori argument, 75, 88
a priori argument, 75, 77
Aquinas, Thomas, 32, 69–70, 89,
    102–3, 121–4
argument, 72–5
argumentum ad absurdum, 78, 98
aseity, 37
attributes, divine, 34–9
Ayer, A. J., 58–60

belief, basic, 130–132, 144–5, 188
brute facts, 142

cessationism, 165–7
Clifford, W. K., 187
code, 7
community, 9–10
conclusions, hard, soft, 74
contingent, 49, 81–2, 91
contradiction, 47, 138–9
cosmological arguments, 88–99
Craig, William Lane, 95–8

credulity, principle of, 131–2
creed, 6–7
cult, 8–9
cumulative argument, 97, 134–5

death, life after, 142–4, 161, 164–76
debate, 72–3
deism, 28–9
Descartes, René, 34
Dewey, John, 22
dilemma, 39–40
divine command ethics, 119–20

Eddy, Mary Baker, 155
Edwards, Paul, 92–3
Epicurus, 152
equivocal usage, 67
ethics, 119–26
evidentialism, 137–8, 187
evil, 152–61
ex nihilo, 28, 29, 91
exclusivism, 148
experience, religious, 128–35

faith, 188–90
fallacy of composition, 92
fallacy of division, 92–3

Philosophy of Religion: The Basics, First Edition. Richard E. Creel.
© 2014 John Wiley & Sons, Inc. Published 2014 by John Wiley & Sons, Inc.

fallibilism, 190–191
Feuerbach, Ludwig, 21–2, 154
fideism, 188
fine tuning argument, 107–8
free will, 49–55, 161

Gaunilo, 78
genetic fallacy, 143
God, nature of, 17–33
Goldilocks principle, 116

Hartshorne, Charles, 27, 50–53, 156
Hegel, G. W. F., 24–5
Hick, John, 158–9
hiddenness, divine, 145–7
hope, religious, 171, 191
Hume, David, 82, 105, 124, 166, 181

identical, 23, 173–8
immanent, 21, 29, 37
immortalism, 167–70
immutable, 38, 44, 48, 52–3
impassible, 39, 53
inclusivism, 148
indiscernible, 174
interruptive religious experience, 129–30
Irenaean theodicy, 158–9

James, William, 187–8

kalam argument, 95–8
Kant, Immanuel, 79–80, 171–2
karma, law of, 155–6, 168

Leibniz, G. W., 70, 82, 89, 93, 153–4

many religions, problem of, 147–51
meaninglessness of "God", 58–60, 138
metaphysics, 85, 165, 175–6
miracles, 179–82

morality, argument from, 118–19
multiverse, 109–10

natural law ethics, 121–6
naturalism, 21–3, 139–42, 165–7
necessary conditions, 173

Ockham's Razor, 135, 139–41
omnibenevolence, 36, 43–4
omnipotence, 36, 42–8
omniscience, 36, 44–5, 49–54, 156–7
ontological argument, 77–86
oscillatory argument, 93–4

Paley, William, 104–5
panentheism, 25–7, 156–7, 166–7
pantheism, 23–5
Pascal's Wager, 185–7, 190
permutations, running out the, 113, 156, 164–5
person, nature of, 30, 38–9, 44, 49, 53–5, 98–9
personal identity and continuity, 173–6
philosophy, 1–2
Plantinga, Alvin, 161
Plato, 27, 101
pluralism, 148–9
positivism, logical, 58–60
possibility, 83–6
prayer, 183–4
principle of credulity, 131–2
principle of sufficient reason, 75, 88–9, 92–3, 111–12, 142
process philosophy
  see panentheism

razor *see* Ockham's Razor
reductionism, 60–61
religion, 11–12
religion, philosophy of, 3–4
religious experience, 129–30

resurrectionism, 170
revelation, 182–3

Schopenhauer, Arthur, 153
Scotus, Duns, 83
simplicity, metaphysical, 38, 84, 169
sufficient conditions, 173
sufficient reason, principle of, 75,
    88–9, 142
suffusive religious experience,
    130–131
Swinburne, Richard, 159–60

Tennant, F.R., 110–115, 118
theism
  biblical, 29–30, 53–5
  open, 53–5
  philosophical, 31–2

theocentric ethics, 120–121
theodicy, 154
theology, 3
transcendent, 21
transcendentalism, 167–70

univocal usage, 66–7

veridical, 131
via analogia, 66–70
via negativa, 61–6

Weil, Simone, 128–9
Wieman, Henry Nelson, 22–3, 154
Wittgenstein, Ludwig, 58–60

ze, zer, mer, 13–14